Beginnings

Cover picture

This Catholic Church was built in the 14th century in Zdar, where my mother was baptized, my parents were married, and where Kazimir Zajicek, my great grandfather, was buried. It is a landmark dedicated to St. Vaclav, also known as the Good King Wenceslaus.

Beginnings

By James Vaclav Frank

"Beginnings" is an account of my early years growing up in the country near Plzen (Pilsen), Czechoslovakia, during the German occupation and World War II. In 1948, as Czechoslovakia became communist, I escaped across the border to western Germany. Across the border, I met my wife to be, Marta, and her young son, Zdenek. We spent over two years in refugee camps in Germany and Italy. Marta and I were married in Italy where our son, Pavel, was born. We eventually immigrated to the USA to begin a new life.

Published by:
ZAP Studio, LLC
PO BOX 1150
Philomath, OR 97370
www.zapstudio.com

Copyright © 2012 by ZAP Studio, LLC
Library of Congress Control Number: 2011944703
ISBN: 978-1-935422-04-4

All rights reserved. No part of this book may be reproduced or transmitted in any form without written permission from ZAP studio, LLC except as provided by the "fair use" provision of the United States of America copyright law.

First printing: January 2012
Printed in the United States of America

ZAP Studio, LLC   www.zapstudio.com

*Dedicated to the memory
of my beloved wife Marta,
who passed away in 2007,
and to all of my family,*

*also with special gratitude
to the memory of my mentor
Mr. Rudolf Voboril.*

Acknowledgements

The Frank, Martinez, and Antoch families, from their collection of photos and slides, contributed most of the photos in this book, including those taken on trips back to the Czech homeland. The manuscript was compiled by Marney Antoch. The layout and editing was done by Zdenek Antoch. The author, James V. Frank contributed diagrams and many pictures of Czechoslovakia, including the cover photograph.

All other photographs used in this book are in the public domain and attributed to the sources listed below:

USAF	United States Air Force / www.af.mil/
USAR	United States Army / www.army.mil/
USN	United States Navy / www.navy.mil/
FSA	Farm Security Administration / Office of War www.loc.gov/rr/print/coll/052_fsa.html/
AG	National Archives / www.archives.gov/
LOC	Library of Congress / www.loc.gov/
USHM	United States Holocaust Memorial Museum www.ushmm.org/
NATO	North Atlantic Treaty Organization / www.nato.int/UKMN
tfi	http://www.totallyfreeimages.com
pda	http://publicdomainclip-art.blogspot.com/
kw	http://www.karenswhimsy.com
pld	Public domain from Poland
pd	Public Domain
cc	Wikipedia Creative Commons http://en.wikipedia.org/wiki/Creative_Commons_licenses
m.a.	Illustrations by Marney Antoch
z.a.	Illustrations by Zdenek Antoch
p.j.	Photos from Pavel Jiran (Nepomuk, Czech Republic)

Table of Contents

Chapter 1:	My Early Family	page 1
Chapter 2:	Farm Life, Work & Play	page 12
Chapter 3:	Wooden Shoes	page 20
Chapter 4:	From Winter to Spring & Easter	page 32
Chapter 5:	Education & Health	page 45
Chapter 6:	Toys and Tasks	page 58
Chapter 7:	Autumn to Winter & Christmas	page 65
Chapter 8:	World War II	page 77
Chapter 9:	Endurance	page 87
Chapter 10:	Apprenticeship	page 98
Chapter 11:	More About WW II	page 107
Chapter 12:	After WW II	page 119
Chapter 13:	Conditions at Work	page 128
Chapter 14:	Preparations	page 142
Chapter 15:	Border Crossings, part 1	page 150
Chapter 16:	Border Crossings, Part 2	page 163

Chapter 17:	Last Border Crossing	page 174
Chapter 18:	Plague, DDT,& Potatoes	page 186
Chapter 19:	Bagnoli and Jesi	page 196
Chapter 20:	Back to Bagnoli & on to Pagani	page 208
Chapter 21:	Pagani to Salerno	page 219
Chapter 22:	Rome	page 227
Chapter 23:	Bremerhaven & the Liberty Ship	page 239
Chapter 24:	U.S.A	page 249
Chapter 25:	Seaside	page 261
Chapter 26:	Portland, Oregon	page 270
Epilogue		page 276
Appendix 1:	Family and Friends	page 278
Appendix 2:	USS General Harry Taylor	page 285
Appendix 3:	Liberator Memorials	page 286
Bibliography and Recommended Reading		page 288
Index		page 290

Chapter 1

My Early Family

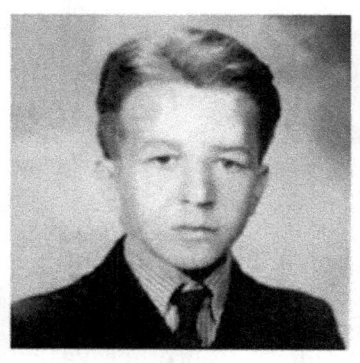

James Vaclav Frank   z.a.

This is a record of my early life, a personal narrative and gift of memories that I wish to share. However, the story begins in about 1860, with a pioneer, my great grandfather, Kazimir Zajicek, who came from Prague. It is possible that as a city dweller and perhaps from a privileged class, Kazimir may have escaped the city because of religious persecution, which was quite common in those days.

He cleared some land, built a log cabin, and named this new place, 'Myt' (from the Czech word mytina, meaning clearing in the forest). This village still exists today. Kazimir and his wife had a son, Frantisek, who had seven children, two boys, and five girls. The last child, a daughter, was Jana, my mother. The following are a few short anecdotes regarding Jana, and her siblings:

1. Frantisek Zajicek II, lived in Prague, and worked in a bank. He was well to do and generous.

2. Vaclav, became a wagon maker, and inherited the original house and shop (the house that Kazmir built in Myt).

3. Frances, was married to Mr. Heidelberg (a tragic family).

4. Anna, was married to Schneberg. Her husband was a railroad worker. She was good and generous to us. We loved her.

1

5. Marie, was kind to us. She lived in Prague. She and my sister Anna had some traits in common. They even looked like each other. Unfortunately, they both died of breast cancer at the early age of 51.

6. Barbora (Beta) was employed in Prague. She was well to do, noble, and good in every way. She was very generous. I remember the beautiful letter that Beta wrote to me when I immigrated to America.

7. Jana, my mother, lost her mother when she was only two years old. Later, Jana cared for her father throughout her school years. He loved her very much. He was a devout Catholic, and sang a song every morning after awakening, "Ava Maria", When her older brother Vaclav got married, Jana became a domestic worker for a well to do family where she was happy and well liked.

   However, her brother Vaclav arranged for her to leave and take care of several children for her sister Frances, of the Heidelbergs. She gave a few good years of her life there, and though she had been promised compensation, she received nothing in return. Vaclav did not fulfill his given obligation to take care of his little sister.

Our father Frantisek Frank was previously married around 1915. He had a daughter named Marie, and then was drafted to fight in the First World War. He came back home with a bad leg wound. Not long after his return, his wife died from an illness. After a few years, Frantisek met Jana. He was employed as a Forester, a uniformed guardian and carried a shotgun. He had been living in a village near Myt. He and Jana were married in 1926, and settled in the little farming village of Zahradka, Czechoslovakia (today the Czech Republic) where they raised their family of five children.

I was the second child born and their only son. We all grew up in this village and countryside, which is located north of Plzen, about 20 km, in the southwestern part of Czechoslovakia, approximately 50km from the German border.

Frantisek and Jana

Our home

Zahradka

As most inhabitants, my parents were small farmers on about twelve acres of land, raising potatoes, wheat, alfalfa, sugar beets (for syrup) and meadows for cattle feed and hay. One field was devoted to cabbage (for winter sauerkraut) and various vegetables, used in the summer months.

Farm animals consisted of two sturdy cows, which were the main source of livelihood, i.e. milk, butter and usually one calf was born each year, which was raised and sold, bringing some income to the family. The cows were the main source of power to pull the plow, so we could plant and dig out potatoes. They were also used for pulling wagons and everything that was needed for the raising and harvesting of crops.

We valued our cows as the most precious possessions because the family's livelihood totally depended on them. Therefore, a lot of the family's effort was devoted to gather feed, which was not easy considering the farm's small plot of land available. This made it necessary to take them out to pasture from spring to summer and into fall.

I took this photo in the 1970s. This same method of plowing was done in my youth forty years earlier.

Because of all the land that was to be cultivated, there was not much left for foraging and pasturing. Only steeper terrain areas next to roads were available. This made it necessary to rope the cows together, and hang on to them to keep them from going into the fields and damaging the crops. After the day's labor of manual hard work, our father took the cows out as much as possible, typically for two to three hours.

The adults as well as children had to work. Whatever was needed, always, and pasturing cows was the task usually designated for the boys, grown enough to hang onto and command them. I was probably about six years old, being told to do this after school, also on Saturday and sometimes on Sunday. As much as I was willing, and glad to do whatever to help my tired folks, pasturing cows I always disliked. This task had great boredom as I hung onto them and watched them munch on the grass.

Later I will address in more detail how my sisters and I, as children, were very important for manual work, to sustain ourselves and to maintain the existence of the whole family. Recollection of these early days relies mostly on my memory, with only a few photos to help, so different by comparison to what we have in abundance today. Quite early on, I was aware that we were a poor family, a condition which persisted into my teen years. Possibly the main reason for this was that we had a large family with five children.

My sisters and I rarely had any new clothing or shoes that had been purchased. For example, in my case, I received shoes about three to four times, and mainly hand me downs. My mother and later my sister could re-sew the used garments to fit. In addition, my mother spent the long winter evenings knitting wool gloves and full-length stockings. In the cold winters, I also wore a full fleece under garment, down to my feet, which was a lifesaver, not having had enough of any other warm clothing.

Our father did mostly farm work in spring and summer. He worked in the forest only in wintertime, cutting pulpwood, which brought some income. His health was impaired, having suffered pneumonia three times, which left some complications in his ability to breathe. He was also severely wounded in the leg, while fighting in the Italian Alps during the First World War, as part of the Austrian army. My mother was very conscientious and caring about his health and helped as much as she could.

From left: Marta, Mother, Drahus, me, Lidus, Father, and Anna

I had four sisters. The first born, was Marta, (I came next), then Anna, Lidus and finally Drahus. My youngest sister Drahus was born when I was five years old. I remember the event. It was at home. An older lady, a midwife came in with a black bag. My sisters and I were ushered into an adjacent room, where we waited all evening.

Later on, when we heard the baby cry, we were told that the "Stork" flew in and brought the new baby. This was a popular fairytale at the time.

m.a.

It is hard to imagine how my mother managed caring for our family, when in need of rest. I believe my older sister, Marta, who was about seven years old, did many of the chores along with our father. Our Aunt Anna, on my mother's side, came in to help with the washing.

As young children, we had to take care of ourselves when our folks were working in the fields. We played together, with Marta, being in charge. She had her hands full and was instructed to report anyone misbehaving, who would be spanked later, as a warning and deterrent.

I was the recipient of spanking a fair amount of the time, not because Marta squealed on me, but because if I played too rough with any of my sisters they cried long enough to mother, who came and would even-out the score. For the longest time, perhaps because I was the only boy in the family, and being somewhat stronger, more was expected of me in regards to behaving maturely and responsibly.

Our young lives in those days were quite primitive: a small house, living, sleeping and cooking mostly all in one room. The size was approximately 25 feet by 25 feet, which had a big Dutch oven built in with the cook stove, all wood fired which measured about 5 ½ feet by 7 feet. There were two adult beds, and a couple of other smaller sized beds. We made special arrangements for sleeping at various places.

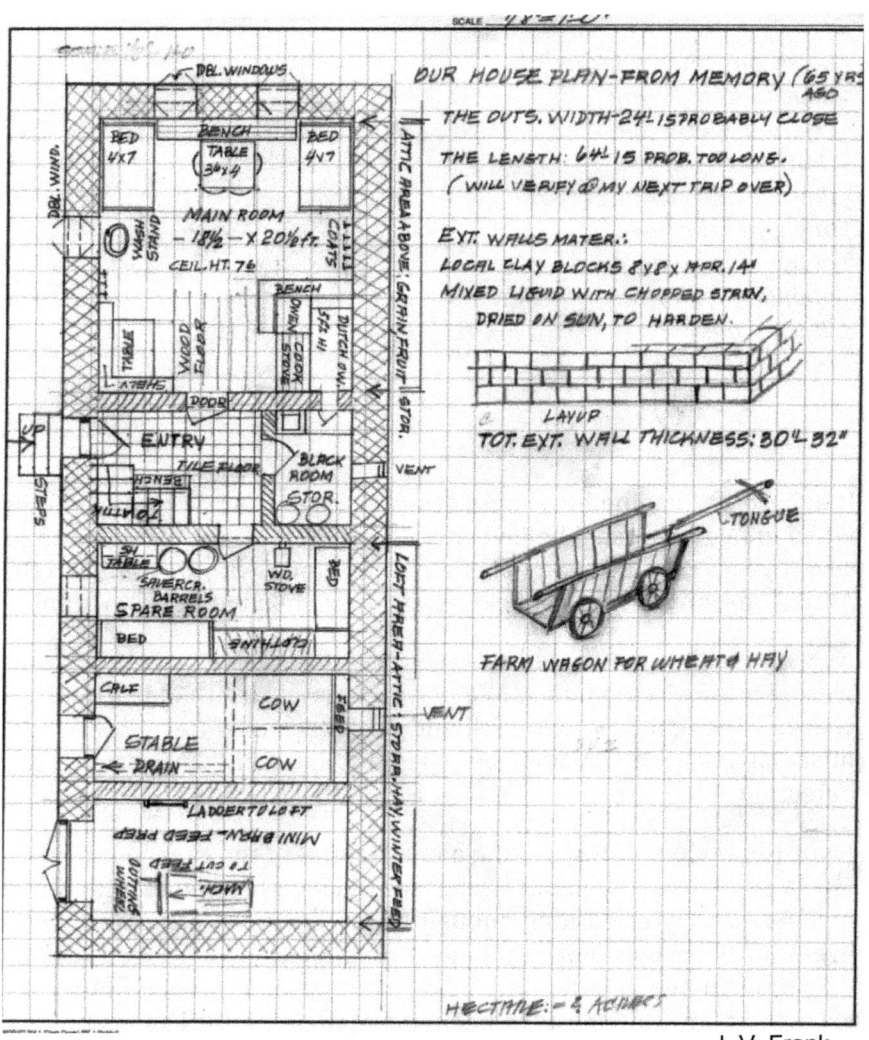

An approximation of the inside of our home.

At the head of the room there was a 3 by 4 foot family table with four chairs and a bench. There was a kerosene lamp hanging above for lighting. When we needed more light, like for reading and doing schoolwork, it was placed in the middle of the table on a pedestal.

In the evening, we usually lined up all around the table to read and do our homework.

There was no electricity, and we were quite happy, and no one complained.

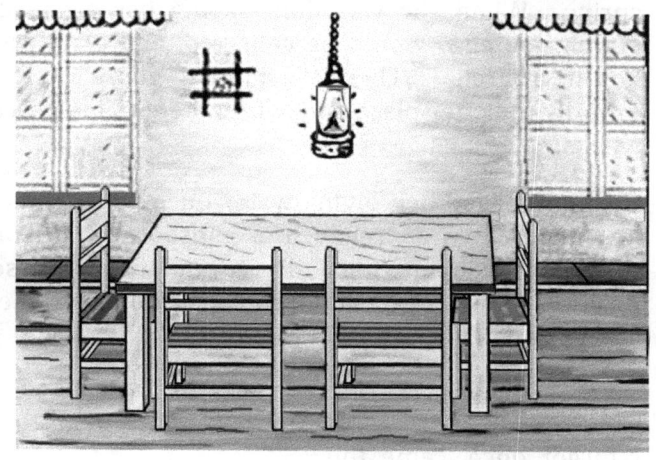

m.a

There were times when our entire family of seven ate the main dinner out of one big 20 inch bowl. The meal was usually non-liquid, such as dumplings with a generous sprinkling of ground poppy seed, with sugar and melted butter on top. We were seated around the table and we would begin eating from the edge of the bowl and we continued to the middle. I at times ate rapidly to reach the center, but my father would tap my spoon with his, a signal to slow down.

In addition, our father did woodworking in the same room, mostly in the winter and early spring during the day. He learned how to make wooden containers similar to wooden barrels from wood slats, which were slightly curved and held together with a riveted iron band. He made all sorts of sizes, mainly for carrying water and feed to cows and pigs. He also made huge vessels for farm use. This, he did outside, weather permitting. He worked hard until passing away in May of 1972.

I never will understand how he could do it, with only hand tools. I often helped him while putting these vessels and various containers together.

If that was not enough, we had a mother goose sitting in one corner on a large wicker pan with hay, on about twelve to sixteen eggs. We always had geese, and that meant another chore, which my sisters and I helped out with. The mother goose started laying eggs in early spring. When she was done laying her eggs, sometime by early March, the eggs would be collected, and arranged in the prepared box in a circle. Then, the mother goose came in the room and proudly took her place and sat on them. This process took about six weeks.

Our mother fed her, giving water once daily, and took her out to do her needs. When ready, the goose came up on the four steps, through the open door like a human, and assumed her sitting position. If any of us children came too close, she would hiss at us and peck us.

I forgot once, came too close, and got pecked from behind, quite painfully and I never came close again.

By early April, the beautiful little yellow geese hatched, one by one. The mother goose contained them under her. When they all hatched we made a small coral in the corner for the new family.

Goose in our back yard.

We put them in their little wooden house as the weather warmed by early April . It was one of the most beautiful sights of spring to see the small yellow chicks waddle around their mother on the fresh green grass. The shelter door was open and when cold they waddled all in line and huddled under their mother's wings to warm up.

This recreation of life was one reward in the country, perhaps compensating for all the hardships. The same joyful occasion came when the chickens hatched, and the baby rabbits were born, and the beautiful new calf took his place in our stable.

m.a.
New life of springtime

Chapter 2

Farm Life, Work and Play

As a young boy, I don't remember very many occasions of great joy, only going along with the simple flow of village life. A lot of my activities were spent outside, beginning with spring, and following through summer into fall, until the fall rains and cold weather set in. Usually spring started with some field plowing, wheat seeding, and potato planting, which were the main events, along with sugar beets, that later produced syrup lasting all winter.

I usually went along with my folks, in the farm wagon, which was pulled by two cows, hauling a plow and whatever equipment was needed for that day. Everyone wore wooden shoes, which my dad made in the winter months. They were sort of hollowed out from flat board, and curved according to the foot size. They were finished with a leather top nailed into the side for the foot to slip in. Work boots were a luxury, and used very rarely.

Many days in late April through May were still fairly cold, and I remember always being cold. The donated clothing was not always suited for the season.

Most fields were bordered by some hedges, and trees. My dad always made a fire, which I liked and gladly fed it.

m.a.

Potato planting I remember the most. First, I helped sort the potatoes, which were cut into ½ or ¼, each part having an eye or bud for sprouting. The cows pulled a plow, creating a series of open furrows where we placed the single potatoes, about 18 inches apart. I had a little child sized wicker basket and also helped with the work.

When all the seed potatoes were in, my dad plowed a furrow between the first ones, which pushed the dirt over the plants. Sugar beets were done about the same. The potatoes were really the most important, and precious item and were stored in an underground cellar, which gave the family most of it's subsistence.

Another job that I could do while very young was killing field mice when my dad plowed the field. Some years they were abundant. The plow exposed them. They ran and I walked behind with a blunt farm implement and hit them. Some I had to chase. We had a dog with us who also helped, but got tired of it if there were many.

Because our family was quite numerous, the older children had to take care of the younger ones during the day, while the folks worked in the fields. As I was growing up, I was left in charge, when my older sister Marta was in school. In early June, the weather warmed and the hay season started. We had two meadows, which my dad cut by hand with a special scythe.

The area was about three to four acres. My mother tried to help, but my dad insisted that he do it alone, to be cut just right. The fresh grass was spread, let dry and turned over once or twice a day to dry evenly before night.

It was raked into furrows, and scooped up into mounds of about four feet round by four to five feet high. The hay was raked on top, so if it rained it did not get soaked. On the second day it was again spread out, later turned over, put up again over night and by the third day, usually past noon, it was loaded heaped high onto a specially rigged wagon, and taken into our barn. When done, it provided a big part of the feed for the cattle all winter.

This season was real nice, being out on sunny days, but there were thunderstorms, which came suddenly out of the blue, with good showers. The folks worked so hard almost to exhaustion, raking and putting the hay into mounds, so it would not get wet. I remember if the hay was left lying on the ground and it rained for several days, it looked sort of bleached out, and would lose most of its nutritious value.

I usually went along to the meadows, which was a very beautiful time of year. On a few occasions, I had to guard my younger sister, a baby, often kept in a wicker basket, usually in the shadow under the trees. Once I vividly remember a frightening experience while guarding her. I noticed something crawling on the ground, close to the wicker basket, something I had never seen before. It was a snake, and it completely stunned me with fear.

I could not cry out to my folks, but recovered enough to run to them, coming in horror, making sounds and pointing in the direction of the baby. They understood and came running.

They moved the basket and everything was all right. Mother later said it was probably a viper snake, which was known to be there, and said they were most likely attracted to the baby's milk.

m.a.

A snake!

It took me some time to get over the shock. Later, when I would go out, I remembered to take a good stick along for that sort of occasion.

With the summer came warm days, and I and other children often wore only shorts, and went bare footed for all of that season. A happy time was to splash around in warm water in a good size wooden vessel my dad had made.

One day while splashing around with most of the family present, we got important company. My stepsister Marie came from Prague for a visit. She brought candy, and we were so overjoyed and performed all sorts of stunts.

Her name was Marie, and she was so nice, especially to the children, always bringing many nice things. She worked in Prague, and was situated real well. Her clothing and manners were completely noble to us. It was always so special to have her come.

She was a daughter from my father's first marriage, losing her mother in her early age to disease. She also brought certain items to the kitchen, changing our diet completely, away from mainly potatoes.

Once Marie wanted to make prune dumplings (prunes stuffed in round dumplings), but it was already late fall and no prunes were left. I was so determined to find some prunes that I walked for about half a day searching for some. Finally, I found a few in the next village, and got about two pockets full. The dumplings were made and served with fresh ground poppy seed and sprinkled with sugar and warm butter. All this happened so many years ago but I will never forget how special this dinner was.

Our summertime diet was supplemented by the food we found through foraging in the forest for berries, mushrooms and whatever it had to offer. Plus, home baked bread was always plentiful, being consumed rapidly while fresh with a very special aroma. Consumption only slowed down as the sixteen inch round loaves became harder. The bread lasted for about two weeks. Sometimes the last loaf was so hard it would have to be fed to the chickens or the hog.

Our mother also made small pretzels with caraway seed. These were so delicious, and they disappeared within two days. A special treat was fresh bread spread with freshly churned butter. One bi-product, which happened when the butter was being churned by hand, was sour cream, which accumulated in the top of the container. I would be given a slice of fresh bread with this delicious cream on top.

Memories from my very young life were of some carefree playing but many times associated with needed chores.

For example, my sisters and I spent many summer days at the public meadow plains, outside of our village, accompanying our flock of geese, about sixteen, on the average, in number.

m.a.

All of the children from the village had their own flock to watch. We were responsible for preventing the flocks from straying into the farmer's fields, which were unfenced. Many of these fields were planted with wheat, which was tempting to the geese. The flocks foraged on the meager grass all day. We normally had some lunch, a good slice of rye bread, sometimes smothered with butter, which was rather rare. We also had a glass jar of water with vinegar and a little sugar added. Our diet was supplemented with berries from the nearby woods, and some wild cherries.

We also sneaked into the nearest farmer's gardens. We climbed the fences to pick pears, cherries, apples, and whatever there was to eat. Our most favorite forbidden food were the fresh peas, which were always planted out of view some distance away, to keep us hungry kids from feeding on them. If one of us found the location of these fields, we would make expeditions there. One boy always had to be on the lookout, because the farmers would chase and whip us mercilessly if caught.

The girls, along with my sisters usually made dolls. They played with them and made wreathes of field flowers. We boys were mean to them sometimes. We would throw stones or mud on their nicely arranged displays. The girls fought back but we were bigger and stronger, so they sometimes started crying and we would then leave them alone.

One of our favorite places was at a creek that flowed through a pasture where we spent many hours building dams, even making a mill wheel, which turned with channeled water.

But picking other people's fruit was our passion.

There was an alley of cherries, a beautiful red color, but there was an old man on guard, and he was not sympathetic to our begging. Once we formed a plan to fool him. A few of us tried to talk to him, using his distraction while others picked like mad. When he became aware of our scheme, he chased us away from there with a big stick. For the duration of the season, we could not go near that old man again.

Fishing was also a favorite pastime. There were little minnows in the creek, and the bigger boys typically caught a bunch of them at a time. Then they fried the fish over a fire hanging from a wire. I was very young the first time I saw barbed fish cooked this way and remember how I wanted some to eat.

The boys obliged, cutting off the heads and tails, which I ate. I remember how they laughed, giving it to me, but I thought that they were happy to see me eat something that they had cooked.

m.a.

Of the many activities, and having long days to ourselves, we'd often build a cabin-shelter out of limbs and leafy tree branches, big enough for three or four of us to crawl in. This was always a major project, which made us very happy, especially when it rained. It kept us dry.

More about the raising of geese: So long as children were around to help, and there was something for the geese to forage, it didn't cost anything to keep them. They really gained weight in August after the wheat was harvested. After cutting the wheat, the farmers allowed us to pasture our flock, picking up the seeds, which had fallen on the ground during the harvest.

The geese had long necks, which also served them as a storage place for their food and this would really swell up by the evening when they were herded home. I also managed many times to pick up a big bouquet of seed-pods and gave them as a present to my mother, who would give me a big compliment for it.

Once I almost got into real trouble, injuring the gander by throwing a rock. It happened at the end of the day. After I had herded them into a pond, which they liked, they cleaned themselves, but then they didn't want to leave despite my efforts. As a final attempt I started throwing rocks close to them, to get them to move and somehow one bigger rock hit the gander in the head. His head dropped under the water and he became unconscious.

Horrified, I waded in, brought him out, and poured water on him. He came to slowly but his neck was noticeably curved. I waited for about a half to three fourths of an hour before he could walk home. I got home late. My mother noticed his uneasy wobble and crooked neck and wondered what had happened to him but did not ask me, to my relief, and I did not volunteer. The knowledge of that would have been a capital offence – whose consequences I did not want to face.

About mid summer, when the geese were real well rounded, our mother plucked all of their feathers, leaving them naked, except for their necks and wings. These plucked feathers were then washed, dried and saved for the long winter evenings, to remove the fine feathers from the stems, a very tedious process.

The finished product was saved in a dry place, to be used later for all the girls, when they were to become brides, as a part of their dowry. It would have been unthinkable in those times for a bride not to have a feather blanket. By the end of August, the geese would be sold to a buyer. I remember seeing a big truck with hundreds of geese on board. They all honked, as if to say good-bye. So it was a somewhat sad occasion to see them taken away, along with our carefree summer days.

Our mother promised us that we would get shoes for school time for our care and work, but it did not always happen when there were other more important needs, like food supplements, or bedding for the family, etcetera. This sale was a major source of income for the whole year and it was spread pretty thin.

Chapter 3

Wooden Shoes

If we didn't get shoes, we did not feel bad and understood the circumstances and besides, our dad could always supplement the foot ware by making us wooden slippers. Because we were one of the poor families, wearing these wooden clunkers was normal, while the better-situated kids had shoes.

This put us to a big disadvantage when running, which was often. Our school was three miles away. It was impossible to run in wooden shoes because the soles didn't bend and they would slip off.

m.a.

If we had to run we would carry them, one in each hand. If the ground was wet, it made our socks real dirty, which was a problem at home where we wore no slippers. Somewhat fortunate was that our socks had a good stiff bottom/sole, called the "devils hide".

I always tried to somehow clean this by scraping and washing the bottoms of my socks so it would not be noticeable. The folks would not have been sympathetic.

Now something about the cows: When the cows were not working in the fields, I had to take them to pasture. Most often, this would be at the common public meadow. Usually there were other boys and we often played soccer.

One time the cows strayed to the adjacent farmer's wheat fields, which could have been bad. If he had noticed it, the farmer could have demanded compensation, which my folks did not have. So I punished the cows and tied them by the neck to a stake, but they pulled it out.

My soccer game was disrupted to everyone's annoyance. I was so mad that I started beating the lead cow with the rope pretty severely. A local man came by and scolded me and slapped my face, and said, "You don't treat cattle this way!" I never did it again. This was normal protocol to teach a boy a lesson, even by physical means. Whatever wrongs were done were corrected on the spot, right then. My parents probably never even heard about it. The same method was used in school.

This kind of physical upbringing of boys was quite normal in those days. I remember another incident involving the same man, the one who corrected me for the cow abuse. My friend Tony and I, were at the public commons with geese, and this man met another man there, who was sort of a comical person.

Whatever he did or said was always funny to us, so we came close to them to listen, but this time he told a sad story about his mother dying. Even though it was serious, it still seemed funny the way he said it. He said, "I know she only mumbles nonsense," and we burst into laughter. Our village man turned around, slapped each of us pretty firmly, and said, "You should have respect, not to laugh at news about death." We certainly understood and left.

By late summer, with the fields harvested and the geese gone, we had more time to play, except we still had to take the cows to pasture. And at this time they were taken to our meadows to eat whatever new grass there was after the spring and summer harvest. The grass was fairly abundant so we didn't have to hang onto them.

Having time in the cooler weather, we made bonfires and cooked potatoes in the hot coals. They were usually all black, but good to eat.

It was always nice to be out, and we stayed out into the dark, with the fire going. There was a mystique about it. Someone always came up with some scary story. When I was very young I remember being frightened, and going home with my sister.

m.a

Often in the afternoons, when the older children came home from school, we played hide and seek. I being the youngest in my group of friends, always lost. We also flew kites on the hills and all sorts of paper airplanes. One game that we played was called the "Robin," which consisted of a one inch diameter by five inch long stick, pointed on each end, with a paddle about twelve inches long.

Taking turns, we were divided in two teams. One of us hit the pointed stick, and it jumped up and then we would hit it, which is about the same as baseball. The stick flew some distance, which we measured, striving for more distance, against the other team. But most popular was soccer, even if two boys got together, some sort of ball, even a tennis ball was found to kick.

By about the age of six years, I was introduced to a slingshot. This I really liked. The older boys showed me how to make one, consisting mainly of a forked limb, with a length of rubber. It was a lot of fun for us to go throughout the country in the fall time of the year. We really enjoyed target practice and hunting.

In the fall we brought in all the fruit. Apples were stored in the wheat bins, pears were cut and dried in home ovens, and our mother made marmalade for later use. Prunes were our favorite fruit, which were dried in special huts equipped for it. This smelled heavenly to us, but again there was an old man in attendance, and he was stingy. Once, my friend covered the chimney with a rock, filling the hut with smoke. The old man ran out to free it, and then we filled our pockets full. He was quite mad at us, and we had to avoid him for some time.

Our domain.

The country was our domain, along with our geese and cows. giving us that wonderful opportunity to be part of nature and enjoy all of its bounty. The fruit of summer was not bought and sold in stores. We only had the fruit from the fruit trees we grew, which were not many. Besides, always scouring the country and farmer's gardens was much more fun and exciting.

We were also given fruit, apples and walnuts by our church and school. In those days, every church had an adjoining parish house and a good size garden, usually well cared for, producing an abundance of food. We were given these treats mainly on religious holidays, like for St. Nicholas day, around Dec. 6th. Despite how generous the priest was, we still found a way to sneak into the garden during our noon recess on school days.

When the right time of the season approached, typically, I along with two other strong boys were selected by the priest to harvest the apples and walnuts. We were given fruit for our labor and really loved it. We were also invited to dinner with the priest in his beautifully decorated dining room. This was very special.

My exposure to the catholic faith was from an early age. This started with kneeling for prayers at bedtime, and giving thanks to our Lord. Our mother was very devout. Along with all the farm work and cooking, and caring for all of us, she still always found time to go to mass and pray for us, and we would dress up for Sunday and go to the church service with her.

Old family church in Nepomuk visited by my granddaughter Alyssa, and son David, in 2009.

My early exposure to music was also from attending the services at church. We had no radio at home, and were not inundated by the sound of music. In the gothic church when the organ played in company with two violins and the young girl's chorus, it was so overwhelming, and so heavenly, it could never ever be forgotten.

In later years, when I started violin lessons, the incredibly beautiful sounds of my early age in that church inspired me for all time. I often think now, in this modern age, how deprived our young children are, many times being exposed to the current vulgar sounds which border sometimes on animal behavior under stress.

Because of later efforts by the communists to bring about the extinction of the church and all its practices, I believe it is especially important to portray our upbringing of those early days. In grade school, we had one hour of catechism, taught by the priest. He was very dedicated to his faith and a good shepherd to his people. There were many church observed holidays, some very festive and glorious, like Easter & Christmas.

About mid June, one holiday celebration was the "Corpus Christy." I would like to describe its glory, from the limited perspective of a young boy: Several days before the event, beautiful altars were decorated with spring field flowers arranged artfully around pictures of saints and placed at several main entrances to the local farms. There was so much greenery, young birch boughs and flowers that the village became a natural wonderland. This was the best that nature had to offer. The church was also decorated in this spring time splendor, often with heavenly music playing.

Around the altar there stood a semi circle of young girls, perhaps as young as 3 to 4 years old, in their best colorful dresses, holding white wicker baskets with field flowers and wearing wreaths of flowers in their hair. The wreaths were also blessed. Later, when taken home each wreath would be placed on a religious picture until the next year's celebration. After more than half a century, I remember vividly these events, as possibly the perfect manifestation of an innocence and purity of life.

At a certain point of the service, the priest and his entourage of altar boys and flower girls walked outside to each of the altars, holding a sermon of blessing and giving thanks to our Lord. The attendance was overwhelming with people joining in from all around, including my mother and father.

My father was dressed in his best. This was only the second time of the year that he attended the church festivities. In the afternoon the adults attended a festive gathering at a local pub, in the presence of a brass band. My father was especially fond of meeting many of his friends, not having seen them all year, and now over a glass of beer.

Again, I would like to stress that my portrayal of this special holiday does not begin to cover the magnificence of this event. These memories remain the clearest among the many festivities of those early days.

In times past the influence of Christianity was an essential part of everyday life, even though not many people were as devout as our mother. In greeting each other, it was proper to say, "God bless you". The reply was something like, "God giveth this to us". When saying goodbye, the phrase would include, "I go with God". While working in the fields, the saying was, "May God help you". And the reply was again, "It's God's given".

There were many statues and small chapels all over the countryside. They were built to commemorate a loved one, who may have met a misfortune at a particular spot. When walking by or riding in the wagon, we always made a sign of the cross, and our mother would pay her special respects by kneeling on the stone stoop and say a prayer.

In later years, when I was an adult, and living with our young family in the U.S., in her correspondence, my mother always sent her prayers for God's blessings for all of us. It was most comforting to know we were being looked after and cared for by the divine power of the Almighty. After this many years, looking back, I believe that these blessings were, and are, obvious in all walks of life for all the members of our family.

The winter months brought a time of rest from the fields, which were covered with a beautiful blanket of snow, lasting from about mid December to mid March. The weather was usually very cold, so a lot of time was spent indoors. Our mother would spend many hours knitting wool socks and mittens for us, and mending or altering clothes for everyone. Since it was all second hand, it is hard to imagine clothing five children and two adults throughout the extremely cold winter months, and never buying anything new.

Whenever I received the freshly knitted socks or mittens, I was overjoyed. Lack of good warm clothing was always felt while walking to the next village, in open country, and it was usually windy. Sometimes, when I carried bottles of kerosene for our lamp, my hands would begin to freeze. By the time I'd get back home, my hands would be very painful, "screaming" in pain. The remedy was to submerge them in cool water to thaw out. Fortunately, I never had frostbite.

Another winter chore was cutting and chopping firewood for our wood stove. Our fuel for heat and cooking was taken from the nearby woods. Our father worked part time in the forest making pulp wood. As a by-product all the workers could take any wood scraps, slash, limbs and stumps. They also cut up sections of trees and hid them in the slash pile to be hauled home, usually on a sled in winter. When I grew up a bit and became stronger, I was part of the pulling power, along with my father. The forest owners were very tolerant of this practice, allowing people to take what they needed.

I remember the routine of our father coming home in early darkness; typically hauling a good chunk of tree on his shoulders. This wood would be split in sections, air dried and later used in making wooden containers for home water use and cattle feeding. Many days in winter I walked with my mother bringing lunch to him. This was usually a fresh cooked meal, including soup, kept warm. Packing cold meals was not done.

One time, while bringing my father his lunch, probably when I was about seven years old, I wanted to prove my strength. So, I told one of the men that I too was able to haul a hunk of wood home. He took me up on it, and said, "You select the wood, but you must not drop it or rest along the way, until you are home." If I agreed, he was to go with me and watch, and he did. I really suffered. My shoulder got all bruised up and it was very painful and twisted under the weight, but I made it. After this sort of crucifixion, I never tried to prove my strength like that again.

I helped our father perhaps every other day to cut and split firewood. Much of it was gnarled stumps with big roots, all twisted up which had to be cut, before it could be split up.

We used a bow saw, about 3 ½ feet long. I pulled one side of it, and he pulled the other. After working for about three hours we would get pretty warm. even though it was freezing many times. My dad once said smiling, "When cutting wood you get warm twice, once cutting, then when sitting by the fire."

Another chore in winter was to help feed our cows and the pig. The cow feed consisted of hay and wheat straw, stored in the attic and a barn. This was cut by a hand-operated machine with about a five-foot iron wheel, with two big cutters. Our dad fed the right mixture in, and I turned the wheel. I enjoyed spinning the big wheel.

I also hauled water out of our hand dug well. The well was about 18 to 20 feet deep and about 4 ½ feet around, and stone lined. It was covered by a wooden shed and a roof, with a heavy wooden bucket and an iron clap, held up by a chain. This would be pulled and rolled up on a round log with a crank on the end of it. The bucket had to be heavy so it would sink into the water when let down. To crank it up was quite hard when full of water. When at the top, one had to hold the crank with one hand, then reach in to grab the heavy bucket out.

A few times, not having enough strength, I let go and the full bucket went crashing down with the chain unrolling and the crank spinning wildly. It could have easily broken my arm. My mother warned me to be careful, and to let go of the bucket if unable to hang onto it so that I wouldn't go down with it. It was quite scary at times, until I got bigger. My mother's prayers and the guardian angel were surely with me.

The cows were housed in a nice warm stable adjoining our living quarters. Every day they had fresh straw or pine boughs for bedding, which had to be cleaned daily and then wheeled out to be dumped on a manure pile. I did not have to do this chore. A chore I did do was to sort out and chop the pine branches into foot long pieces, making kindling for the stove and cutting the boughs into small pieces to be used for the cows bedding. The pile was about six feet tall. It felt that this chore was endless, taking two to three hours. I hated to do this, but orders were firm: no play until it was done.

The pig was easy to care for. We fed him table food scraps and potatoes with some bran in water. Sometimes, I took the feed to him and remember how he indeed "ate like a pig", gobbling it all up in the shortest time possible. Mucking out the pig stall was done about once weekly, and was a dirty job, which I rarely had to do.

We often had a new calf born in the late fall. He was such a nice beautiful addition, very loveable, and I liked to take care of him, cleaning his stall and feeding him after the period of nursing. It always felt cruel, that we had to take him to the market, which was approximately by the end of March.

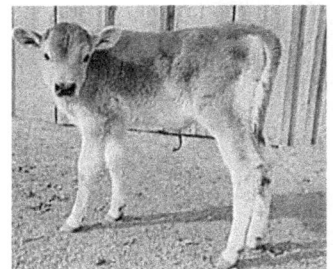

FSA

It was always an emotional time of parting with the calf, especially for my mother and sisters. I usually went along with my father for the trip to market, about 5½ miles. I had some sort of switch, and while walking behind him, prodded him along. It must have been real hard for him to walk this distance, especially since he had been cooped up all winter.

After selling him, we bought ourselves some ground horse-meat, mixed with heavy garlic and grilled. It was really good. Later, we went into the local pub, to have some strong beef soup and a beer. To my amazement, while recently visiting with my daughter Marta, son Davy and granddaughter Alyssa in this town pub, I recognized a painting on the wall, after about 66 years. We sat at the same table as I had in my early days.

This picture still hangs above the table where I sat with my father.

Another important chore in January, was plucking goose feathers. Having four girls in the family mandated that they must have feather blankets for their dowry. Usually, several neighbor women came to help. All the women would be sitting at a table, with the unplugged feathers in the middle, under the light of a kerosene lamp. They usually entertained themselves with someone reading a book of stories about country life or gossiping.

The men did not take part in this, so our dad usually read a book. Children also had to help. I disliked doing this for it was very tedious work. One had to take the feather by the tip and peel it off the feather from the stem, leaving the smallest amount on the stem, the waste.

I was constantly corrected by my mother, who told me not to leave too much waste. This task was also done during the day, which I hated because other kids were outside sledding and playing. My dislike for this work was so strong. And, one day, just as I expected, my mother gave me a pile to un-plug and said that when it was finished that I could then go out and play. The allotment would have taken several hours so I thought of a method to get done sooner.

Unseen, I stuffed a portion of feathers into my pockets, and went out to the outhouse to unload my pockets in the woodpile. Months later, while using the wood, the feathers flew all over. I got into trouble to have wasted something so precious, and could not repeat it the next season.

m.a.

We did manage to enjoy the winter, after completing the chores, usually sledding down low hills in the village. We could be out all evening, yet never really dressed for the cold, but being so lively and active, we were quite warm. I remember how our cheeks turned red.

There was a side road going up-hill on which we liked to sled. The snow and ice on it became thin, so we poured many buckets of water on it, and it would freeze over night. By the next day it was great. At the top of the road there were two houses. One place had milk cows, where folks carried the milk in buckets to a truck each day.

This one time a big lady was carrying two buckets and slipped on the ice and took a bad fall, spilling all the milk. We were reprimanded to have created such a hazard. Ashes were sprinkled all over the road to prevent it from being so slippery. After a few days, we came right back, poured water over the ashes and sledded again.

Many years later, my sons, Jimmy and Davy, enjoy the snow, like I did in my youth.

Chapter 4

From Winter to Spring and Easter

There was abundant snow on all the surrounding hills, and the kids liked to go skiing. Those who were more affluent had normal skis with slip-on bindings, which would have been a luxury for me, so I made my own. I used my dad's woodworking tools.

I found two boards about 4½ feet long, and smoothed the bottoms and on someone's advise, boiled one end in water and then bent it while hot in the crack of a stable door. The end was not good enough in some respects, but it was adequate to glide.

The shoe attachment was quite simple. I cut up an old leather belt, looped it around the tip of a shoe and nailed it with small shingle nails into the edges of the board. It was probably while running into hard snow that the leather belt tore off and I would take a spill. I remedied it by keeping a rock in my pocket with some shingle nails and simply reattached it. After it happened too many times, it was hard to fix, so I gave up skiing.

Once, I thought of making sort of a railroad using our wood sled. I piled snow on a mound, and made a curved runway and carved in a groove for one side of the sled runner. I poured water on it to freeze overnight. By the next day I was so proud to show it to my sisters, and took them for rides. They liked it and it was fun. The groove had to be repaired and reformed every day until the weather got warmer, with no freeze, which ended it.

One of the big events in those days was to butcher our hog. This was a welcome event, since we only had meat once a week if at all.

I recall, when he was led on a rope out of his stall, he really squealed in terror, probably sensitive to his fate.

tfi

My mother and sisters went into a corner of the room and buried their heads into a feather bed, not to hear his cries. The day of butchering the hog was real hard on my mother, who fed him daily.

After the cruel but necessary act, we had a feast. Sausages were made, and meat was placed in salted brine to later smoke for hams. One most important item was the lard. There was probably six to eight gallons of it, which was often generously served on a big slice of rye bread. This supply normally lasted until spring and was especially valued during the cold weather.

In addition to the pork products, we made our own pickled sauerkraut, using our own cabbage. It was grated on a special cutter, pickled in the fall of the year, and put in a 45 to 50 gallon wooden container. We did not have any other vegetables except carrots, which we stored in the cellar, lasting typically through January. This was a real good source of vitamins. The big container always had an abundance of juice, used as the only remedy for all sorts of ailments, such as an upset stomach.

When the ham was cured and smoked it was hung in the attic. It was really good and I snuck in often, cutting a chunk of it. By having this sudden abundance of meat and sausages, we were generous to our relations in Prague, often my uncle, his family, one aunt, and our stepsister with her family.

My folks certainly reciprocated for the generosity of our relatives to our poor family, such as the welcomed packages of Christmas treats. And, as I grew older, probably about eight years old, I could travel on trains. I would take gifts to them, and remember being treated like royalty upon my arrival.

Winter and its snow kept its grip into about mid March, with longer days and some sun which was now warmer. The awakening of nature and our activities in anticipation of spring was really noticeable. This was the biggest contrast of any season of the year.

In preparation for the Easter celebration, it was traditional to cut twigs of pussy willows and other hedges to keep inside for about six weeks, in the water in which they sprouted and leafed out. By about the end of February I often walked in snow in the country to find the most prized species.

Aside from normal church services there was a pilgrimage made to a shrine in the woods, commemorating St. Vojtech. He was a Catholic bishop martyred at the end of the 10th century. He supposedly traveled through our region, leaving distinct footprints in the rock. There was a quaint little chapel where a catholic service was held every year.

On the anniversary of St. Vojtech's death, we walked about five to six miles to the shrine, usually having some sun, with somewhat a warmer day. There were concession stands, and merry-go-rounds, in a circus like atmosphere. My sisters and I were usually given some coins for some of the rides. Again, the folks enjoyed meeting each other, after a long period of winter. It was an occasion we would have never missed.

With nature awakening, snow mostly gone, there was work to be done in the fields. In early April, we had to go to certain fields where clover or alfalfa was to be planted, and had to pick the abundant rocks off the surface.

The reason given was that the crop had to be cut with a hand scythe, which would have been hard with rocks present. This was really hard work, using pointed short sticks to dislodge the rocks, putting them in a wicker basket and then carrying it to a pile, to an unused part of the field. Sometimes the wheat crop had to be reseeded, if it did not germinate, due to bad weather conditions.

Potato planting was next. Fields had to be not too wet to plow the furrows and close them. I helped always, first quartering the potatoes, with each portion needing to have an "eye" spot that sprouted. To plant, we walked along open furrows carrying a basket with cut potatoes, and while bending down, we placed them about 18 inches apart.

When all seeds were in, our dad came with a plow that was rigged specifically to push the soil on top. Potato planting was of a major concern to be completed and difficult sometimes in the spring and fickle weather. If there were prolonged rains delaying the plowing, perhaps the growth season would have been short, creating a serious shortage in almost every day consumption.

As the time rolled through the end of March, close to Easter, nature's awakening and the full glory of spring was evident. Walking between villages through open farm country, the transformation of field and meadow colors was spectacular.

From bleak browns to fresh greens was a great joy to see, especially when the occasional sun came out, magnifying all of God's creation. It has remained in my memory, this joy and happiness, being warmed up by the first sunrays of spring. Even with the lack of adequate clothing, the persistent chill seemed to disappear.

At home, our baby geese were growing. They were corralled inside in the corner of the room. The chickens had their young ones outside in the chicken coup. We also had rabbits born by this time, which were my duty to take care of. I gave them water, hay, and a little grain, when they were nursing about twelve to fourteen young ones. I remember how clever and skilled the mother rabbit was, creating such a nice cozy pocket of hay for them to be warm. In the corner of our room, my pussy willows and various twigs were blooming and leafing out with everything pointing to Easter.

There were traditions associated with this holiday of spring, which we really enjoyed. One tradition started on Thursday. All the boys marched in formation with the oldest boy being in charge, making noise, using a special crank operated contraption with a toothed roller, and a thin wood blade, jumping between the teeth when rolled making a racket. We loved it, making sure it was heard at every house. The reason was that the church bells quit ringing and had been flown to Rome, so we substituted this way, announcing the morning, noon and evening hours. It was done on Green Thursday, Good Friday, and the day of Resurrection on Saturday morning.

As a reward for our services, we were usually given eggs, and sometimes a piece of ham after the Saturday march. We usually made a bonfire in the country and cooked the eggs, fried the ham, and really enjoyed the feast. There was much light everywhere. It was truly a serene and glorious celebration. On Saturday evening we went to church to celebrate the Resurrection. There was the traditional wonderful and heavenly music mixed with the sight of fresh decorations of birch and other tree boughs.

The holiday's tradition included baking special sweet bread with raisons and almonds. We also decorated our eggs using onion skin. Coming home, we ate the sweet bread for the first time, and drank tea with rum.

On Easter Sunday, our mother prepared everything for the big dinner in the early morning hours, to be able to attend the main big mass. We walked over three miles each way.

I carried the sprouted pussy willows and leafed out branches with colorful ribbons with me which were blessed and sprinkled with holy water. Going home, I visited many farms and families, giving them about three branches each. They placed these branches in their fields, and because they had been blessed, it was believed that the fields would have a bountiful harvest.

kw

As a reward, we were given colored eggs and other holiday treats. On Easter Sunday, there was bounty everywhere. This was one of very few such lavish times. We'd have a big noon meal of roasted pork or ham with sauerkraut and dumplings (Given the rare freedom to eat so much, I remember actually over eating once). The rest of the day was spent enjoying the company of relatives, who also sometimes brought some tasty surprises.

In those early years our family and many others were self-sustaining with food, milk and whatever was raised. During periods that our cows did not give milk, we never bought it, but would go to the next village to our relations to get it, if possible. We had mainly two supply sources: my mother's birth place in Myt, where her sister Anna and brother Vaclav lived, about six miles away, and Lounova, where another sister, Frances lived, about five miles away.

I went with my mother to Myt very early on, bringing fresh bread in exchange for milk if they had any, or for any other exchanges, whatever they had. My mother's brother, my Uncle Vaclav, was also my godfather and was relatively affluent, being engaged in the craft of wagon making.

He was very skilled, making wooden wagons, wheels with wooden spokes, skis and other things. They had a large garden with many fruit trees, and about sixteen to eighteen hives of bees. But he was very stingy, rarely giving us some honey, and maybe some fruit when in season.

They had one son, who was about the same age as me, whom I played with when visiting. He was quite spoiled and had many toys that I wouldn't even dream of. He was also stingy and was usually not willing to share anything with me. He had a working train with tracks, which I really liked. Once when he was in a cheerful mood, he gave me one car to take home. I later made my own railroad tracks out of wood and spent a lot of time playing with it.

My Aunt Anna, was just the opposite, very generous, and was really nice to us. Her husband worked steady on the railroad, so they were fairly well to do, compared to us. She often gave me a little change to buy candy, which was quite special. Usually when I came home, my sisters flocked to me in anticipation of the gifts of candy to be shared.

Being little, the trip with my mother seemed real long and almost without end.

We walked through a forest, which was a shortcut with all sorts of pathways, and trails. We crossed over wood fencing (containing wild game).

The scariest part was when we crossed over a river on a log bridge, made of two logs side by side with a flimsy hand rail. The river was pretty wild, looking very dark, deep and with a rushing current.

m.a.

The first time, I didn't want to cross. My mother kept reassuring me that it would be all right and asked me to walk slowly in front of her, with one of her arms resting on my shoulder. I was totally petrified, and still remember that while in the middle of crossing, severe freight overtook me and I could hardly move. How we got across, I don't remember. Later, as I crossed this way many times on my own, I admired her bravery and care.

There was another route to take using normal roads, but it was probably two miles longer. Sometimes, by the time we would be walking home, it would already be late and would be getting dark, and I think that my mother was a little frightened walking through the darkening woods. It is possible that even as little as I was, my presence provided some feeling of security for her. I can still remember how she kept talking to me while we walked.

Having made quite a few trips with my mother, by the time that I was about six years of age, I went there on my own. I was asked to take the long way but I chose to cross through the woods, finding my way. When arriving at my aunt's, she was a little amazed at my courage and complimented me.

She had a heart of gold, and liked to bake. I still remember her "kolace" (Czech, for a dough that is sort of like a pizza dough, with prunes on top and sprinkled with ground poppy seed and sugar). I loved it. Everyone there made the same thing, but hers was the best.

Her supply and source of milk was from two or three goats. I of course always took the milk home, but I never liked it, even if there was nothing else to drink. We added this milk in the morning coffee (fried wheat with chicory), and when used also for other cooking needs was more tolerable.

After this visit with Aunt Anna, she urged me to take the long road home, but I thought that I would save time by taking the short way instead, and went through the woods. Darkness in the woods is denser somehow, and it was a little scary. I also missed my trail, and had to back track, losing more time. Finally, I came home in complete darkness.

To my surprise, Aunt Anna was there, having taken a train and getting there much sooner. Probably suspecting that I would go through the woods, she worried and became so concerned for my safety that she had to make sure I got home.

Even though I got mildly scolded for not taking the better route, there was a huge relief by everyone that I got home safely. I now know that my dear guardian angel was with me all the way.

As part of our family's existence, there was the trekking over to my Aunt Frances' home, which included the exchange of bread, milk and sometimes flour. This route was also across some woods, but on forest roads, more defined, and was only about four to five miles. This aunt was nice, but her husband had sort of a gruff nature, which I thought was unfriendly, but later got to know him better and understood him.

By about the age of eight years old, I had learned in school how to graft fruit trees. He had about six wild apple trees, which he mentioned to me and I offered to graft them. He didn't have much confidence, since someone else had tried it before, but got the grafts and supplies and I did it. He was beside himself, and praised me, saying how handy I was. A few weeks later, the grafts took, and sprouted.

When I came in after that, I was his favorite boy. Up until that time, this was the most satisfying and rewarding experience of my life. After about 22 years when visiting this place again, the trees still produced fruit. It gave me a big sense of gratitude, touching the trees that I'd given a fruitful long life to.

Yet, there is tragedy that overtook this Heidelberg family. They met the cruelest fate when their four children's lives were taken by the Nazis. The youngest and first to die, was shot by the Gestapo shortly after he was taken. My other three cousins survived for about ten months in the concentration camps before they each perished.

Marie, Jan, Josef, and Stan Heidelberg

Their father, my uncle, was also imprisoned, but was later released so that he could go back to work on the farm. He came home a broken man. I remember visiting them after that tragedy, seeing this previously robust and positive man, now so hollow, who spent all the rest of his time in grief until he died.

Our Aunt Frances was so affected by the loss of all of her children, that she became withdrawn and uncommunicative with everyone, only seeking peace and seclusion. When her husband, our uncle, was also taken away, she had been left alone.

She had a heart ailment and could not do any of the small farm chores, especially carry water and feed the cows. This was also felt deeply by our mother who had helped raise these children with her aunt while they were very young.

I believe the neighbors helped her until our mother's resolution to send my older sister, Marta, to live with her and take care of the household, along with the farm chores. I am sure it was not Marta's choice since she was about thirteen years old, and still had to finish the final year of school.

I remember going with her to Lounova and helping her carry her belongings. She was sad, and did not say much, just quietly accepting her new role as a housekeeper. As I left her to return home, I remember the sadness in my heart, and that I promised to come and visit as much as possible. It is hard to imagine a girl at that age, being the sole housekeeper, and responsible for the caring of our aunt.

The cows had to be fed daily and watered. This house did not have a well, only a surface water pond, which dried up in summer. So, all water had to be carried from the neighbor's well, which was about 300 to 400 feet away. Poor Marta, she was only average in stature, and certainly not strong enough for such a burden.

While visiting them, I hardly ever saw my aunt, who was in seclusion. Marta was also notably reserved, certainly not a happy and open-minded young girl. Becoming an adult with all of the responsibilities at that young age left its mark. When our uncle returned from prison, her situation did not improve, even though he was able to care for himself, and do some chores. But the loss of his children weighed on him so much that he was apathetic to his surroundings.

Perhaps a brief respite came after some time, when our Aunt Betty came to live there, from Prague. She was very well to do, and had worked as a secretary. She was very bright with a wonderful disposition, making the household more bearable. But being well past 60 years, which was old in those days, she had to go into a rest home, a sad occasion for Marta. This sadness stayed with Marta, and remained as part of a personality trait into adulthood. She got married and had two sons. Her husband was employed as a blacksmith. She herself eventually worked at the collective farms.

When visiting her many years later, I always found her to be much more negative minded. This was a big contrast to my other three sisters. By the time Marta was 72 years old, retired, and a widow, she moved into a rest home, where she died at age 82. These are some painful recollections, but also part of an acknowledgement to honor a sister's life, as seen by her brother.

An abandoned collective farm

Note: Prior to 1948, before the communist takeover, all land was privately owned. Many fields of various sizes and kinds were predominant and looked like a colorful mosaic. It was a joy to see from late spring to early fall. However, after the takeover, thousands of farms were taken and were replaced by large scale collectives, with much less variety and lack of individual choice available. After the confiscation of land and livestock, farm equipment was brought in from Russia.

In later years, when visiting my homeland, I was sad to see that the beauty of the small fields has never returned. This criminal transformation of the land is most obvious when entering the Czech Republic from Germany and Austria.

The awakening of spring was darkened by the rain in April. Sometimes all of the streams and the creeks overflowed. When we were children, to busy ourselves, we made wooden ships or little boats made out of thick tree bark, which we floated and would have to run fast, to keep up with the swift stream. Our wooden soled slippers often made it a little hard to catch and retrieve the boats. Some would get away from us.

Also, I helped my dad make birdhouses, which we would put on trees for the robins. I remember how much jabbering those birds made. Our dad was busy, making wooden buckets of all sorts, and wooden slippers for us. This used to be a trade of its own. He was very skilled and had learned this from an old neighbor who had given him the necessary tools.

He undertook even the making of big vessels, about thirty inches around by seven feet long. He had no power machines and did it all by hand, splitting the boards from a log and shaping them. At times, I helped him with the assembly. And, later as I became involved in the woodworking trade, it became even more amazing and unbelievable to me, how he could accomplish what he did.

If the rainy season persisted, it created a real problem to feed the cows, since the winter supply of hay and soft straw was exhausted. The saturated ground made it difficult to pasture the cows outdoors.

Our mother would cut some grass at the edge of the forest, which survived the winter. It was coarse and had to be fine cut and mixed with something else, so the cows would eat it. Usually, hauling feed, like clover later on, was done by use of a single wheeled cart. There were times that the cart was not easily accessible so she hauled it in a big wicker basket on her back.

I often went with her and helped with the cutting and pushing of the heavy loaded basket.

m.a.

By age 84, my mother had to have an operation for a hip replacement. She was a very hard worker, incredibly strong, and lived until her 96th year.

Above: I am visiting my mother with my wife Marta in 1974.
Below: My mother with Marta and our daughter Marta Ellen.

Chapter 5

Education and Health

Here's more about the history of my early school years. Our grade school was at the adjacent village, Cizkov, about three miles from home.

Attendance was from about 8:30 a.m. to about 3 p.m., with one hour for lunch, Monday through Friday, with half a day on Saturday. Starting at six years of age, the walk was quite long, but always being in the group with my sisters and other children, sort of fooling around, we managed.

The school was about 200 years old, two stories, and had three classrooms, and living quarters for the principal on the ground floor. I don't remember how they divided the students to be able to teach each group separately, but vaguely remember that we were seated separately and grouped by grades.

The teacher outlined the daily subject to a group, and gave them an assignment to write or read, then she would attend to the next group.

My old grade school.

These are the same steps in the same building.

It is now used as a day care through kindergarten school.

The biggest classroom held three grades, a seemingly impossible task. They probably lumped the subjects together. The discipline was very strict, with corporal punishment quite common. If a child acted hazy or not quite awake, getting one's face slapped would quickly bring them to attention.

Probably to compensate for the lack of classrooms, we were given a lot of homework. Our teachers were usually young ladies, from Plzen or the vicinity. They tried hard to control us, mischievous country boys. One of their goals was to teach us to use a proper language and not the dialect of our region. Some words were quite slanted or totally different.

The teacher would sometimes make us write the proper word one hundred times within a sentence as homework, which consumed the biggest part of our evening. I recall one time when the teacher was correcting a boy to say a word properly. After repeating it three times, he still said it wrong. She then slapped his face and walked away.

A good portion of the time we spent singing country folk songs, which we really liked. By the fourth grade, while under the German occupation, we sang a lot of German songs, in the German language, including the die-hard Nazi songs.

These were sung on a daily basis, and so diligently, that even after seventy years, I still remember two songs perfectly. About twice a week we walked into the country to learn about nature's wonders.

We were also taught the Catholic religion by the local priest once a week, who did his best to imprint the church's Christian doctrine. He was very sincere, doing his utmost, but the school was state run with some past history of conflicts with the church, which gave us some contrary view points, often directly opposed to it's teachings. Despite it all, we received a good Catholic upbringing and attended the church with all of its rites.

I and the other boys did our share of mischief, especially during noon recess. Our lunch usually consisted of a big slice of homemade rye bread, occasionally smeared with butter or lard. By early fall season, we often scoured the countryside, looking for ripe fruit, or just went wandering around.

Once, we got into trouble while we were playing hard and jumping from bench to bench in our classroom. Our principle stormed in with a stick and really gave us a good whipping. He was really mad.

We later found out that chunks of plaster had fallen off of his ceiling, right on his dinner table, which was right under our class room. As per the norm of those times, he dealt with the problem right there on the spot and no more was said or done.

In early December, on about the sixth of the month, there was a traditional holiday, "St. Nicolas" day, a Catholic saint, who was associated with charity. Gifts were exchanged among children, similar to how Christmas is celebrated in the USA. We exchanged small things, but the big present was the gift of walnuts and apples by the priest. The amount was quite generous and was loved by all.

m.a.

"St. Nicolas" was dressed as a white bearded bishop, and was accompanied by an angel with wings, and a black devil with a tail and horns on his head – ferocious.

Traditionally, the angel pointed out who the good children were. St. Nicholas had gifts to give. But, if a child had a bad history and was pointed out, the devil would spank him, with a braided switch. I was never exactly a saint and had my encounters with the devil a few times.

Some of the bigger boys in the eighth grade were quite rowdy and used this to cause trouble. Once someone gave a gift to a girl which was a box containing two mice. When she opened it she started to scream. The mice jumped out and ran under the benches. All the girls were screaming, and it was a pandemonium.

No one admitted to the act of course, but the teacher sort of knew. Another time, some boys sent a box to a girl, containing wet sand from the creek. Somehow, it did not soak through the box, until St. Nick presented it and it came all apart, with wet sand all over.

At this time of year, the weather turned colder with freezing conditions, and we enjoyed ourselves on the icy roads and ponds. One of the subjects we had been taught, was about grafting fruit trees, as previously mentioned. I learned so well about grafting, for not only my uncle, but also at home grafting two apple trees and a cherry tree in front of our house.

The trees that I grafted grew for several decades.

By about my second grade, there was a big distribution/delivery of apples from America, as some sort of gift. Each of us got a certain amount, but I mostly remember how big they were with real nice color. Our local apples did not compare to those. Another time, a shipment of cocoa came from America. This was cooked in big kettles with milk and I did not like it. Even though being told how special it was, coming from far away.

Generally the grade school education was adequate and sufficient for normal life. What we missed the most though was the history of our own country, which stretches back to the sixth century. A deciding factor most likely was the German influence during the war years (my third to eighth grade).

Their plans for our country was to be Germanized, and/or assimilated at best, so any history was of no value to them. We had classes in the German language with a good portion of their history included. As some compensation for our knowledge of history, we read history books, during our long winter evenings at home and learned some basics.

My graduation from school in early June of 1944 was preceded by one major event in European history which was the Allied Invasion of France. About June sixth, our principal gathered us around a big map of Europe, and pointed to Normandy in France. He explained that the Allied American Forces have landed, and that it will profoundly alter the course of the war. We all shared his enthusiasm.

Walking from place to place was part of everyday life. Plus, there were many excellent opportunities for running and racing each other when in groups. In spring and summer, we were barefooted and quite mobile but this presented some problems, such as stepping on bees in the meadow, and being stung, or stepping on thorns, which stuck into the foot. Once I stepped on an ugly frog, which was horrible. I jumped about five feet high. I avoided that spot for some time afterwards.

When I was about six years old, I walked with my mother to town, which was about five miles away, and had a new pair of shoes, a very rare commodity, and probably purchased from the geese sale, for school.

I was asked not to wear them, and to put them across my shoulder and walk barefooted until we approached the town. Then I put them on, for walking through town, and repeated the same routine when returning home, so as not to wear the shoes out. Upon my old country visits to this town, Nepomuk, where one of my sisters lives currently with her family, I could still remember about the spot for shoeing up. During our recent visit, in 2009, with Marta, Alyssa and Davy, I pointed out this spot with an explanation.

Walking between villages through the open country in summer, there were dangerous thunderstorms, which came real sudden like. Once, I walked with my sister from our aunt's place through the forest and a storm came upon us. It was at the dusk time of day, and semi dark. The lightening lit up everything white, the thunder was real loud, and resonated throughout the forest. We thought it was the end of our lives!

Another time that I will never forget, is when I walked in the early evening from Cizkov, three miles away from home. A powerful storm came. I was in the middle of the road, when everything around me lit up, blinding white light, one flash after another, with extremely loud thunder.

m.a.

I could not move. I stood in the middle of the road screaming, until it let up. There were telephone and power poles, also trees which were probably struck, close to me. I remember all the power poles had lightning rods attached. We were taught in school to never go under a tree during a storm and to crouch down, or to lay on the ground.

In those days most of my travelling was by foot. Some affluent people had bicycles, but they were not geared for going up hills, making them marginally practical. There were also some cars, mainly trucks, belonging to folks in town. My first ride in a car was at about age seven, while walking from school through snow slush on the road. On the way home a villager asked if we wanted a ride. We were wet and cold, and the car was warm and we were overjoyed, except the ride ended abruptly after about two miles.

About the best way to travel in winter, when snowed under was by a horse pulled sled, used by farmers. They always let us hop on. It was pure joy, so quiet and smooth. Only the sound of the bells that were attached to the horse's heads were heard.

There was always a need to bring vegetables from our field, (and rarely from the store) about half a mile away on a daily basis. Our mother would never ask us to walk over there, but always "run over" and I did. Our vegetable field was about over a quarter mile away, accessible by a narrow trail through the meadows. I remember running as fast as I could without a care or worry.

In our modern world, much emphasis is given to physical exercise, which we had a full measure of. Yet, healthy nutrition, we did not always have, with perhaps the exception of summer time. Typically, meat was only eaten once a week, and rarely purchased, having our rabbits, or one of the chickens, if she was too old for laying eggs.

In winter, the main source of vitamins and minerals was limited to the use of apples, which lasted until about mid January, along with carrots, being stored in the root cellar. The main staples that we used were: potatoes, meat with lard from our hog, and sauerkraut, which was stored in fifty gallon wooden containers. We were encouraged to drink the kraut juice, for all sorts of ailments. Despite the shortcomings, we grew up quite healthy, owing to constant exercise. I think the meaning of the word obesity did not exist in those days, especially among children.

Winter time did bring its portion of child ailments, like the colds, and tonsillitis which was probably contagious when accompanied with a fever. The home remedies were: soaking one's feet in hot water, inducing perspiration, and massaging the back, rubbing by our mother. When necessary we laid on the floor and she pushed and worked on all the muscles. The main thing that I remember was that my rib cage felt that it was about flat, after this treatment, and at that time did not know how effective it was.

My favorite cure was to lie on top of the Dutch oven, in the corner of our family room. It was quite warm, after the baking of bread, every ten days or so, and the oven bricks stayed warm for two days.

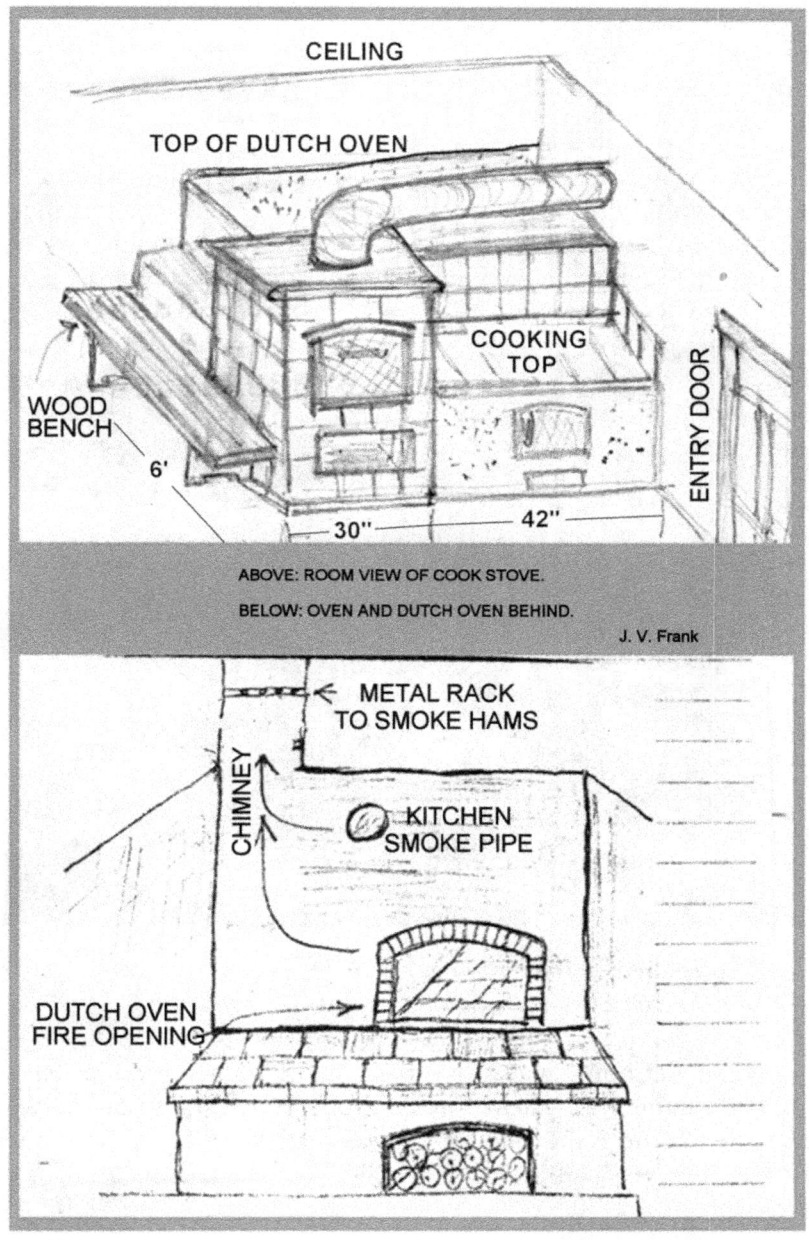

ABOVE: ROOM VIEW OF COOK STOVE.

BELOW: OVEN AND DUTCH OVEN BEHIND.

J. V. Frank

Recouping on top of the Dutch oven for about one day and night helped a lot. Our mother also made a sort of pancake from rye dough, with a good portion of ground horseradish mixed in. This was placed on the chest overnight and wrapped warm.

The folk's belief was that it drew any infection out. Our father had many episodes of chest ailments, having had pneumonia several times, and this remedy seemed to keep him going.

Tonsillitis was much more miserable, taking more time to cure. We had to gargle salt water, or some sort of purple solution. Our mother was very caring, knowing if a high fever came, it could be strep. I only saw the doctor once while my father was being treated.

Today, the main room is no longer heated only with wood. Plus in-door plumbing has been added.

Our hygiene at home was in big contrast by today's standards. One important habit was that we washed our feet in warm or hot water before bed time, especially in summer when walking barefoot so much.

We bathed once a week on Saturday, in a big wooden trough about the size of a big bathtub, using heated water and soap. The smallest child was first, followed by all the rest by age. I don't remember how clean the water was when I got in, but it seemed o.k. We washed our hands before meals in the washbowl.

There was a serious lack of health care regarding how we took care of our teeth, with hardly any care given at all. Even though we were given tooth brushes from some of our urban relatives, no one at home seemed to care. As a consequence, we developed tooth decay, and bad tooth aches. Sometimes these toothaches would last until the tooth probably died. The only time that we went to a dentist was to pull out a bad tooth.

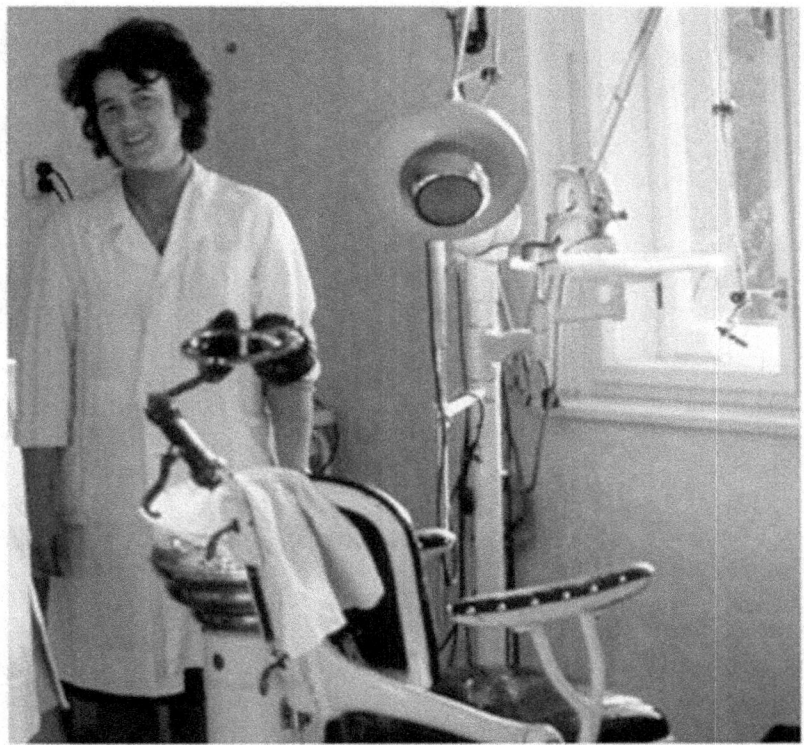

My sister Drahus, later went to work in the dental field.

There was no insurance to cover any care, and to pay for it was out of the question. Lack of the right vitamins in winter probably played a big roll in our dental health as well.

When I was about thirteen years old, I made my first trip to the dentist in town. After all the pain I had been going through, I thought it would be a saving grace to go and have the bad tooth pulled. I didn't know that no anesthesia would be used when extracting the tooth. In our case, probably due to lack of money I was given none.

What followed, I do not want to describe, remembering the occasion as being barbaric. Going through this, I can't understand being left all alone, and having to walk home for about five miles.

Another major episode of health that happened to me, was scarlet fever. This was a most serious disease that children died from and I was nine or ten years old. I was unconscious for about seven days with a real high fever. It was the worst type of a delirious nightmare in my memory. The remedy included placing cool packs on my forehead and arms, and my mother's prayers. I know my life was hanging in the balance.

The doctor was never called perhaps a cure without antibiotics did not exist. Being so close to death, I believe, it was by a special grace of God that I survived. After seven days, with the fever subsiding, I sat up, but couldn't stand up. Slowly, I recovered, with good nutrition, though my heart did sustain some damage, which doctors sometimes still detect. My mother and sisters, except for Anna, were blessed by good health during their formative years.

When Anna was about twelve years old, she began to have severe pain in her right abdomen. I remember she really suffered one whole day and night, with the pain becoming more intense. Sensing that it was something serious, our mother asked me to run to Nepomuk to get the doctor. There were no telephones close enough to call from.

Knowing how urgent it was, I ran as fast as I could. Coming to Nepomuk, it occurred to me that getting the doctor would not be good enough, and that she needed to get to the hospital quickly. So, I found a telephone and called an ambulance. They promised to go immediately. This was the first time that I had ever used a telephone.

By the time I got back home, my father had already accompanied my sister to the hospital in Plzen. The next day we learned that Anna had a burst appendix, and it was infected. They operated, but the infection was a real problem. In those days there was no penicillin or any wonder drugs yet available. She was kept at the hospital for three weeks to cure this infection.

We were also told that if we had waited another day that she would not have survived. Thinking back, I wonder what made me call an ambulance, instead of having the doctor go to our home? If he had, it would have prolonged her suffering, or maybe worse. Several years later, whenever we visited each other, we knew that we had a special bond, always feeling the blessing which had saved her life.

Chapter 6

Toys and Tasks

With the onset of fall and the slowly approaching winter, I would like to portray the activities of my friends and my childhood era during the seasonal idle times. Most of our outdoor activities were not practical now, due to the weather, and all of our houses were too small to play any games in, so what was there to do? One of us had a bright idea, to create a puppet show, emulating the productions that visited our village from time to time. It was perhaps one of the most enthusiastic endeavors of our time.

We made the puppet stage, drawing and coloring the various fairytale scenes, and copying pictures from children's books with these stories. We particularly loved drawing the castles with motes.
To make the puppets, we took various sizes of plastic dolls, the hollow ones, and split them in half. Then we waxed the inside and poured in plaster of paris, and closed the forms. We painted the dry figures, adding mustaches and beards to some and adding horns to the devil. All of the girls were busy sewing costumes of all sorts, again using pictures from books for ideas. We all had our jobs to do, and were quite serious with our tasks.

m.a.

Kings and queens had their ornate attire with tiaras on their heads. I think we had an instructive booklet, showing us how to attach the strings to each body limb, so it could be manipulated to wave its arms, walk, sit, and do whatever was needed.

After much practice, we put on a performance for the local kids, using mostly fairytales and stories, which someone had bought in Plzen. All the kids loved it, and we thought we would eventually charge for admission, and even go to other villages to perform.

After playing all the written plays that we had, we asked one of the boy's father, who worked in Plzen, to buy us some other stories, which he did. These were entirely different from the previous ones.

While rehearsing, we noticed that the direction and slant of each play was totally anti-Jewish, anti-Semitic, even though it had comical portions, we knew it was not what we wanted to be doing.

Some puppets used by others today.

I still remember the names like, "Klein" and "Levis" and they all had long noses, beards, and their dealings were remarkably shady. After a few performances, similar in motif, and lacking any appeal to a child, we went back to the old ones. We maintained this show on and off, but there were not enough kids to continue coming, so we lost interest. Its a pity that no photos were ever taken.

Children's toys were never bought for us. I made my own, usually making trucks with wheels that were sliced from approximately three inches of round logs. Another item involved the making of airplanes, with a carved propeller, which actually turned in the wind.

The whole plane was elevated to about ten to twelve feet off the ground on a pole. At the beginning of the war, about 1939, I saw a picture of a big four engine bomber, and really liked it. So I made one, with all of the propellers turning, I was very proud to see it, as a dominating feature in our back yard.

We learned about the functions and mechanics of motors and engines in school, and I became fascinated with the steam engine. I never missed an opportunity to watch the trains, powered by steam engines on my way to town. The road to town crossed the railroad station, where they ran one engine going back and forth.

A real steam engine was my model.

I watched and watched, forming a plan in my mind to copy the mechanism. I learned about the principles of the steam pressure, pushing out a piston, which turned a crankshaft. I then spent many days looking for parts, like the boiler piston, at various scrap yards, which I later adapted to function.

I spent much time experimenting and assembling, when finally I just needed some sort of fire to boil the water. I found a little kerosene burner that we used for light. It did fire up, creating steam, and enough of it entered the piston, pushing out the rod, which turned the crank, but it did not keep turning.

Later, I learned that the steam had to enter each side of the piston in order to return. There was the new problem of valves, exhausting the spent steam. This was too technical to figure out, especially using my limited resources, so I let it be. I thought that I had been partly successful, but knew my limitations.

One of our early technical endeavors was to rig up a telephone with my friend, between our two houses. The boy's house had electricity and a radio, which he always fooled around with. He got hold of some wire, probably about two hundred and fifty feet, connected it to a transformer, and added a switch to it. It worked like a telegraph. We learned some basics of the Morse code, and actually received signals at each end, but we didn't have very much sensible communication.

One spring, about 1941, while at war, the German navy sunk the biggest of England's battleships, the "HMS Hood". This was a big victory for the Germans and its pictures were in the news papers. So we used those pictures and made our own powerful battleships.

A lot of our idle time was spent playing games. One that I readily recall was hockey, played on dry land with a tennis ball. We of course had to make our hockey sticks. It was quite difficult to find a tree limb shaped just right, to look and function correctly. By early spring, I would walk in the woods even through snow with a saw, looking for these bent sticks.

My father always let me use his tools to make toys, and for whatever I needed for our sports. Our involvement in whatever we did was always so intense that any sort of boredom did not exist.

Before I finish this chapter and begin the next regarding Autumn through Winter, I would like to add a brief recap and a few notes about the tasks needed to be done during the seasons of Spring time through Summer.

I would like to describe more now about our many childhood responsibilities. We were being counted on to help. Each of us had a part or several parts for making our small farm function so that we could maintain our very existence.

The spring time started with the picking of the dreaded rocks off some fields, raking meadows and fertilizing them with liquid cow manure, planting potatoes, cabbage, sugar beets, and clover. Plus, sometimes sowing spring wheat was necessary, if the field sowed in the fall failed to germinate due to unfavorable weather.

As always, the ground conditions had to be fairly good, which at times caused delays if spring rains persisted. By mid to the end of April, spring work usually was done with everything growing with a new life. During this time before early summer hay season, our dad worked in the forest, making pulp and he also worked at home. He was quite busy making a variety of wooden farm containers for people and wooden slippers for our family.

As I previously mentioned winter feed for cattle was by then depleted. Pasture grass, which had not yet developed enough, made it almost an everyday necessity for us to scramble to find enough feed for them. Forest grass, was one alternative, which our mother carried on her back in the big wicker container.

Not having enough of our own milk was an ever-present concern. This would bring the need to walk to our two aunts to barter or borrow from them. With a rapid improvement of warmer weather, conditions became somewhat easier. Most important of all was to be able to pasture the cows again.

The transformation of nature from spring into early summer was really a wonderful welcome time, bringing new hopes forward. Even in my early youth, I remember how we shared the good mood and feelings with everyone. One of the most memorable beautiful changes in nature was the lush flowering of meadows. The colorful flowers started to appear in late May and by the beginning of June it was all ablaze in color.

Walking through the pathways, I vividly remember the wild red poppies, carpets of yellows, white flowers with yellow centers and the most beautiful shade of blue, as if the spring sky descended upon the land. Growing up among all of this beautiful nature and reflecting deeply on all of my long ago memories I believe that these blessings of nature were so incredibly rewarding that they gave everyone a renewed strength for the future struggles of existence.

Carpets of yellow fields (today, used for bio-fuel).

Growing up in a small farm environment where much of our time was given to helping our parents, we did whatever was needed. My sisters and I never objected or rebelled in any way, knowing that there was always more than they could do.

One important item was that our family needed to help other farmers as a compensation for the lease of some fields and for helping at wheat thrashing times for the loaning of farm implements. For instance, a machine was used to sow wheat. Plus, a machine with an electric motor which used a fan to move air to separate the grain from the chaff was used as well.

I worked with my older sister, Marta, in the beginning of September. We were helpers loading bunches of wheat which pushed through the threshing machine loosening all of the grain. This work lasted for about three days. It was done in a big barn and we really had to move fast to keep up with the machine feeder. It was customary that we would be given a big meal at lunchtime and we were always very hungry.

There was a constant cloud of dust from the machine in which we all worked all day long. No dust masks were available then and we were coughing and spitting dust for some time. This was very unhealthy but no one was concerned about it and it was just considered to be a part of that sort of operation.

We were not paid for this work, not even knowing at that time what the agreement was, knowing only that it was for the benefit of our family. My sister and I had worked another two days for another farmer, also under the same arrangement. We always received compliments from the farmers who praised us for our hard work and this made us feel good.

Another method to separate the grain was by flailing. This is the original primitive method, going way back in history. The flail is a wooden pole, hand held, about six feet long, with an attachment of about two inches by about thirty inches long, made of round hard wood, attached so it could swivel with strong leather straps. Only rye was done that way. It is long and doesn't get all meshed up like when using the thrash machine.

This long straw was used to stuff our mattresses for our beds so just enough was done to fill the family's need. The rye was spread in a circle of about eight feet diameter. About four women standing in a circle of about ten to twelve feet in diameter swung the flail hitting the grain to dislodge the seeds. The biggest trick was that they had to work in unison, with each hitting solo, so as not to hit the other flails.

Once as I watched them, I asked if they would let me try to participate. I had never done it before and I could not get the rhythm of one, two, three, four and disrupted everyone. So they threw me out. The rye straw really smelled good in a freshly filled mattress and lasted several months when it would then be refilled. Most of the rye was thrashed by machine, being about half of our entire crop. This was used to make bread, which was so good, and was one of the most important parts of our daily diet.

Chapter 7

From Autumn to Winter and Christmas

During the advancement of fall season, after the completion of harvest, the grain was stored in the big bins in our attic. The potatoes, and some carrots were stored in the underground cellar. We were ready to face the long winter, except for the remaining task to make sauerkraut, and cook sugar beets for syrup.

We also had a good supply of pears and apples, which were sliced and dried in the oven, so they would keep through the winter. We loved all the pastry with this cooked dried fruit on it in wintertime.

With the slow change evident everywhere in the countryside, starting with the colors of trees and all foliage, it was as if nature were saying goodbye to all of us, and preparing herself for a long winter's sleep. Looking over the rolling hills and wooded valleys, there was a dramatic change from spring and summer greens and yellows, to dark browns of the plowed fields.

With shorter days, showers came with a noticeable chill in the air. It gave us a sort of melancholic mood.

Perhaps this was one of the main reasons for a holiday such as that of November 1st. This was celebrated by honoring the departed, with the graves at the cemeteries being richly decorated with evergreens and holly wreathes.

After St. Nicholas Day on December 6th, wintertime announced itself with an early frost and a dusting of snow. We loved this but we were also cold due to inadequate clothing. It always helped us to walk fast or run to warm up. As children, we usually could find more time to play since there weren't many chores left except for the gathering and making of firewood.

The beginning of the Christmas season in my earliest memory was somewhat mysterious with wonderment as if knowing something was in the air but not knowing what. Perhaps this was due to the change of behavior in our parents and my older sisters, but not from any gift shopping among the country folk which was perhaps done only in the cities.

Because of our economic situation, we received gifts of money and packages at such times from our step sister Marie and our Aunt Betty (mother's sister) who was well to do in Prague and was always most generous. I believe she was consistent year after year and never failed with such kindness.

Prague skyline

One custom was that our mother baked all sorts of special pastries, and cookies. It was forbidden to eat any at all, until the "Little Jesus" came (similar to our children's anticipation of "Santa" here, in these current times).

We only had one adjacent room, where these specialties could be stored and it had no lock. Despite the orders, I occasionally snuck in and filled my pockets and would then rearrange the pile so it would not be noticeable.

On Christmas eve, the mystery and anticipation deepened with the whole house being awash with the wonderful smells coming from the cook stove. Finally, when it became dark, we were ushered into the small room. Then the bell rang and we were told that the "Little Jesus" had come. In the semi dark room there was the beautiful lit up Christmas tree on our table.

m.a.

A soft warm glow.

We stood there in awe and couldn't believe our eyes that this, like a miracle was happening. We would go closer after a while to look at it. It was a spruce tree with cookies and colored paper ornaments attached with clamped on little candles which gave a soft warm glow. We sat awhile around it, looking at this wonder, until our mother called us for the evening special meal.

The meal was a type of cooked porridge of barley with spices and garlic. It was really good, and we enjoyed having it only on this special evening. Then we had "buchty", (these are like normal buns) filled with prune and ground poppy seed preserves, dipped in syrup and sprinkled with ginger bread crumbs. To drink, we had tea with rum added for flavor. To us, this meal was fit for royalty (Upon my numerous visits back home, and once at Christmas time, my sisters tried, but never came close to making the porridge, which I have wanted so badly).

The rest of the evening was typically spent with the traditional time of charity given to domestic animals, owing perhaps that Christmas eve is called the "Evening of Charity" in Czech. Every animal, starting with the family's dog, would have a piece of ham, then grain was given to the chickens and then the rabbits. The cows each got a big slice of salted rye bread and some special drink which they liked. The hog was also rewarded.

m.a.

Evening of Charity

A while after suppertime a local watchman came, who announced himself with a trumpet. His wife came along with a wicker basket strapped to her back which was used for collecting gifts. These were very poor people, who lived in a little community house. He limped badly due to a war injury and was supported by the village as a night watchman, mainly as a lookout for fires.

My sisters and I busied ourselves with traditions and games only done for this evening. One involved standing in the middle of the room with our back to the door. We threw a shoe over our head towards the door. If the tip of the shoe pointed to the door it meant that that child would soon leave home.

My sisters now tell me that most often my shoe pointed out. This fulfillment took about seven to eight years in my case, first by going for apprenticeship training. and then living away from home by age fourteen.

Another tradition was to float empty halves of walnut shells in a big washbowl. We glued little tiny candles into the shells and lit them. The shells were placed in the center and formed a circle of five little ships, one for me and one for each of my sisters. The water was calm but the little ships moved somewhat. Again, my sisters told me that my ship always went out the most.

All of these traditions, including the one of the "Charitable Evening", are the recollections of my memory from my later boyhood years, not the very first years, probably four or five years of age, whereas the earliest years are of recollections of only the magic of the Christmas tree. The "Little Jesus", our Santa, was invisible, never to be seen, as was the Christmas tree, only to be revealed on the magical evening.

Our father of course put it up in the barn secretly, out of sight. If there were any presents, they were homemade like the knitted socks and gloves. Our stepsister and our uncle in Prague sent us some chocolate and other sweets. We were quite happy with what we had, enjoying the feasts and the wonderful spirit of Christmas.

In addition to the traditions of the season, we also sang Christmas carols. Our mother and each of us children could all sing well, being musically gifted, taking after her. Now, after more than half a century, having my own kinds of struggles and supporting our large family, I think I can better understand my parent's deep feeling of gratitude in those days. Being thankful for enduring another year of struggle, seeing all of us together, being healthy and happy so much of the time. I remember now how we collectively said our prayers and concluded that special evening.

We did not attend the midnight mass because of the distance, which was over three miles. Plus it was very cold out and we could not have dressed well enough for that. Only once in my later boyhood do I remember going to church in the late evening with someone, and hearing the church bells, whose melody rolled across the snowy hills.

On Christmas day, our mother would get up early and make preparations for our big dinner, which was normally held at noon, and then she would go to church. Some of us only went with her occasionally, again because of a lack of proper clothing for such cold weather.

There was also a concern about not having enough festive looking attire for such occasions. In small villages, like ours, people would notice these things and gossip about it to entertain themselves. Sometimes we felt left out when some of our friends got gifts, like ice skates or skis. Fortunately, there were not many such times, and we would soon get over it.

Our Christmas dinner was usually the best we could have. It was really delicious: roast pork with sauerkraut and dumplings. There were celebrations observed after Christmas day as well. We usually had one more elaborate dinner and spent a lot of time playing outside in the snow. For the adults, this was a time for visiting our relations and neighbors for a friendly get together, sitting and reminiscing around a warm stove.

A final holiday of winter was the "Day of Three Kings", celebrated on about January 6th. It was in honor of the three wise men, who traveled to Bethlehem guided by a bright star on their way to visit the new born holy child. Traditionally, this was observed with an enactment of the "three noblemen" as they visited each household.

Three of us boys dressed in royal exotic looking garments and went from house to house. We sang a greeting like: "We three kings come to you from faraway lands and are wishing you happiness and good health with many long years." We wrote our names on the door or door jam with black charcoal, "Caspar, Melichrand, Balthazar", followed by three crosses. We were sometimes rewarded with some sweets for this service.

The balance of these cold winter months was spent mostly as a time for relaxation. Only our father worked in the woods, and continued to bring wood home. It was my chore to split it into firewood and place it by the cook stove. The evenings were taken up with feather plucking, singing songs, and reading books. At the beginning of January, we butchered our hog as I previously mentioned, giving us sausages, ham and other cuts, providing much appreciated food.

Throughout the winter season, it was a time for many happy activities with folks entertaining themselves. They held dances accompanied by some very talented local bands. There were also performances of theater plays by local volunteers. These cultural events were actually part of what was called a "National Awakening" which began back in the early 1800's and were used as a means to bring the Czech's identity back with our native language, etc.

Our village was really quite culturally progressive, having a good public library, good meeting hall, and a few talented people who could organize and direct theater performances during the long winter months. The themes were usually depicting the nice, simple county life, sometimes with a good portion of humor, music and also making fun of the city folks, the starched perfumed ones, who occasionally visited us. Most scenes had an abundance of the country's greenery, flowers and beautiful girls in colorful costumes.

There was music on occasion accompanying the play or its singers. The performances were repeated two or three times, usually at the end of the winter months, so people could travel easily from surrounding villages. Because all of the actors were local folks, sometimes it didn't happen as per script.

Once two actors were on stage, one sort of scolding the other one in a funny way, for some misdeed. The other fellow receiving the scolding was supposed to look serious. Only the audience should have laughed and did. But the actor lost his self control and also burst into laughter, infecting the scolder as well.

The audience had gone wild, and were laughing so hard that the director had to drop the curtain. After a few minutes, with everyone apparently composed, the curtain was raised again for the scene to continue but it happened again. Someone in the audience made a loud remark and the laughter was again contagious. So, down goes the curtain, giving more time for everyone to recover, and they finally performed as planned.

It ended with such high spirits that people didn't want to go home, until some parts were repeated. It all made everyone feel so happy that they remembered and talked about it for a long time. These wonderful staged plays were performed almost every year. They were advertised by hand printed notices and delivered to all of the surrounding villages. They always created great crowds with halls jammed full. Each play would usually be repeated several times.

It seemed like all of the country people liked the dancing events and went from village to village for added spice in their lives. Our parents also went on occasion. One memorable time they came home sometime past midnight from a firemen's ball. Because we all slept in the same room, we woke up and saw that they had brought us oranges. What a treat it was, being the first time that we had ever seen any. Each of us ate one and loved it. Even now when I eat an entire orange this joyful occasion comes to my mind.

Another activity held sometime in July involved outings to selected places throughout the beautiful countryside. There would usually be a brass band of about eight to ten members from the surrounding regions playing at these sites. They had received their training in the

Austrian military school. They were so disciplined in timing, so well harmonized and a great pleasure to listen to.

People's birthdays were not overly celebrated but name days were. One such day was September 28th, the St. Vaclav holiday (Wenceslaus).

Vaclav is my given name; one of the more popular names and celebrated widely on this day.

Saint Vaclav was the first Christian king of the then Bohemian empire or kingdom in the ninth century and martyred in 925 AD.

He is revered as a "prince of peace", having created great prosperity among his people in times of the constant ravages by wars in early Europe.

pda

St. Vaclav, King Wenceslaus

He is also highly respected in Germany and Austria for his special unique abilities to create livable and peaceful environments. In Germany he is known as "Wenzel", and in America, there is a song about the "Good King Wenceslaus". Due to the high reverence to this good king, among all the people, there is a hymn in his name, which was an important part of the Catholic Church service, especially during the difficult times of the war. I remember the entire congregation singing it with so much enthusiasm, that the entire church seemed to vibrate with the encouraging words.

Statue of Saint Vaclav, the good King Wenceslaus in Prague

As previously mentioned, my uncle, our mother's brother, was also my godfather, and was also named Vaclav, the same name, a necessity to be my godfather. He was a wagon maker who made wooden farm wagons including the spoke wheels. He also made wooden skis. Once, I thought that if I brought him the wood to make skis that he would make some for me. So, I cut down a hardwood tree, probably elm, about six inches thick and hauled a chunk about six feet long on a sled in winter, about six miles away.

My uncle told me that he would think about it, but never did do anything towards it. As I mentioned before, I made my own skis with nailed on leather straps for shoes. The first normal (not home made by me) skis that I had was at about age fifteen, when I was an apprentice cabinetmaker. This was a gift to me from our boss, for the performance of good work.

To conclude the recollections of all the holidays through the year, a thanksgiving was held at the conclusion of harvest time, and in Czech is called "Posviceni", which loosely translates to the meaning of enlightenment. It was held at different times at every locality. In our village, it was held sometime at the end of August. The highlights of it again included a feast. We sometimes had roast goose and a lot of pastry. "Kolace", is a favorite treat, a round eight to ten inch white flour pancake, with a topping of prune preserves, ground poppy seed, sweet cottage cheese, and almonds. This was really loved, and every housewife outdid herself to make the best.

In the evening there was a dance at the local pub (Hospoda in Czech). The band of about six to eight members were very good. This happy time was enhanced by beer. Because of the alternate times that these events were held, our relations often visited each other.

One such time, when I was quite young, we visited my mother's birthplace in Myt. Again, we walked across the woods for about two hours, and met the neighbors of my mother's birthplace. After the greetings, which included statements about how much I looked like my mother, we were invited in, and we sat at a table. They put a big platter of "Kolace" in front of us, and then we were told to have some. I really dug in and ate and ate. My mother became quite uncomfortable and sort of nudged me from under the table, which I didn't quite understand, being totally engrossed by its great taste.

After more than half of the platter was gone we left. I then heard how I had embarrassed my mother by eating so much, as if I hadn't eaten for several days (which was probably not far from the truth). I was told to never again eat so much, and to only have one or two pieces at the most. She really felt bad about the gossip that was to follow. We visited this village of our mother's birthplace quite often.

Once I walked over there with my father through the woods. About half way there he found a little hidden cabin which to me looked like the ginger bread house in the fairy tales, but had a different reason. In one corner, cleverly disguised, was a trap door covering a pit in the ground which held bottled beer. It was nice and cool and my father helped himself. In his younger days, when my father was employed in the forest service as a guardian, he knew about these places. On my subsequent trips over the same route, I tried but never found the little cabin.

In later years when I commuted by train to work, as an apprentice, I still liked to stop in Myt from time to time, especially to see our Aunt Anna, perhaps because she was so generous, and I never left empty handed. Her daughter Fanny, who married later, had a little boy who was also named Vaclav. I liked him and enjoyed being in his company. Being there on a visit in 1945, an American army jeep went by. At age four, he knew who they were and called them "Hamericans", since he couldn't pronounce it properly. Sadly, he died after age four due to an illness. Many years later I visited the local cemetery, found his little grave, and said a prayer. My memory is all that remains of so many special people and events in my early life. By God's grace I hope it will never fade away.

Prague Astronomical Clock. Installed in 1410, it is the third-oldest astronomical clock in the world and the oldest one still working.

Chapter 8

WW II

I would like to portray a summary of the main events which occurred, and affected my early life to the time that I left my country, with the following focus on WW II. 1939, March 15th was the date of the German occupation of our country. That day there was a big snowstorm making roads impassable. Our local village Mayor (Elder) came to our house and asked me to go from house to house wherever there were able-bodied men, and tell them to come immediately to shovel the snowdrifts.

There was snow on the road on March 15th, 1939.

This order was from the German command, wanting all roads everywhere free. By giving this message to some of these men, I heard some peppery language, some of which I had never heard before. By evening all of the roads were passable. By September 1939, Germany invaded Poland. England and France declared war on Germany. The Germans renamed our country at its takeover in 1939, from Czechoslovakia, to Protectorate of Bohmen Und Mahren, meaning Bohemia and Moravia.

In May, 1941 the Germans announced the sinking of the British battleship "HMS Hood", the biggest afloat, with 2,200 men lost, by the German battleship "Bismarck" in the North Atlantic. The ship exploded, being hit at the ammunition magazine. My dad explained to me about the huge size of its guns, sixteen inches, which he was familiar with, during the First World War. Several days later, the British navy sank the battleship "Bismarck", with 2000 men. That ended the German's elation of victory.

In 1941 the Germans were attacking the Soviet Union. There were the biggest propaganda efforts made by the media, the radio, and newspapers, depicting the many victories of their early success, and the taking of hundreds of thousands of prisoners. They also described huge victories in European countries, including France.

I remember the enormous and relentless propaganda of all their "glory", placing big posters everywhere showing a big "V" for victory and being invincible. I also remember seeing pictures of countless hordes of Russian prisoners, and pictures showing the New York skyline and the sinking of ships in its harbor by submarines. It was the most depressing of times with everyone feeling that the Germans were unstoppable.

Because of the world's events, so unfavorable to our existence, I being about eleven years old felt the deep worry and anxiety of our elders. Not completely understanding all of the events, I knew that it was most serious. At about that time, being home alone, looking for something in our table drawer, I found a letter from America, which had a stamp with the Statue of Liberty on it (This was probably from one of our uncles, who worked at "Skoda Works", and traveled abroad, installing water turbines and generators at dams).

The Statue of Liberty, looked glorious and divine. She portrayed the message of freedom and had the appearance of such complete faith in the future.

I remember being totally engrossed by the feeling that everything is not lost, that there is a nation more mighty and powerful than our oppressor, which will save the world.

pd

With so many years gone by, when I see the beautiful Statue of Liberty, the symbol of freedom and hope, that moment in those difficult times flashes through my mind.

Left: Photo of Adolf Hitler.

Hitler declared war on America in the fall of 1941. The United States entered the war after Pearl Harbor was bombed by Japan in December. There was now more hope that America with its might could stop the Germans.

LOC

In May of 1942 the Nazi Deputy Reich-Protector of Bohemia and Moravia, the German governor Reinhard Heydrich, was assassinated by Czech paratroopers, who'd been trained and were in cooperation with England. What followed was absolute terror unleashed against an unarmed and defenseless population. The scope of which was unprecedented in our nation's history.

Reinhard Heydrich was a SS General, a sadist, and Hitler's pet, and the principle planner for the extermination of the Jewish population.

He was one of the five Nazis, and a principal planner at the Wannsee Conference in Berlin in January 1942. It's purpose was to lay out plans and directives for the extermination of the Jewish population in Europe.

Photo: Bundesarchiv, Bild 146-1969-054-16 / Hoffmann, Heinrich / CC-BY-SA

Reinhard Heydrich

I remember one main detail of the absolute importance: The transport of these people to the extermination camps by trains, must not be interrupted, taking precedence over any military transports. It reveals their enormous monstrous importance of the annihilation of all Jews.

I learned more about this many years later. His ruthlessness was certified upon the assumption of the office of Governor in the fall of 1941, by ordering the execution of 250 Czech political prisoners. The post war history revealed that Heydrich formulated plans for conscription of Czech men to fight with the German army in Russia.

The Germans were at the peak of their success, and felt totally supreme and invincible, this assassination triggered revengeful terror without bounds. Immediately martial law with a curfew was declared with thousands arrested daily. Radio announcements and newspapers printed hundreds of executions. Most of the condemned people were charged with: "Agreeing with the assassination of Heydrich". They did something unprecedented in Czech history, which was the liquidation of "Lidice", a village southwest of Prague, on a pretext of their collaboration with the assassins.

It was announced by radio that 186 men, sixteen years and up, were executed, all women were shipped to concentration camps where many perished. All children about as young as two years old were separated from their mothers and were taken to a camp in Poland and later killed by gas. Several children which were deemed to have Germanic features were given to German families to raise. Later, after the war many were found and returned, speaking only German.

A memorial stands today in honor of the Lidice children. This shows 82 of those who were killed. Sculptured by Marie Uchytilova and completed by her husband Jiri V. Hampl.

It took over twenty years for Marie to study available pictures, compiling all images from memories of their mothers, to portray all of them as they were exactly at that time, before proceeding with the final plaster models. The child's innocence in all the individual faces is so revealed, being life like speaking to us. All the statues are sculpted in "the round" meaning the entire figure, not just the front portrayed.

The sculptress worked tirelessly for twenty five years to exhaustion, with full support of her husband, Jiri Hampl, until her death in November 1989. There was no official government financial support, being totally indifferent and negative to this monumental lifetime work. The rescue came from public donations and many countries, including the US.

It is noteworthy to mention the support from the German government resulting from the state visit by Premier, Helmut Kohl, who, upon seeing this great work in the studio was so moved, he declared that Germany would undertake the entire project, and see it to completion, if the Czech government refused to help.

The memorial of 82 of the Lidice children who were killed by the Nazis. Sculpted by Marie Uchitylova and completed by her husband Jiri V. Hampl. Marie Uchytilova said, "I give these children to this nation and the world, to look deeply into the consciousness of mankind, that this or similar acts will never, never happen again."

They finally provided some help after being shamed by the gesture of a foreign power. A big problem emerged before the final casting: where to find the many tons of bronze required. Again the people came to the rescue by dismantling and donating many communist era bronze statues to the foundry.

Back in 1942, after Heydrich's assassination, in addition to what happened in Lidice, the following is an account of some of the details of the tragedy that happened to my cousins in the Heidelberg family, as told to me by my sister Drahus.

That terrible and dark day began when their youngest son Stanislav (twenty one years), also known as Slavek, stopped at a café with two other friends. It was the day of the (assassinated) German Governor, Heydrich's funeral. It had been proclaimed to be a National Day of Mourning. Sitting at Slavek's table, someone (it was reported) had wondered out loud, "Why was there no music playing on the radio?" Another man, close by remarked, "Don't you know? It is in honor of Heydrich's funeral."

Slavek's friend then muttered with satisfaction in his tone of voice, something about there being one less tyrant. The man who had been observing them, got up and showed his Gestapo badge, and asked them for their ID's. He wrote all three of their names down and told them, "You have five days to turn in the one who was just speaking with the negative comments. If you fail, you will be arrested."

Though none of these friends turned on each other, Stanislav was arrested and executed within two days. The shock was complete upon everyone and of course our parents.

On the left: Plaque in Lounava to Marie, Jan, Josef, and Stan Heidelberg.

USHM

Arrivals at Auschwitz concentration camp. This was one of many extermination and forced labor sites where several million perished.

I remember hearing for the first time: "Barbaric, and Barbarians." My family was affected directly with the arrest, by the Gestapo of our cousin. It would be difficult to describe the grievous shock upon us all, especially my mother. It was her sister's son, whom she had helped raise as a baby, in her younger days.

A few days after his execution, the Gestapo came, and picked up two of his brothers and one sister, all in ages twenty three to twenty nine, along with their father, who was about sixty. The reason they gave for the arrest, was the charge of suspicion of having agreed with the assassination.

After these many horrible events, still another was to come. We were visited by the local regional police officer, who told our mother that the arrests were not over and that we probably would be next. After all that had happened, this was almost beyond endurance.

Our mother cried deeply and uncontrollably, especially when she looked at my sisters and me. It was known how cruel and barbaric the Nazis were, and that they had absolutely no respect for human life. In view of what they had done so far, each of our lives would have been a very small and insignificant matter to them.

As the days went on, the grief and fear never subsided. Once, in the evening our mother called us all to prayer. We knelt on the floor and prayed for our safety.

m.a.

In a little more than two weeks the paratroopers were found in one church in Prague and shot it out with the German soldiers. After that, the terror slowly subsided. Martial law was lifted, yet the memories remained like a dark shadow. The balance of 1942 became more or less, a routine of hard work and unending labor. Perhaps, after the "Heydrich Era of Terror," nothing could possibly compare to its intensity.

So, in that respect, life seemed a little easier for us, without the predominant fear of those atrocities. One event I remember from about that time, happened in late fall. It was the process of regular review and strict enforcement of selling all farm products (wheat, potatoes, and eggs, etc.). The amounts were dictated by the acreage of a farm, under cultivation. The Germans dominated the supply system and were extremely well organized, knowing about every plot of land, and what crops were to be produced.

All food was rationed with the use of coupons. The rations were meager but always available. Any farmer who produced a crop such as wheat could keep the allowed amount per person and eliminate the flour coupons for a certain amount of time according to its weight. The same thing happened with the raising of pigs which we could butcher. Its weight was certified and strictly controlled by the village Elder (Mayor). According to this system we were not to receive any meat coupons for as long as six months.

This procedure was supposed to be equally fair to everyone. However we gave so much of our meat and sausages to our relations, mainly in Prague (to our uncle, one aunt and our stepsister, to reciprocate for their support at Christmas, and other times). Being generous to others and with many mouths to feed at home the smoked hams didn't last for as long as the specified time of the allotment according to the ration cards. We usually ran out in about three months.

I don't know how much I contributed to its diminishing quantity by sneaking into the attic where the hams were hung from the rafters; cutting off small chunks. The hams were smoked almost cooked and so delicious. I would have been disciplined for this so I rubbed some black soot on the cut portion since it was mostly dark from smoking and it wasn't noticeable. With no ration card being given for some time we ate mostly rabbits, once a week. It was my job to kill, skin, clean, and cut up the rabbits.

Perhaps this duty was a little pay back for my earlier over indulgence on hams. The rabbits were not considered to be a controlled commodity and our number of them depended on the available space in the shed.

m.a.

This reminds me of the times when our mother prepared a most delicious meal (one of my favorites) with paprika, root celery and other items. It seems that still no one else can duplicate it.
It was so memorable and good, that upon my first visit to our parents in 1970, our mother prepared this meal for me. I watched her every move, wrote down everything in detail and gave it to Marta, my wife, upon my return to my home in the USA. I helped her with the preparation, but it was only remotely close to my mother's. Two of my sisters also tried but had the same disappointing results.

Another story that Drahus described to me from those early days concerns a time that she and our mother went to a flourmill to exchange some grain for flour. By about 1943, all of the flourmills were sealed and forbidden to operate. But one, which was about four miles away from our home and in a remote part of the country, was probably overlooked somehow by the Germans.

My sister, Drahus was about eleven years old at this time. It was evening as they walked cross-country, through the snowy fields, carrying their heavy loads. Our mother carried about twenty five to thirty pounds of grain, and my sister carried about eight pounds. Upon their departure from the mill with their new heavy loads of flour, the miller asked them to walk exactly back in the same steps in the fresh snow. He gave my sister a tree branch and asked her to walk backwards, swishing the branch over the snowy ground to obliterate all of their steps. She did that for quite a ways and became utterly exhausted.

Chapter 9

Endurance

As mentioned before all farmers, even the smallest ones, had to produce and sell to the governor supply depots whatever was produced including chickens and eggs, and cow's milk. It is incredible how efficient this system was (no computers involved) to keep records for example, such as when cows gave birth and nursed a calf for a certain period of time and then how much milk would be produced to sell.

Perhaps the information given regarding quantity was under strict guidelines, and reinforced by fear of prosecution. People still under reported the number of chickens and amount of wheat. Then they had some eggs and wheat to sell privately. The excuse being that some years are not as good as others. When the officially measured allotment came in short they sent tough inspectors into the villages to find out why and could impose penalties or even jail time.

Once, an inspector came into our village. These inspectors were mostly Sudeten Germans. They lived in the border region with Germany and were a part of Czechoslovakia and aligned themselves with the Third Reich in 1939. They spoke Czech and had been rewarded for some special deeds by the Germans.

One time my father got into hot water for a shortage of wheat. Our dad's excuse was that the crop simply came up short that year. The inspector didn't buy it and gave our dad a certain amount of time to think about it, and admit the mistake. If not, he would turn our house upside down to find anything hidden.

This meeting was in a pub. The inspector was given a lavish dinner with plenty to drink to soften up his official posture (in other words, this process may be called bribing). During this period, someone who was present at the meeting came to our home to tell us that we would probably be searched and discovered unless we could somehow get rid of the hidden wheat in the attic. We had to act fast.

There was probably a ton in the bin about eight feet by eighteen inches deep. There were three of us, me, our mother, and another neighbor. I remembered we had a big wooden vessel, a round cylinder, which was about thirty inches in diameter by eight feet long, and was made to haul water. We had one, not yet delivered and still on hand. So we took it into the country, about 800 to 1000 feet out, and hid it in the thorn thicket, camouflaged it, and hauled in the wheat. We loaded it into sacks of about sixty to seventy pounds, and carried it down the steep attic stairs.

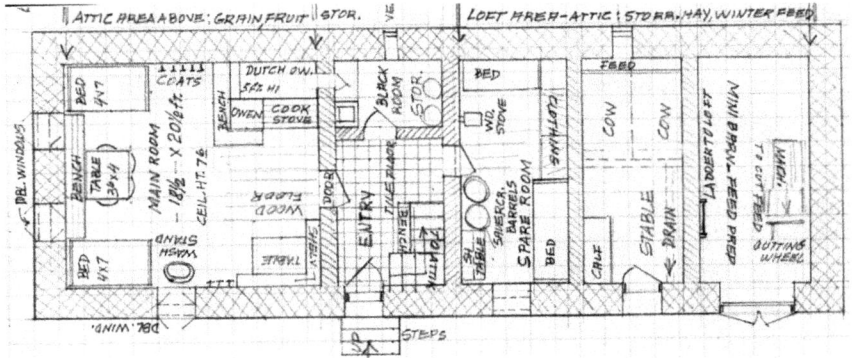

Note the upstairs storage area J. V. Frank

Then it was put on a single wheel type cart and was poured into the vessel with a cut at the top opening. We worked frantically not knowing if or when they would come to search.

I was almost fourteen years of age. This was the hardest and most strenuous work that I had ever done. I was totally drenched in sweat and bending under the heavy sacks. We emptied all but some, leaving it so it wouldn't be so obvious.

The same man, who informed us, took our message and snuck in close to our dad. He informed him that all was done. In this period of time of about two hours, our dad said convincingly again that we had nothing to hide and the inspector dropped it. The good meal and liqueur in those two hours probably played a part in the affair.

I can recall another one of these inspections, the beginning of which was almost comical. Every house had chickens, which by law had to be counted give or take some for their ages, with regard to their ability to lay eggs and the tallies had to be turned in. Everyone knew that the Germans were not about to crawl in every chicken coop to verify the amount, so people listed about one half of what they had despite the dire threats.

The problem came when the inspector's car arrived one day. The folks all knew if they would come and count them that they would be in deep trouble. So they started to chase the chickens, which were all currently outside, and this made it pretty hard to try to put them in sacks to be carried out of sight.

The whole village was enveloped by this chicken cry, plus all of the dogs started to bark creating a pandemonium. This would have been an easy matter for the inspector, had he been aware in the least. A saving grace for all was most likely again that he was being kept inside while grilling every one and enjoying a good meal and drinks.

Being raised with my formative years and experience taking place during the period from 1939 through the 1940's, most of my memories of major events are those associated with war. One of the biggest informative tools of that period was the radio.

We now know that the German minister of propaganda was a highly skilled Nazi, Joseph Goebbels, who could turn any situation around, sounding positive with glorious over tones. No other means of information, except for the radio and newspapers, were available. The illegal foreign broadcasts, mainly the BBC, were available on the short wave band, which most radios had.

Bundesarchiv, Bild 183-1989-0821-502 / CC-BY-SA

Joseph Goebbels

The news from BBC (British Broadcasting Corporation) was a direct contrast to the German propaganda and people believed it. It was very comforting to know the truth. However, every radio had a special notice with the tuning knob that said: "Remember that listening to short wave is punishable by long imprisonment, even death."

People did listen discretely and then told one another so the contrary news traveled like lightning. Our neighbor had a set like that and informed our dad. It was customary in those days for neighbors to visit each other in the long winter evenings. The main topic of conversations was about the war of course. Because we were all in our main big room, my sisters and I were present to most conversations.

After the German's "glory of victories" of 1941, came a slowdown in pace. The biggest BBC news was about the German defeat at the battle of Moscow in January, 1942. Their army froze in their summer uniforms in extremely freezing cold weather. The Germans announced their dire need for winter clothing and a big drive was started. Even our school engaged in the "winter hilfe" (winter help), collecting every discarded sweater and anything with fur or wool, even old items.

One significant war news story came from Russia again, and it was the first time that the German news acknowledged the huge struggle at the battle of Stalingrad, hinting at possible defeat. The climax came in early January 1943, when the German Sixth army was defeated. Scholars estimate that the German armed forces and its allies suffered from 500,000 to 850,000 casualties. This was the first time that the radio portrayed this kind of defeat. They banned all music, dances, and any entertainment as a sign of mourning.

We all knew this was a turn around, and it was. Many years later, as I read a book about this battle, it was described how the Germans were extremely tough soldiers, despite the freezing conditions, and that they were low on food and ammunition. One account stated that there were so many wounded that they couldn't be treated, so the most hopeless cases were put on stretchers and placed in the windowless hospital and let freeze over night.

We learned of the first German defeat in Africa. They had been chased off the continent by the British. Then, the Americans landed in Africa at the beginning of 1943, scoring victories. The balance of 1943 was evident of a turning tide, with all of the oppressor's arrogance totally gone. The neighbors at our evening get-togethers were being more hopeful and enthusiastic with the end in sight.

I must add a story concerning the forbidden radio and any illegal activities that were life threatening. There were cases when the Gestapo, the dreaded police or their agents, would approach school children. They would ask about their family's evening activities, especially about listening to the radio, hoping to get a reason to make an arrest.

We were specifically told by our parents to not say the truth about the gatherings and discussions, but to say that our folks were tired and go to bed early. This was a necessary life saving thing to do but in essence we were told to lie, to fabricate a story, which later affected our character as if it was o.k. to be deceptive.

Although I was brought up to be honest by good people, this wartime request established itself enough that at times, especially later as an adult, while starting a business and being under great stress, I might give an evasive story to get out of a difficult situation. I know it wasn't right, but the situation of the moment simply demanded it. So it seemed until one time.

In the course of my business I talked to someone that I knew well enough and he knew me. I gave an explanation to avoid some situation and he said: "You are not being forthright." He was a simple man, direct, thoughtful, and absolutely honest. I turned red and was embarrassed to the limit, knowing that he was right and honest. I corrected myself and apologized to him.

At work in my cabinet shop.

At that moment, I resolved to myself that I will tell the truth even if it hurts. This changed my conduct for all time. Often in dealing with customers most of them have been in well positions in life, i.e. doctors, lawyers, wealthy people, and I have felt their sincere respect. I have had to say things as they were, nothing deleted or added. Without exception I have felt that their respect and trust in me has grown stronger as time went on and is enduring to this day.

In traveling back to my homeland, especially while still under the communist oppression, I felt an inherent change in people's character and conduct. They appeared to weigh and analyze every word before speaking to estimate what power, effect or direction it will have. At the beginning I couldn't understand their hesitancy and carefulness, until I came to realize that I was simply different after living in America, and acquiring American values. Today most people over there, especially ones with higher education, do sense this and know it is the American way. And, I am proud to portray it.

Early in 1943, I started taking my violin lessons in Cizkov which was the same village where our grade school was. I believe it was my mother who wanted me to do it, because she had great musical talent and liked music. I probably acquired my musical ears from her.

Years later my daughter Marta and I played violin and piano together.

My teacher, Mr. Benda was a part time farmer and a bandleader, playing a clarinet with the violin as his second instrument. In those wartime days higher schools of education were banned. My folks felt that because I was a boy that I would be learning some kind of trade. Music was considered to be a privilege and an exceptional addition to have in one's life. The once weekly lesson had to be held after the farm chores in the early evening. This meant that I walked three and a half kilometers home from school, and then walked back for the lessons for two and a half hours. All of this walking meant about a total of fourteen kilometers on a lesson day.

In 1944, after about one and a half years, while beginning my cabinetmaker apprenticeship, I started taking lessons in Plzen at a regular music school. My teacher, Mr. Vlcek, was a music conservatory professor. There was a huge difference in school standards and I had to study and practice hard to continue. I studied in this school for about two and a half years, playing to a certain level and was able to play in an orchestra, which I really enjoyed.

To continue further would have demanded too much time for practice, which I didn't have. Advanced violin music with all of its intricate techniques demands nothing but time until perfect. The violin virtuosos devote thousands of hours in study and even when accomplished never stop and are always practicing.

The balance of 1943 and into the summer of 1944 was marked by the continuing decline of German might. It was quite evident in the demeanor of most of the German officials, who were shedding more and more of their persona of superiority and arrogance, which they previously displayed.

About the beginning of 1944 there were quite frequent over flights by American bomber squadrons. They always flew from south to north, being extremely high, leaving white trails behind. Once I was on a hill with a friend pasturing cows when we heard a real horrible sound coming down. We started running down hill, thinking it was a bomb and then there was a big explosion. When we felt that it was safe enough we ran to the site of the explosion. There was a crater in the fields, about twenty feet in diameter, and about ten feet deep.

USAF

B-24 bombers on a bombing mission.

Later, in 1944 I was working as an apprentice close to Plzen, near a big industrial town, which had "Skoda Works" and employed about 40,000 people. It was a prime target but to our amazement they just flew over high up enduring all the artillery fire as if they were invincible. During the air raid alarms, we ran outside to play soccer and watch the many explosions, which were close to the planes. We wondered whether they had enough sense to stay clear of the fire.

Note: It was about June 1944 when our teacher had announced that the Allied Forces invasion in Normandy, France brought high hopes for the conclusion of the war. And as it turned out, the liberation really took place from 4/27/45 to 5/5/1945 (More will be said about those days later).

The summer months of 1944 were the last months of my boyhood which were spent at home working with my folks on the farm. September was the month when all apprenticeships began. By then my family and I knew that I had only three choices available. I chose the cabinet-maker profession. Fortunately, my mother knew someone connected with the furniture factory, Mr. Rudolf Voboril in Old Plzen, and asked him for my admission.

Upon receiving news that I should come and introduce myself in the second part of August, I took a train there. I was astonished by the size, general neatness, and how everything was in order. It happened to be one of the most modern places and was reputable for quality with separate departments for apprenticeship training. They already had one big shop with about twenty boys going on their second year. I was to be included in the younger group in a separate shop also with twenty boys.

I filled out all of the paper work. One segment regarded what they called a physiological and physiotechnical test which was timed. It included some tricky puzzles to see if I had enough common sense to fill the spot. In a few days a letter came stating that I was admitted.

A new era had started in my life and I was conscious of the privilege to be in one of the best facilities in the country. Our instructors were so special, upbeat, and gave us beginners much encouragement for our future. We could not be in a better place that with our consistent effort we would be masters of our craft within three years.

Also from a continuation of 1943 and as the years advanced, even as children we could do an almost adult amount of work. So at the beginning of August my sister Marta and I traveled to the area cultivated in the northwest part of our country which was approximately sixty five to seventy miles away from home, to harvest hops (used in brewing beer).

We left by train with a local group of about ten women who did this every year. After transferring to different trains twice we arrived in the town closest to the hops growing farm by evening. There wasn't any other transportation so we walked for about four plus miles. We both carried a suitcase with our belongings which were pretty heavy. After some distance, I helped Marta with her suitcase while she rested.

This entire area was called Sudeten Land, whose inhabitants were predominately German and had chosen to be a part of Germany. Previously a portion of the Czech population, which was about fifteen to twenty percent, included many mixed marriages with Germans. They often moved out or were severely intimated and forced out leaving most of their possessions behind.

They had a choice to stay and become Germans. Only a handful did, which meant their children would be going to German schools and all the adult men would be taken into the army, probably fighting in Russia. Later it was obvious that moving out would have been a better choice considering the high percentage of losses in the war.

I remember as we were walking to the hops farm, meeting some of these young people who made unkind remarks to us (Czechs). Their superiority complex and arrogance was astounding. We arrived by late evening, very tired and were given a meager meal and then sent to sleep in a common area on straw filled mattresses, placed on the floor. This floor was on top of hops drying kilns and the strong drying smell was really present. It is a fairly pleasant smell, but somewhat toxic and drug like, which of course no one told us. As a result we slept real well.

The next day we were driven part way. Then we walked the rest of the way to the field, given a leather apron, and a small stool. The hops plants grew tall, about ten to twelve feet and were attached to a wire grid above us. We were shown how to pull the plant down, moving it slowly across our lap, picking the hops flowers and placing them into wooden containers. We were given a coin for each full bucket.

I was sitting next to an old man who had done it for many years. He showed me what the best way to do it was. The plants have some sort of coarse surface that was hard on soft hands, which cracked at the beginning. We were given a lotion to be used over night to help the skin heal. The hop flowerets are about the size of a dime and nickel, and took a lot of time to fill a container.

We were quite slow at first compared to the older pickers but gained speed every day, becoming almost equal in a few days. They told us that the more we pick the more money we'd make but we never knew what the pay was and never saw it because it all went to the family.

Our mother arranged it all with the woman who was the group leader. Marta had a much harder time than I did, not being as competitive as I was. For a few days I knew it was stressful for her, but she did not complain, and eventually got used to the regiment.

Our day began between five a.m. and six a.m.. We had imitation coffee with milk and dark bread for breakfast.

Lunch was served in the field, a big pot of some sort of thick soup, called in German, "eintopf" (one pot), having just about everything thrown in. Many times it was heavy with cooked milk and raisins, which I hated. The choice was clear. Eat what there is, or starve. After trying hard, I learned a method of eating and not tasting the food; sort of shutting down my taste mechanism. Evening meal at the farm was the same, eintopf, with maybe some potatoes and tea.

The owners of this farm were two middle-aged ladies, with husbands who were probably in the war. One lady really liked me for some reason and was always saying "Hello," even saying something to me on occasion in German which I understood and could answer.

Upon our leaving after two weeks of ten hours a day labor, she gave me a nice farewell and a money bonus and invited us to come back again next year. As it turned out I did come again in 1944, though that time with my other sister, Anna who was one year younger and who adapted better than Marta to the routine.

Chapter 10

Apprenticeship

After getting home from the hops harvest, the time was fast approaching to begin my apprenticeship, perhaps in a week or two. A good portion of time was spent doing farm work, making hay, the late summer crop, if the weather was favorable. There was also the task of plowing the wheat fields which I enjoyed doing.

This was done slowly, at a leisurely pace, as I walked behind the cows, hung onto the plow, and turned the earth. The cut field being turned over had a particularly good smell. This kind of work was considered to be man's work and it made me proud to know that I could handle it, but also I knew that it was probably the last time.

Starting my new journey in life required some reasonable clothing and shoes suitable for a country boy. I walked to Nepomuk to buy a pair of shoes, quite a special occasion. However, I don't remember getting any clothing.

Things were made by altering older hand me downs. Looking back, considering the income from hops picking and the sale of geese, there should have been some reward, but other more pressing items had to be taken care of.

The decision to learn a trade was quite simple due to the official rule, mandating learning a trade, and not requiring any higher education beyond eighth grade level.

It was about mid August when I made an introductory visit to the factory. I was well received. After taking the tests, I was notified of the starting date to proceed further.

Previously, my boyhood recollection of various shops, such as cabinet shops, was that they were always dingy, poorly lit, and often in some basement, but this place was another world. All the office girls were always helpful and caring, as were all the shop's foremen.

The factory: "Rudolf Voboril Furniture" was the most progressive and modern in the country. The apprenticeship program was a separate division and was run like an institution.

Many years later I visited with friends from the apprenticeship program.

As I previously mentioned, in my beginning year there were twenty boys. The second year, more advanced also had twenty. We each had our own instructor. Mr. Vileta, was a very kind elderly man and a master from the old school.

Mr. Reisl, was a young principal and was also a cabinet maker. He instructed us in all theoretical matters, as well as the importance of issues regarding our personal behavior, cleanliness, and personal appearance. I am sure having a group of twenty country boys was quite a challenge.

He had a high position in the local boy scouts and taught us all the main scout principles such as being truthful and honorable; being helpful to those who are disadvantaged and to love and respect our country, God and nature. He was most persistent and all of us soon fell into place.

The method of teaching a trade at this shop was especially designed to develop progressive steps in all the aspects of the trade like structural joints while using hand tools only the first year. All the work was graded and displayed on the board for all to see. This gave the slackers good incentive to improve.

We spent days doing some tedious tasks over and over until we mastered the lessons. Looking back, it is clear that this strict training paid off because some of us were definitely able to produce the finest furniture by our third year. One of the rigid requirements regarded the neatness in everything we did. At the end of every day our work station had to be spotless. If it was not clean then we stayed over until it passed. This rigid discipline has remained with me to this day. Sport was also encouraged and we all received a set of skis the first Christmas.

Mr. Reisl lived by boy scout standards for instance, he believed that we should run; not walk whenever possible. This exercise would produce a healthy body with a healthy mind. One of his favorite routines came at the end of the day. After everything was cleaned up all students would line up and then listen to an important lecture.

Most of us took a train. The station was about six blocks away (the trains were steam engines). Standing there we could hear the train chugging while approaching making the lecture feel endless. When dismissed we ran as fast as we could to catch it; sometimes jumping on while it was moving. Eventually, the station master complained about a hoard of stampeding boys so we were given more time to get there.

The daily commute was most difficult and time consuming. Without the use of an alarm clock, my mother would wake me up by four a.m. for a breakfast that she had already prepared. The walk to the railroad took me about an hour. The train's running time also took an hour and then I worked for nine hours and I would get home by about eight p.m.

At times, due to poor wartime quality of coal the train engines ran out of steam, moving slowly so I would get home by about nine p.m. The result was a lack of sleep. If I was able to sit down, I would immediately fall asleep. To be able to get off at our station, I would ask a fellow passenger to wake me if he didn't fall asleep himself.

Train Station in Old Plzen

Once, I was awakened late; the train already had left our station. Running to the exit-outside-door I jumped out, my first time ever and did not realize how fast it was going. What probably saved me was hanging on to the hand rail as I was jumping and making huge strides until I could safely let go.

Cold winter months added to the commute problems so sometime after January, I rented a small room near the factory; coming home on weekends, Saturday afternoon after five hours of work.

At my new place the nice landlady would give me breakfast consisting of coffee with goat's milk. Dark rye bread was cut up and put into the coffee. I never liked the goat's milk but had no choice so I (again) learned to swallow without tasting it. The supper was simple but adequate. I think money was a big problem but we earned enough to pay for transportation and some lunch. Fortunately, being one of the able boys I later earned more money by being sent out as a helper installing furniture.

My parents probably could not help much financially except when it came to supplying food. Every Monday I packed enough bread, pastries and essentials to last for a few days. Another way that I received food after my mother baked something was when she'd give it to a man, who was taking a train passing through my way. I would then meet him on Wednesday or Thursday at a certain time and he'd pass it to me from the train's window.

Having more time after work I started attending a music school in Plzen taking violin lessons. I practiced as long as I wanted in our shop not disturbing anyone. Also, supporting myself took extra time and effort, and being sent out for installation jobs really helped.

Recalling one such occasion: After delivery of some expensive furniture to a prominent attorney in Plzen, I was trusted to do the installing all by myself. This was quite an honor, and not typical, so I worked really hard. With all going well, the lawyer was extremely pleased with my performance. Upon completion he gave me a tip and asked me how far I had to go to get home. When he learned how late it would be, he offered to drive me there, which I loved.

The next day, my foreman told me how extremely pleased the lawyer was with my work. Unfortunately, the lawyer also commented that the trip taking me home was the roughest that he had ever taken.

I was sorry about our rough roads. I was used to walking on them and they seemed to be o.k. but apparently that was not the case for driving.

As mentioned previously a good part of the teaching of this trade included cleanliness in all aspects such as how we organized our work spaces, material, and storage, etc.

After a few months we were given additional tasks to sweep and clean the main shops, being organized into segments for each student and given about half an hour to do it. We worked very hard, running and not walking. When completed our foreman approved the work. Every Saturday afternoon we were allowed one hour to do a more complete clean up including dusting. Our efficiency had to be super organized and quick to be able to finish on time and take the train home.

This strict part of our training gave us strong traits of character which lasted into our adulthood. Many years later while running my own business I felt respect from our customers, for being neat, clean, and organized. This was a reflection on one's overall reputation. These customers were professional, successful people who would probably not have succeeded as well for themselves without similar required rigors and needed discipline.

Sometime in the early spring of 1945 some students with good progress reports were assigned new positions in the main shops. This also brought a substantial increase in wages especially if the assigned segment of custom furniture was done in good time and well crafted.

My position was stationed in the main and best quality shop, working next to old time masters, who kept an eye on me and gave me valuable tips. It was remarkable that some of us were advancing incredibly far in only nine months.

I have the highest respect for Mr. Karl Krysl, the master craftsman who worked next to me, in those early days. During my visits over there, I always visited Mr. Krysl. He was about 90 years old when he passed away.

Our training included that we attend a special building crafts school once a week in Plzen. This was a fun and easy day and it coincided with my violin lessons. The music school had high standards and I had to practice hard to keep up. The trade school also graded our assignments with a portion of a final cumulative effect on our passing the final trade test by the third year.

Once, about one and a half years into our program, the school asked each of us to make a small piece of furniture, which would be displayed, evaluated and graded. At that time being engaged in fine custom furniture, I was making a fancy entertainment cabinet. It consisted of a built in radio and had a record changing compartment, which could be opened up and slid out.

The whole thing was quite complicated and was almost finished when my boss, Mr. Voboril decided to submit it to the contest upon receiving the customer's permission. This was done but I did not receive a score. The evaluating commission ruled that no one could have made it with only one and a half years of apprenticeship training.

Mr. Voboril appealed, and submitted all the proof but to no avail. At least I got a high compliment and felt very good about making something that was so unbelievable. Later we found out that because our excellent reputation gave us the highest standing in this profession, there was a lot of envy. Some of the evaluating members represented the small shops that could never measure up to us.

At about this time I was elected to be the representative of our apprenticeship class. I was to be a spokesman for my co-workers in case anyone felt that an injustice was done by the management. It was mostly an honorable position of title with no one having a reason for complaining.

War was still going on in the spring of 1945 with food and all commodities rationed. Yet, our economic situation was markedly improved due to advancement in our work positions and in my case my farm background brought some precious food that could be shared with others.

I witnessed some co-workers existing only on the meager rations. One was a lady helper, who was very kind to everyone and always worked very hard. She appeared exhausted, worried and unable to smile. I found out why. She had three small children and no husband and was having an extremely hard time. Her kind and worried face is still etched in my memory. I mentioned her plight in a very passionate way to my mother who sent eggs, bread, and all that she could spare from our meager household. My mother sent it all with me on Monday morning.

As I gave it to my co-worker, she had to recover from her shock but very gratefully accepted the food. It is something I will never forget. She cried and thanked me and asked me to thank my mother and said something like, "You, a young boy, care about my family." She lovingly stroked my hair and uttered something about God's mercy. (Hugging here was not a custom but stroking one's hair was.)

I was brought up to be humble and helped people on occasion but had never personally experienced anything of this magnitude outside of family matters. From this I received so much deep satisfaction which never goes away; always remaining a most memorable occasion.

So in connection with the meaning of generosity I would like to add a note about some feelings I have regarding the USA. It is known by too few of us that it is one of the most charitable countries in the world and often by a huge margin. Its generous help reaches millions and is done quietly without fanfare or even any public acknowledgment and is just one of the things it normally does.

How gratifying would it be to so many generous souls to see some mention of this on occasion. There seems to be a bias for mainly and even exclusively the negative news, and very little of the good, the success stories.

For example, there are many remarkable stories regarding the heroic and helping nature that is at the core of the USA. One account that stands out involves the Merchant Marines during WWII and the shipping of supplies and many thousands of soldiers across the oceans. Tragically, this includes the huge carnage in the North Atlantic and Arctic Oceans while shipping war materials to Murmansk, USSR.

This aid was so vital to the Russians at their most critical time that the Germans did their utmost to choke it off. Many ships were sunk. The losses of so many ships and lives led to consideration at one point to abandon it altogether, but it was continued. I respect and admire the courage of all those who bravely served knowing these odds. There are many other examples of similar kinds of aid given by the USA, including the post WWII generosity of the Marshall plan (more on this later).

Only a few years ago, during the huge disaster in Thailand, the United States sent a big aircraft carrier to their aid, to give medical help and produced thousands of gallons of drinking water. This was shipped by helicopter day and night. Thousands upon thousands were saved. Yet, I only saw a small mention in the back of our newspaper about it.

Similar help was given recently in Haiti. There were fortunes of billions spent for aid by many concerned and caring people, such as: Bill and Amanda Gates, Oprah Winfrey, and Warren Buffet, who pledged over fifty billion dollars of donations. These are acts of compassion during a crisis and only one example of several others in past and present times.

Locally in the USA, while working for the prominent Schnitzer family, I learned that much of their daily effort is spent in support of charities, mainly in causes for children. This generosity is done quietly and unpretentiously. How noble. As an American I share the belief of many Americans, that we are a giving and compassionate nation, and often try to help wherever and however we can, and wish we could do more. Indifference will not be a deterrent. I also share the hope that our schools and institutions inform and teach our children about this American greatness.

My son David and grand-daughter Alyssa walking down a road in the old country in 2009

Chapter 11

More about WW II

Back to the time of my youth and the ongoing war and how it affected our lives. Besides the meager food rations in the cities there was an increased fear of being bombed, especially in Plzen because of Skoda Works. It was known to have had one of the biggest productions of armaments there under German control. We all knew that the German cities were becoming rubble and it was just a matter of time till the end would come.

Perhaps one of the most feared conditions and one directly affecting families, was the forced employment in Germany's war production of weapons. I believe it started in early 1944 affecting anyone born in the period of 1923 to 1924.

It was known that these workers were living in factory compounds working long hours and because of producing war material, they were also heavily targeted and bombed. It was agony for many families to have learned which cities were being bombed on a daily basis if their loved ones worked there; either announced by the Germans, or the BBC.

Our factory was spared, due to the effort and skill of Mr. Voboril. He spent a few years before the war, in Berlin engaged with the prestigious "Berlin Philharmonics Orchestra." He spoke perfect German, and knew their ways. He was able to establish contact with high labor officials, and bribed them with expensive furniture. The result was that no one was forced to go.

We were visited by high ranking German army officers on quite a few occasions. Not known to us it was part of a scheme Mr.Voboril used to save our people. No one would have imagined at that time that Mr. Voboril's effort would be used later by the communists to persecute him.

In December 1944 the Allied bomber groups came about three times per week. A loud siren sounded and all work stopped. We had no air raid shelters, so we just ran out on a meadow nearby and played soccer. The planes always flew high and sometimes numbered up to thirty.

They looked like small silver fishes up there. We could see them approach Plzen and then all the shooting started. The town was heavily defended because of Skoda Works and its war industry.

USAF

They just flew over straight right through the fire, time after time. We couldn't understand this needless exposure but thought because of hearing about the flying fortresses (B-17 bombers), that they must be invincible. When reading now all of the accounts by the airmen of how they feared this fire, it makes no sense.

Time of war usually produces shortages of everything but not in our factory. We had expensive materials stored for many years. Mr. Voboril took advantage of the world economic downturn in the 1930's and purchased huge piles of exotic veneers (thin sliced wood) from all parts of the world.

Once while I was working in rearranging this warehouse I was amazed to see wood from China, Brazil, Honduras, India, Africa, and Scandinavian countries. The production never slowed down and was of the highest quality. People paid a lot of money. Our apprenticeship shops with all the equipment and staff were surely a part of this business procedure.

By about Feb. 1945 I had to start commuting home by train again. The trains were packed, slow and cold. My trip, which was about twenty miles long, lasted for two hours at times because of the poor quality of coal, unable to generate sufficient steam.

We were also held up by passing military and Red Cross hospital trains, which had preference. Not untypical, after a long day's work I'd be coming home late and would have a hard time not falling asleep while eating supper.

As the hard winter slowly went away the spring announced itself with all of its glory and the renewed hope for a better future. My work progress was very good. I was working in the best shop making some fancy furniture pieces in exotic veneers. They were finished in "French Polish", which is of the highest degree, with a mirror like finish and is all hand polished.

It took a lot of patience, much practice, and the constant vigil by my surrounding old masters. Finally, there was a huge improvement economically with the pay scale pegged to the allocated time to produce the items.

I knew Mr. Voboril was very happy with me. I started to feel a new sense of pride and an improvement of my mental frame of mind. Also, I was finally able to buy clothing and slowly began shedding some of the downtrodden beginnings of my life. On occasion, I was still asked to go out to help deliver and install furniture. This was a different routine, an added freedom and I liked it very much.

A few times, we delivered even to Prague. I remember how exceptionally nice and hospitable some of these people were.

After a delivery we were given a nice lunch, even with a pitcher of draft beer. Once unfortunately, I broke a piece of a glass panel and was horrified. I tried to assure the nice lady that I would replace it. She was so pleasant and told me not to worry about it in the least because broken glass brings good luck, I was overjoyed.

Because our training and spectacular progress was so unique in the country, it was noticed by some occupational institutions in Prague. Upon notice they sent a filming crew; filmed us and our shops including our work in progress. It would have been great to see this film with all of my buddies together but we never saw it. Perhaps the end of war and great changes in the country made it impossible.

I was still able to bring my mother's fresh bread to my co-worker and I enjoyed this very much. My young life was not all about work since we had our week-ends to congregate. We'd sometimes go to dances in the surrounding villages and this was fun. By Saturday often after coming home at about five p.m., I would just rest and catch up on sleep, sometimes for twelve to fourteen hours.

Sunday morning was spent putting my things in order, bathing and generally cleaning up and then I'd go out at about two p.m. At that time I had a little more money to spend so we could buy food and beer. I don't remember ever drinking in excess but liked to dance with the pretty girls all night.

Once at about age seventeen I didn't come home to go to bed. I only showed up, had breakfast and went to work. To my relief, my mother did not scold me at all. Perhaps, because I came home sober and she appreciated it. That Monday was a real drag, being half asleep; it was noticeable. My foreman told me, "You don't want to do it very often." I never did it again.

Sometime in mid March, the advancement of war from the west was getting closer. In addition to high flying bombers, smaller fighter planes appeared more frequently. One of their favorite targets were moving trains. Since the morning shift train ran in daylight, it was attacked twice. The planes came real low, circled the train as if to signal it to stop which it did. Everyone, including the engineer would run away from it and they opened up on the engine, leaving a big plume of smoke and steam behind.

My train was not attacked because while I was going home, it was usually dark and they didn't attack at night. It was becoming more and more difficult to commute, greatly decreasing our work schedule. Mr. Voboril recommended that I should again find a place to stay in town but I did not want to. We did not deliver any furniture because we were unable to hire truck drivers who feared they'd be shot up.

About April 24, 1945, Plzen was bombed at night. I was home, at about eleven p.m. while the bombing was happening. The whole sky was lit up very bright, even from twenty miles away. The Skoda Works armament factory was about fifty to sixty percent destroyed. This late date made little sense, not affecting the outcome of the war in the least. During the election campaign in later years, the communists made a heyday out of that, calling it an unnecessary destruction by the west.

Because of its senselessness the opposing parties didn't have any grounds to justify it which gave the communists a big advantage; a big boost but not enough to win which later did not matter.

By about April 27th or 28th, I and other workers and students had gone by train to Plzen to attend our trade school. Shortly, while walking, an air raid alarm started, and in a few moments there were multiple explosions all around, especially in the skies which became very smoky. Somehow we knew that this was not just bombs going off but the anti-aircraft guns. It was morning around eight a.m. and fairly light but it started to get much darker, like early evening, sort of ominous and strange. There were bright flashes in the skies; everything really intensifying.

Three of us decided to quickly get out of there and head back to the railroad station with hopes to get a ride out. When we got there all drenched in perspiration, we found out that our train going south had left only minutes ago and no other train was scheduled. So we started to walk on the tracks heading south.

We had a lot of company of German soldiers, walking in groups of six to ten also heading south. They did not seem to be armed and looked harmless. A few kilometers out of Plzen, having had a clear sky we noticed several fighter planes circling everywhere. When they came closer, the Germans laid down on the embankment. We quickly realized that this could be risky so we got away from them and lay down also.

This happened several times and no shooting occurred. After walking for about seven to eight miles we came upon a train that was standing still. Walking along the vacant cars toward the front, a man with a black bag walked out of one of the cars. He said that he was a doctor and told us sternly not to go in. But, in a few seconds we were up the steps and going in. What we saw was sheer horror.

In two compartments there were about six to eight men, all dead with body parts missing and a lot of blood with wood splinters all over the floor. One man whom I had known had the top of his head completely blown off. I became real sick and felt like I would pass out so I quickly went outside.

We later learned that the engineer disregarded the fighter's warning and tried to make it into the deep draw. When they opened up on it, about three cars received the fire along with the engine because it was moving. *It was the very same train that we had previously missed.*

About half way or more I parted company with my two buddies who lived closer than I did. My total walking distance from Plzen was about eighteen to nineteen miles. Not being prepared for this trip, I became very hungry and thirsty. There were small concession stands along the railroad stations but were all closed up due to the situation. Being hungry and thirsty, I remember the urge to get home that day. I know now that it was adrenalin and will power that helped me get home.

I remember not losing hope that I will make it. Just another mile beyond that bend and so on. Finally at the home stretch, from our railroad station to my village at a certain crossroads behind a grove of tall trees, I walked upon some military vehicles. Coming close, I saw the white stars painted on and knew they were Americans.

It seemed unreal after so many years that this could be happening. Coming closer, I saw people around, all happy and smiling. Then, looking up, standing on top of their vehicles, there were the weathered friendly faces of the Americans. Sorting throughout all of the wonderment, I remember the feeling of friendship, closeness, like meeting old friends, bringing us freedom. It became all so real, the mighty America, of which we had heard so much about was represented here, by these friendly unassuming good natured guys. I was amazed to see all of the advanced equipment, radio antennas everywhere, and radios squawking continually.

My exhaustion with thirst and hunger came back, after all of the excitement, and I slowly started walking home. I was so happy as if the greatest nightmare had gone away and there were now, new horizons and a better future ahead. My parents were much relieved to see me come in, since they already knew about the air raid and also knew that I had school that day. They accepted the news about the Americans with deep gratitude. I am sure that our mother thanked God for all of his blessings bestowed upon all of us.

After a very good rest at home I had some free time and was enjoying all of the excitement of the changing times. All the folks, including my parents were happy; uplifted in spirit, knowing this was for real.

Because of the complete collapse of the German military there was a lot of movement of their soldiers. I had seen about three columns on different days of about 150 men each walking south.

USAR

Waiting for Germans to surrender in Vseruby, Czechoslovakia, 1945.

They were sort of lined up with an officer and accompanied by a woman in the lead. Later it became known that the American army was coming from the southwest and that they wanted to be taken prisoners by the Americans. They feared the Russians to death, knowing that they wouldn't see their home for a long time. Then about two days after coming home we heard about a big German armored army unit. Another boy and I went to see and found them parked in neat rows on the hill in a nearby village. We were amazed to see so many tanks looking fresh and new. We walked into the group and then realized it was their most elite force the, "SS Toten Kopf." They had black uniforms and told us that they had been fighting in Russia and now they waited for the Americans to surrender to. An American jeep came with three officers.

They drove in and told us to get out of there, so we did. It seemed strange that such a huge elite force would come our way since it is well off the beaten path, but surrendering to the Americans was probably their motive. If the Russians got them, being SS, the most fanatical dreaded unit, they would probably never see their home. They mostly died in eastern Siberia of extreme hunger and cold. In the same camps there were many hundreds of thousands of Russian political prisoners who died in the "Gulags." In one case at the battle of Stalingrad, only 5000 of the 91,000 men of the German Sixth army who surrendered survived. Most of them died in the Russian camps.

Also at this time with hope for a better future for the Czechs, one would feel that all the cruelty and all the horrible acts of war for our small nation would have ended. But it was not to be. When times change, when the accused victims get the upper hand, they sometimes mistreat their oppressors more without any mercy.

In our surrounding woods there were mainly small groups of German soldiers from broken up units, hungry, disoriented; only wanting to get home or be captured by the Americans. They traded their weapons or whatever they had for some bread. On one such occasion three of them in uniform were captured by local vigilantes and led through our village. One bully ordered them, in German, to walk in high goose steps called the "parade march".

They were hungry, weak, and could hardly walk. Then one of them was picked out and beaten very severely. It was the most sickening thing to watch. I don't remember how the poor man picked himself off the ground and got away in his condition. I can't believe he could have gone very far. This cowardly act was done by the village's most ignorant and next to worthless bully, while the people watched silently. As history later unfolded, these same people became the communist leaders.

Another such cruel act was witnessed by my mother who came home very disturbed, almost in shock and crying. She had returned from working in the fields. Again, three uniformed men came nearby and were captured by some local vigilantes who were armed and hostile.

The Germans pleaded for their lives. One was a young doctor. Our mother understood some of his words, that he was a doctor and had never killed anyone. But suddenly they were all shot without mercy. There were more of these senseless killings in the woods that we later heard about.

One that stands out involved my grade school teacher who lived in another village in the remote area where the valley and the roads converged. This man had a good view of the surrounding country and captured some Germans at gunpoint; forced them to dig their own graves and then shot them. No one knew, because of the remoteness of his house, how many people he had killed. After I lived through the communist deceit I became aware that his teaching was communist inspired. He lived the part.

Note: It is estimated that during that year, when President Benes issued a decree, over 2,500,000 Sudeten Germans and 500,000 ethnic Hungarians were expelled from Czechoslovakia.

Photo: Sudeten Germans civilians leaving Czechoslovakia

[Sudetendeutsche Stiftung – cc]

As you will see in the next chapter, broadcasts were made from Radio Free Prague regarding the portrayal of the expulsion of the Germans. The events were described with extreme and inflammatory language.

This period of time, May 1945, was also experienced first hand by Marta Antochova's sister, Zdena, who had married a German-Czech. The following is their story.

Zdena was married before the beginning of the war to Arthur Mervart. He was born at the Czech-German border to a prominent family, having a Czech father and a German mother (common in this region). He studied medicine at the Charles University in Prague. His higher education was interrupted by the German occupation. The Germans closed all Czech schools of higher education. He faced the dilemma to either drop out and become a common worker or finish his doctorate degree at the German university.

He dearly loved medicine, his lifelong dream, so he chose the second option. He spoke both languages, finished his doctorate degree but was soon drafted into the German army. He did not have much time during his studies nor after his departure to war, to enjoy his young family. He and Zdena had two daughters, Dasa and Marta, and he was able to be with them for only a few times while on furloughs at home.

He was immediately engaged in the war in Russia as a doctor, primarily at Stalingrad, the worst of all places in the war. Fortunately, he returned to Prague to work in a German hospital.

Photo: *Zdena and Arthur Mervart*

It is important to note that he along with a group of German doctors made it possible to ship many Jewish families to Switzerland, under a medical disguise, arranged by those who were sympathetic within the Swiss and German governments. He also helped many people obtain medicine which would have otherwise been unavailable in those hard times.

With the war coming to an end in Europe by the end of April 1945, Arthur joined the Czech side as a doctor, during the liberation uprising in Prague. He sent his family to their country home with his mother, for their safety.

Arthur saved many wounded people, working days and nights without any rest. At the waning end of the conflict, he wanted to go home and was also concerned about his mother in law, Mrs. Smidova, who lived in Prague. Some Czechs warned him about his safety during the mayhem out there in the streets and gave him a railroad worker's uniform to wear because he had been wearing a German uniform. He believed that because he had been doing his utmost to help the wounded that he would be safe. He only needed some sleep. He finally made it safely to Mrs. Smidova's home to rest.

On the street there were all sorts of armed vigilantes, the revolutionary guard. Close to Mrs. Smidova's home, someone yelled, "There is a German in there!" They rushed in past Mrs. Smidova and seized Arthur. They said he was to be taken for interrogation, to their headquarters. Arthur showed them his safe passage conduct paper. They ignored it and led him outside. Again, someone called out that there was a German and people started to throw heavy cobble stones at him. Some struck Arthur and he died right there on the street, witnessed by his mother in law, Mrs. Smidova.

It was later revealed that the apartment building's maintenance woman was probably the one who pointed Arthur out. She was the only one who knew him and had previously even been given medicine by him for her and her family, which would have been unobtainable otherwise. He was a good person who had helped so many and never harmed anyone. And though Zdena has since passed away, Arthur's memory is also forever cherished by his daughters, now also living in the USA. They honored their father by placing his name on the tomb next to their mother's name.

These were very intense and difficult times that very often did not bring happiness or peace even to those who finally found freedom from concentration camps as I found out while walking with my mother one day in early May, 1945. While we were on our way to Nepomuk, we passed the railroad station and came upon two people who walked ahead, very slowly. When we got closer and were about to greet them, seeing their faces we were overcome by shock and utter disbelief. They were extremely skinny, like skeletons.

Their clothing hung on them like loose rags. Looking at them, my mother started to cry and I stood there in shock. As we exchanged greetings, we learned that they were mother and daughter. The daughter was about seventeen years old. They were Jewish and returning home after being freed from a concentration camp. That image will never leave my memory, seeing their faces; pale skin over bones, their dark eyes deeply set were completely without gloss and seemed to be devoid of life.

Looking at them in continuing disbelief, I began seeing torture and unspeakable horrors as if it were projected on a screen in my mind. It is remarkable what I saw and imagined by looking in their tortured faces right then, since the concentration camp's horrors were not all revealed. My mother hugged them but they were unable to express any emotion, no tears, nothing. We said our goodbyes and wished that we could provide more comfort as we walked on. We knew this terrible emptiness and sadness was similar to the tragedy that took my four cousins from the Heidelberg family.

Note: I have heard that approximately 80,000 Czechs of Jewish faith died in the German concentration camps. It is also estimated that 213,000 Czechs were killed during the Nazi occupation. Among the many groups that Hitler targeted the casualties were highest among the Jews. Raul Hilberg, in the third edition of his three-volume work, "The Destruction of the European Jews", estimates that 5.1 million Jews died during the Holocaust. Some sources estimate that the number may be greater than 6 million.

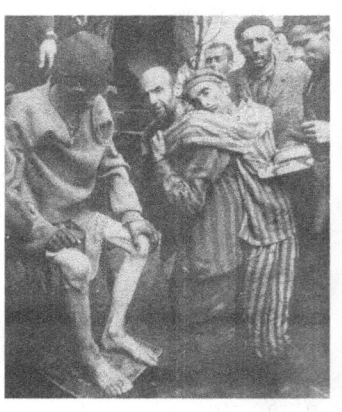

Above: Holocaust survivors at the Wobbelin concentration camp, 1945. [USAR]

Holocaust survivors at Auschwitz, 1945.

Chapter 12

After WW II

USAR

All of the events evolved quite rapidly. The Americans arrived in Plzen, around May 2, 1945. About a day later they arrived in Nepomuk. I walked there and spent the entire day looking at them admiring everything. The town square was full of vehicles of all sorts. I mostly admired the small jeeps and how they scurried around.

In about three days after the Americans, the Russians arrived. A group of big tanks came rolling in with everyone greeting them, offering food, and the best they had. They wanted Vodka, or any alcohol which no one had, only beer. They were friendly enough; somewhat reserved, but nothing like the Americans. We asked if we could have a ride on the tanks. We hopped on top; hung on and rode to the next village. I remember riding on top of this huge powerful monster machine; going up a steep hill effortlessly but quite loud.

Russian T-34 Tanks

They moved on and later established a position before Nepomuk, where there was a "Demarcation Line," separating the two forces. We and everything south of us were in the Russian zone, Nepomuk and west, were in the American zone. It was one of the most unfortunate events that the Americans stopped at Plzen and were not allowed to go on to free Prague, the nation's capitol.

When the Prague citizens believed the Americans were close by, they revolted against the still German control with needless killings. The hatred and pent up feeling of the six year rule was understandable.

There were stories that the commanding General George Patton started to advance, responding to the plea of the Prague Radio and Czech citizens. But he was stopped about half way there on orders from the supreme commander, General Eisenhower to stop or be relieved of command.

Gen. Bradley, Eisenhower, and Patton.

The Russians knew why the capital was so important for future political reasons. In later years the communists made a real hay day about being their liberators. The design to control Europe was on. The cold war had not started yet and the Americans appeared to be trusting Stalin.

USAR

The uprising in Prague lasted for about three days, before the Russians arrived from Berlin. The entire country was understandably most concerned about the situation and was informed about the events by Radio Free Prague.

As I recall the news stories were mostly negative; pleading with everyone for help, being broadcast also in Russian and English. They also announced in a very strong language that the Germans committed a lot of unspeakable atrocities, especially against children. This was readily believed with utmost rage knowing what they were capable of. The effective pitch of this insanity was so powerful, that everyone wanted to kill Germans out of revenge. In my case being fifteen years old, I remember the hatred that I felt when considering what they had done over the last six years.

I know how this totally transformed my mind, wanting to kill, and get even. Fortunately, I never had the opportunity and it was later learned that even though there was much killing, most of this broadcast was not true (deceit due to the communist presence).

It seems likely that some of the killing and brutal acts were probably influenced and committed after these kinds of announcements. Though some of this vengefulness as in the case of my school teacher, was apparently done before the broadcasts.

Knowing what power this hatred had over me back then I think of how history has been shaped to a large degree by this power. For example, it is similar to the power Hitler used to persuade, influence, and totally indoctrinate so many thousands of his countrymen to carry out these atrocious kinds of crimes.

Regarding the conclusion of our liberation, one important factor affecting the outcome was the "Vlasov Ukrainian Army," which was of Ukrainian origin; wore German uniforms, and used German equipment; were stationed just outside of Prague. Even though they were in German service, they could communicate with the Czechs. Through similarity of their language, upon pleas of the uprising leaders they were persuaded to move into the outskirts of Prague to block the movement of the huge German armored divisions.

The Germans were stuck there with the war almost over and the Russians were coming, whom they had a real good reason to fear, so they were hoping to be able to surrender to the Americans. The official line influenced by the communists was that they were traitors against their country. No one bothered to explain the reason for what they did and why they did it. Ukraine, a country west of Russia, having a huge national wealth and the biggest farm regions in the world of about thirty million people, did resist becoming a part of the Soviet Union and was historically at odds with the Russians.

This conflict can be seen in the efforts to subjugate these people by the Russians through its dictator Stalin and his red army who totally starved them out causing millions to die. It was the biggest crime and humanitarian disaster up to that time. The press of the world ignored it completely. So the invading Germans had been welcomed as liberators, who took full advantage of the opportunity & incorporated the Ukrainians in their army.

By the end of WW II, after responding to the Czech's plea for help in Prague to free themselves of the Germans, Vlasov's army also made it out of Prague toward the US side and surrendered. But General Vlasov was later betrayed and given to the Russians who hung him as a traitor. Upon demand by the soviets the US army began to ship these soldiers of unfortunate circumstance back to Russia. Applying undue force to make them go, many committed suicide, by any means. Eventually those shipments stopped. Later, when I escaped the communists in Czechoslovakia in 1948, there were over two million of these Ukrainians in detention camps in Germany. Many were able to immigrate to Australia.

Back to the end of WW II for us in 1945: The Russian red army finally entered Prague and received much gratitude and welcome from its citizens. Life was slowly returning to normal and everyone went back to work including myself.

An aspect of the US army's presence was that they were continually admired, and the other boys and I loved to wear any pieces of their uniforms. If a boy had a US army field jacket, he had everything. Much of this was exchanged with the soldiers for alcohol and also fresh eggs. We couldn't understand wanting eggs, not knowing then how commonly they were served for breakfast in the USA (in a later time when I was served the left over US powdered eggs, I realized that I could not blame anyone for preferring fresh ones).

With the commencement of working again, and everyone being enlightened by new freedoms, we had great hopes for the future and a new beginning. After a week or so, I rented my old room in town which gave me also more time for a variety of things including going to violin school.

The school was quite prestigious, having a music conservatory educated professor. He required strict discipline and a very dedicated commitment. At this point, it was no longer a beginning but a really serious study with a lot of practice. The freedom of being able to practice in the shop was great and gave me a good feeling of accomplishment. If for some reason I practiced less than required the professor knew it right away so I tried real hard.

In those days, learning to play an instrument was considered to be going hand in hand with learning a trade and this was typical at our factory. This was especially true regarding Mr. Voboril who was most accomplished; had previously formed his own orchestra with a few of the cabinet makers playing in it. They were very good and had no equal in our region.

With the Americans introducing their type of light dance music, mainly jazz, almost all music played started with Glenn Miller's songs. This great band leader was widely admired all over Europe. Mr. Voboril's band also started practicing this new type of music, by popular demand. The American Army also adopted a Czech song, the "Beer Barrel Polka", and played it as their theme song on festive occasions

They practiced in the shops where it could be watched, and listened to with great enjoyment. I still remember some songs like: "In the Mood," and "Chattanooga Choo, Choo". With new music, new dances also emerged, like: "Swing", "Boogie Woogie", and others with body movements totally different from the traditional kind, and the older people frowned on it. The young people liked it of course as if for no other reason than being American. It established itself far and wide, and was a big part of many of our week-end dances.

In the praise of American music and its influence, I must mention the most memorable military band of Patton's Third army. It was a farewell celebration for the Americans in Plzen in late August of 1945.

General Patton was known to be a stickler on dress code, and equipment. This parade showed it with possibly no one ever seeing anything like it since that time.

It was awesome to see perfection in everything; most notable was the military band. They marched about eighty strong in rows of about eight to ten, being dressed impeccably and wearing white helmets, white leggings, and white gloves.

USAR

General Patton

Each row played the same instruments, in the front row were the drummers. The unbelievable part was that they all were of the same height, as if shaped by even lines. There was no difference in height or shortness. They played a march, "Sousa" which sounded great and was almost too much to absorb.

One of the most poignant moments was when they played the Czech national anthem "Kde Domov Muj" (There is my home). This song was and is so dear to everyone; resonating with a beautiful melody and deep tradition. Not having heard it for a long six years, and now to be so beautifully rendered by our American liberators, this could not express a greater love any better for our new freedom. I cannot fully describe the applause and ecstatic pleasure of this enormous crowd.

Liberation is celebrated in Plzen.

During the few weeks after the liberation, with notable improvements in many walks of life, we were feeling good and upbeat. Unfortunately, Mr. Voboril's life turned around because he was arrested as a German collaborator. It was incredibly shocking to us, not knowing how to help him and his family.

The governing structure of the country was not stabilized yet, which allowed many hot headed groups in, positioning and making a name for themselves. It is sad to say that very few of the people that were saved from going to Germany came forward in Mr. Voboril's defense. Perhaps this was because the drummed up charges were presented forcefully as facts so they were afraid to speak out or were influenced by the hatred of those times.

An effort to obtain a favorable testimony was made by Mr. Voboril, Senior. He was quite old and frail and wanted so much to help his son. Unfortunately, it wasn't enough. Collaboration with the Germans was a favorite red topic and the one, which was the easiest, sold to the public. Local newspapers published slanted accounts. As in Mr. Voboril's case, it pointed to his involvement with the Germans. Yet if the truth had really been told it would have been explained clearly that he had been helping his people avoid the dreadful forced labor in Germany.

And though I don't know the details, I am sure the factory's leadership hired good attorneys who were still clinging to the hope for some justice and protection. Despite the fact that the accusations against him did not stick, while he was in prison he had been beaten and mistreated. Eventually, they were able to intervene and Mr. Voboril was freed. Also during that time, a temporary manager, Mr. Tichy, took charge.

Unfortunately, it turned out that Mr. Tichy's main function was to steal whatever was in sight. Due to the high demand for furniture, he took many deposits for orders, with poor accounting, and lined his pockets. He also sold some of the valuable veneer stock.

When Mr. Voboril returned, he was shaken and discouraged, especially when he saw what had happened to his company. Mr. Tichy disappeared without a trace. It is possible that the lingering stigma (done in collaboration and sanctioned most likely) imposed on Mr. Voboril made it next to impossible to find and prosecute the kind of criminal Mr. Tichy was.

However, with renewed energy and hope in the future Mr. Voboril got everything going, owing to a large part to the skillful competence and loyalty of his leading personnel, mainly Mr. Skarvan and Mr. Safranek. A notable item also was that this factory could produce and deliver the highest grade of furniture. Mr. Voboril was able to draw on the still good reserve of materials that most of the competition did not have.

We all pitched in with a new fervor and things began to improve rapidly. The same was evident in the entire country, having a huge industrial base with a skilled work force. Another factor was that the cities had industries that were spared much of the war time damage, being able to produce much needed goods.

Since its founding in 1918 to the wartime years, Czechoslovakia was one of the most prosperous countries in the world with everything pointing in the same direction. The renewed spirit that we were experiencing was later darkened by the communist presence and the intrusion into the nation's fabric.

Generally unknown to most of us ordinary citizens was the fact that we had been aligned with the Soviet Union during the war through a friendship treaty and other factors. We were being drawn closer and closer into the communist Russian orbit.

US Dept. of Defence
Churchill, Roosevelt, and Stalin at the Yalta Conference in 1945.

The wartime head of state Dr. Benes, then in London initiated the fateful chain of events favoring the Russians called the, "Big Eastern Brothers." This man's incompetent and reckless moves later produced the beginning of the country's loss of control which intensified until it was swallowed up entirely in 1948.

It is very painful to recollect how the country's leaders naively trusted the Russians who gave false hope and ultimately betrayed all the people. The Czech people were western oriented and known for sharing their culture and values. We were unaware of the criminal genocide that was being committed under Stalin. As in the deaths of the Ukrainians, he was also responsible for killing millions of their own Russian people and many others.

Note: Joseph Stalin (in power 1922 to 1953), from Wikipedia.

"Historians working after the Soviet Union's dissolution have estimated victim totals ranging from approximately 4 million to nearly 10 million, not including those who died in famines. Russian writer Vadim Erlikman, for example, makes the following estimates: executions, 1.5 million; gulags, 5 million; deportations, 1.7 million out of 7.5 million deported; and POWs and German civilians, 1 million – a total of about 9 million victims of repression."

Note: Holodomor, from Wikipedia.

"On 10 November 2003 at the United Nations twenty-five countries including Russia, Ukraine and United States signed a joint statement on the seventieth anniversary of the Holodomor with the following preamble:

In the former Soviet Union millions of men, women and children fell victims to the cruel actions and policies of the totalitarian regime. The Great Famine of 1932-1933 in Ukraine (Holodomor), which took from 7 million to 10 million innocent lives and became a national tragedy for the Ukrainian people. In this regard we note activities in observance of the seventieth anniversary of this Famine, in particular organized by the Government of Ukraine."

Chapter 13

Conditions at work

As a part of the post war prosperity there was a big fair in Prague. This was called the "Sample Fair" which displayed most of the best goods produced such as a lot of machinery, machine tools and furniture.

Our firm was also represented. I and two other students were sent to the fair for two days with all expenses paid. We really had a great time running through the city.

It was a rare event to be there and reminded me of my earlier boyhood days when I delivered sausages and meat to my uncle.

Prague

Our factory was progressing very well and coupled with Mr. Voboril's ability to be a visionary, plans were being made to expand by purchasing adjacent property. I had also learned that if all continued to go well some of us would go beyond the apprenticeship program and receive a factory sponsored education perhaps in architecture or a field related to furniture design, thus advancing along with the future expansion of the business.

I was having a wonderful feeling about the progress in my life which gave me all of the confidence I needed to go forward. This great light faded as trouble returned with the same people, now more and more communist oriented who had previously persecuted Mr.Voboril and still wished us no good. One of their destructive acts was that they set fire to a hardwood material storage building, burning it to the ground. This was a grievous loss. The wood was rare, season dry and perfect for chair and table manufacturing. It was widely assumed who was responsible but no one was ever charged.

The field of fair enterprise and the country's direction was being compromised. Out of concern that this crime may be repeated, some of the older students were stationed throughout the shops at night as watchmen. I was the first in line and was stationed in the advanced apprenticeship shop. The first night I got into a bad accident due to my own ignorance. There was a big stove fired up with coal which stayed red-hot way into the night. I thought that if I put this fire out that I could go home earlier.

So, courageously I poured a big bucket of water onto the hot coal. It almost exploded into my face. Hot steam burned my arms and face which became blackened. I had no access to a telephone to get help. Somehow, I managed to make my way out of the building and to the neighbor's house.

I don't recall how I got there but was seen by a doctor who treated my burns, after cleaning all the suet off. He told me how fortunate I was not to have lost my eyes. He was also upset and scornful of our leadership to have exposed an inexperienced student to that sort of thing. I now know that with so many risky events in my life, especially later in life this was an intervention by my dear guardian angel.

With so many post war developments that I have here described, one still remains, an important one which had an effect on my future personal life. In about the fall of 1945, our training program group accepted another student to train and work with us. However, he was unlike anyone of us.

He was notably skinny, with deep set, dark eyes, so piercing and intense. He seemed to be looking at everything around him as if to make sense of everything he was seeing. His name was Arnost Bloch, who only a few months earlier had returned home from a concentration camp. We were told he was Jewish and to be helpful, and understanding so that he could blend into our program.

By this time, we knew about the published accounts of the deprivations of the concentrations camps, which exposed itself in Arnost's appearance. Also, I felt that I could sense more with the memories from my previous meeting of the two women by Nepomuk whose appearance was unmistakably similar.

I wanted to help him in every way, and was in the best position because his work station was next to mine. We became friends right off the bat. But it was a different friendship, so dear and sincere; unlike anything I had ever experienced.

As time went on, our friendship became even stronger especially after I learned of the loss of his entire family, his parents, two sisters, and most of his relations. He had no one in the world and I being about fifteen years old perhaps didn't comprehend the entire depth of his tragedy to understand the intensity and sincere nature of his friendship.

Even the sanctuary of his family home was diminished by the indifference of his neighbors. His incredible tragedy was overlooked because of his background. He was Jewish and his parents once had a successful business and had been viewed as well to do.

Yet, despite the struggle and hard work of his parents, despite their persecution, and tragic destruction, the town's people; his neighbors often showed no sympathy toward him. Whether it was envy or bigotry, it seems they were fit for the communist mentality.

As a result of my friendship with Arnost, I later formulated my escape plan. He lived close to the border. This will be narrated later.

The post war period up until the end of 1947 was rolling along very well with everything promising a good future for many of us. That is, until the dreadful destructive influence by the communists.

Being well financed by the soviets their relentless drive through the media never slowed down from the end of the war. The national elections did not favor their party so they tried harder to prevail. The majority of the young people of my generation were not influenced by it but the older workers were slowly swept into their orbit. In evidence of this, I remember those older men always reading the communist newspapers, which used a big format with many bold letters with extremely clever messages. This had a big appeal with the worker's minds.

One very big international affair, consuming all of the media's attention was the "American Marshall Plan". By about the end of the year of 1946, it was evident to the U.S. Leaders that Europe would never recover on its own, especially Germany, which had been totally devastated.

Waldenburg, Germany, April 16, 1945.

Czechoslovakia was also offered this aid, perhaps out of courtesy with regards to the fact that they had always been loyal and friendly to the west though not really having as dire a need as other countries. It was there on the table probably for political consideration to derail the country out of the communist takeover. The socialist-communist slanted government made an all out effort to denounce and slant the good intentions of this generous and humanitarian aid. This resulted in a refusal to accept it.

As an additional reinforcement of their rejection, an offer of equally or greater proportion by the "Big Brothers" the Russians, consisting of wheat and other grain came shortly after. All media showed this "generous brotherly help" being distributed. I remember seeing newsreels in the movies, which showed large Russian women shoveling grain from one box car to another. The reason for this was that the Russian rails are wider spread, which made it necessary to transfer all shipments.

I thought to myself, upon seeing this, that it was quite primitive. How much grain can these women realistically transfer by this process? I knew enough about the soviet's deceitful master of persuasion and figured that not much grain probably even came across but was used only to give the Russians a good political score with our people. No doubt the US government had considered this also since the help was not really necessary.

Having lived in the US for many years now and having a keen interest in its history particularly the war and postwar period, I have the greatest respect and admiration for George Marshall, a five star general. Of all the good and brilliant leaders of that time, General Marshall was the top of the crop by far. When one recognizes his great achievements which includes being in charge of both the Pacific and European wars, it was possibly one of the biggest endeavors in all of recent human history. Yet he was a humble and an unpretentious man only doing his level best.

Historical documents reveal that President Roosevelt offered him the top commander position in the European war (European theater). Yet at the same time reminded him that should he not accept he will be forgotten by history. This great man did not accept regardless of his achievements. This brought President Roosevelt a great relief who agreed with him that he knew where he was needed the most.

We now know how accurate the historical prediction was i.e. all the acknowledgements, ticker tape parades, etc. that were bestowed on General Eisenhower, commander of the European theater, as well as Generals MacArthur, Patton and others but rarely a mention of General Marshall.

A few years ago, in the midst of the bashing of America abroad, the Premier of Austria told the hostile news people: "Don't be so harsh on America. They are always generous to all and I was one who was saved from starvation after the war due to the aid of the Marshall Plan."

AG

"Leaders of the Marshall Plan: Truman, Marshall, Hoffman, and Harrimann ..." November 29, 1948.

The Marshall plan was implemented from 1948 to 1952 to help Europe recover from the war. It was also used to help the victims of Stalin's Berlin Blockade (June 1948 to May 1949). This was considered to be the beginning of the cold war. Millions of lives were saved from starvation because of the Marshall Plan.

1947 surely would have been a great beginning in the overall development of the Czech nation if it weren't for the communists constantly creating turmoil among the people. One of their insidious drives was the nationalization of industry held in private hands.

First, they zeroed in on the big factories like the "Skoda Works" with thirty to forty thousand people, and the "Bata Shoe factories" in Zlin, and other big businesses in Prague and elsewhere. Many of these industries were publicly owned by shares of stock which because of the war changed and I have no knowledge who was left in charge.

With biased media coverage, this gave them a foot in the door but they went further suggesting the nationalization of any business of fifty or more people. Our Mr. Voboril's factory also became a target. Mr. Voboril argued that we had about forty full time employees, not counting about thirty five apprentices which were a separate entity. They did not buy it, despite all efforts. It was obviously a communist trap to eliminate all private ownership which of course later happened.

The country was still a Democratic country having a parliament with a house of representatives not yet overwhelmed by the communists. But there was a very big and strong labor union which was unified and heavily infiltrated by communists. This supposedly impartial labor union was involved in orchestrating many of these drastic changes in all companies of manufacturing. We all knew the union was a spokesman for the communists but it was still voluntary. This union also had international ties, giving aid and support for labor unrest and strikes in other countries as well.

On a few occasions we were approached by the union henchmen to donate our time for strikes. One was in France. I was still the apprentice representative and was not afraid to speak out on any issue. I told him that the strikers can go to hell; strike till they're blue in the face and that they would not get a dime from me. The same henchman approached me again about joining the union and the communist party. I told him what to do with his application and where to stick it in no uncertain terms. He told me, "Don't be foolish, you are one of us. This is our new big movement and besides this factory will someday be ours."

One major occurrence in our factory's future came sometime in August of 1947, when a very important official of the union came to speak to all the employees regarding our status. He was an obvious communist henchman. He was also a concentration camp survivor and knowledge of that was probably shared to give him some additional respect.

Under the disguise as an independent union organizer he was an obvious communist public liquidator. Soiling the name of Mr. Voboril, he claimed that our employer was an exploiter of workers and a fat capitalist that should not have a place in this new workers society. He went on and on explaining all the glory of the new order. Listening to him, I couldn't believe the nerve anyone would have to come before all the workers of such an incredibly successful company with such a highly competent and very respectable owner and heap all manners of abuse on him.

Finally, when he was making his important strong point I jumped in and blew up. I told him that he had no cause or right to slander our boss because he was a good man; extremely competent and who accomplished so much which could be clearly seen. What did he have to show by comparison? So I said, "All you have is your big mouth, and I will not listen to any more of it." I was angrier than I had ever been before. He was shaking and looked at me in disbelief.

Somehow, the session ended quickly with no vote taken. No one else spoke but those close to me nudged me to calm down, worried that I'll have serious problems. But I was too furious to worry. I didn't care about anything but to let him have it come hell or high water because I was speaking the God's truth as I knew it.

I later heard from my coworkers that he told the factory henchmen that because of my attack on him he would have me arrested on the spot if I wasn't so young. In retrospect, thinking about why more people didn't speak, I think they were afraid and already knew it was a done deal regardless. And that any objections would have been pointless with a possible stain on their record.

Another possible consideration is that most people lived through so much turmoil in seemingly endless years of war. Now two years with a glimpse of hope marred by this constant orchestration of unsettling problems, that maybe after this action is settled it would be good and calm again. It could be a part of human nature or I am just being apologetic for my coworkers.

On stamp: Klement Gottwald, Prime Minister of Czechoslovakia from July 2, 1946 to June 15, 1948. He was succeeded by Antonin Zapotocky. On February 28, 1948, the communists took over the country's government and Gottwald became president until 1953. It was the beginning of the tyranny behind the iron curtain which lasted for forty years.

pd

Note: Thomas Masaryk was the first president of Czechoslovakia from November 1918 to December 1935. He was succeeded by Edward Benes from December 1935 to October 1938. In 1940 a Czechoslovak Government-in-Exile was established in Britain. Benes became president in exile from 1940 to 1945 and Thomas Masaryk's son, Jan Masaryk became foreign minister in exile. During the war Jan Masaryk made broadcasts over the BBC to occupied Czechoslovakia.

Jan Masaryk remained Foreign Minister after the liberation of Czechoslovakia. The Communists position strengthened after the 1946 elections but Masaryk remained Foreign Minister. He wanted to retain the friendship of the Soviet Union, but was dismayed that they vetoed Czechoslovakia's participation in the Marshall Plan. In February 1948 most of the non-communist cabinet members resigned, hoping to force new election.

Jan Masaryk loc

Instead a communist government under Gottwald was formed in what became known as the Czech coup. Masaryk remained Foreign Minister. In March 1948 Jan Masaryk, was found dead in an apparent suicide (possibly murdered).

In 1947, the communists representing the country's nationalization process wasted no time to steal Mr. Voboril's property and business.

They believed that before Christmas it would be in their hands. I don't recall any farewell meeting for Mr. Voboril when he left for the last time. His persecution though had not ended but culminated in his arrest again in about six months.

After all that he'd been made to endure, all his incredible accomplishments must have felt meaningless to him. He must have been bitter; feeling betrayed by the majority of his workers. It was because of Mr. Voboril that we had received the best possible training in excellent facilities, all provided by him. It was his influence of good upbringing in our young lives, which had given us a solid foundation for our future. Looking back now, I see him as a martyr.

A few years after my escape, I learned that he died in prison. I have also learned that his father who was very advanced in years, visited most of the people which his son had helped during the war. He had hope for some favorable words to be given to the authorities on his son's behalf. Yet, as much as it is hard to believe, no one came forward. I knew these people and would like to cling to some small hope that they only acted out of fear, remembering the almost mass madness of the country's preoccupation to prosecute even a hint of any collaboration with the enemy.

On my visit in December 2010, I learned more of these tragic events from my old and dear co-worker, then 90 years old, Mr. Kryzl. He explained that upon the confiscation of all of Mr. Voboril's property, he was arrested and tried several times, and accused of drummed up charges. Eventually Mr. Voboril was sentenced to prison with a unknown term to the uranium mines of Jachymov. It was the most notorious prison in the country, forcing prisoners to mine uranium ore, underground, in primitive conditions.

Because this ore was of an extremely high quality, it also emitted dangerous amounts of radiation, causing serious sickness over time. Many people, primarily individuals of high caliber, educated people, all those that never compromised their beliefs and who could not be converted, thus were an excessive burden and marked for elimination by the communists. Even, if anyone was freed, after some time the deadly effect of radiation caused cancer, usually fatal. I have personally known people here in Oregon, immigrants like us, but survivors of this prison that died as a result. Mr. Voboril also died, eliminated as a victim of socialism.

How could this all happen in the last century in a so called civilized nation? The deepest cloud of shame on all those thousands of perpetrators, who willingly carried out these deeds will remain forever. It should also be noted that this uranium ore was given to the Soviet Union in gratitude for liberation, who used it to build atomic weapons.

Note: When communism fell in 1989, laws were enacted by the free Czech government dealing with restitution of all confiscated and stolen property, giving it back to remaining heirs. As in many cases, these properties were ruined, bankrupt, or mismanaged and plundered by the thugs in power. Having been back a few years ago, what I saw of what was left was sad to see.

Back after the takeover in 1947, I felt like I had been orphaned and like a big avalanche had rolled across me. I also sadly felt a considerable amount of detachment by some of my coworkers toward me. It was as if I was an outcast because of my outspoken expressions of events as I saw fit. They quit trying to convert me and just kept their distance. We all kept on working, still producing fine furniture but I began to realize that my future would not be as promising as it once was and that something would definitely be changing.

The communist conspiracy being so well planned and expertly orchestrated by their dedicated henchmen had its desired affect on the working class. This was effective after one and a half years of pointed exposure by the media, newspapers and posters. Being the western most oriented country the Russians spared no expense to gain control. From my recollection, trying to engage these people in discussing some important issues was pointless. The popular saying was that their heads became stone hard with no penetration possible. Even people who were fairly accomplished; normally having good common sense were swayed.

It was so hard to believe that they could buy into that nonsense. Later, when the iron curtain came into being, one prominent western statesman called the Russians, "The Masters of Deceit". How true that was. I witnessed the full effect of its power. One such episode stands out from my personal experience. I was becoming fairly accomplished playing the violin. After about two years of studies, I thought that I could play in the country orchestra, the one which played at our dances on most weekends. So I asked the bandleader who told me o.k. and to try it. The first time out, the beginning was fairly hard having sheet music which was relatively simple but the tempo and rhythm gave me a problem. In playing the violin, one does not only create the exact tone but it must be delivered precisely on time. Any split second hesitation cannot be allowed.

After a few pieces were played, I caught on and really enjoyed it. I was also warmed by the feeling knowing that we were being watched by the girls. After one such dance, the bandleader, Mr. Stika, who was very talented and whom I had admired asked me: "I understand that you work for Rudolf Voboril? Then you must get rid of him, even destroy him, and take over his factory." Of course I never answered. I was quite shocked to hear this coming from him. I couldn't get it out of my mind having heard similar things from smaller minded people. I again began to realize that to exist within this society would be unbearable and that perhaps seeking a way out was the only choice left.

As mentioned previously, the effect of a planned and intense concentration of hatred can take its toll while targeting so many minds. I don't know if it is fair to compare this to the mass hysteria in Germany under Hitler where so many thousands did the unthinkable but I believe an explanation is not possible, except with regards to the power of hatred.

If everyone was not shocked, they were really surprised about the struggle and culmination of three democratic parties. This included those opposing the communists with the submittal of resignations of their leaders to the then President Benes. This was in protest to the communist power grab of certain vital segments of government. The general public knew about this struggle.

LOC
President Edvard Benes

Most of us had high hopes in the President not to accept the resignations. We were hoping that the situation could be reversed with a refusal which might correct this serious situation. The President signed and gave the communists the power to form a new government. They packed it with their people in all of the most vital ministries.

The fate of the country was well sealed, helped by the weak president, who was never a leftist or communist but ill at the time and not in possession of a strong will. He was who we needed to save the nation. This tragic man who was a wartime leader, was looked up to by the majority of the people as one who had the best interest of the nation at heart. He went to Russia in 1943 to sign a friendship treaty with Stalin, the soviet dictator. This was his pay back from the "Big Eastern Brothers."

AG

Attlee, Truman, and Stalin at the Potsdam Conference, 1945.

There was no noticeable change in the daily life, except that all of the communist henchmen became much bolder. They praised the victory of the so-called "Proletariat," for their ultimate goal was accomplished. My detachment at our factory became greater and I started to think very seriously about getting out during this period in time. People started escaping to the west to freedom.

I did form a strong alliance with my two coworkers, Joseph Taluzek, and Stan Mann and of course my friendship with Arnost became even stronger. I remembered an earlier warning given to me by one of the factory's new leaders, the one who always had tried previously to convert me. During our heated discussion, he threatened me saying, "You wait, your time is coming. We can do nothing now, but in due time..." I felt like I was their enemy and knew it was mutual.

This kind of harsh reality does not happen overnight, but when fully evident one knows dire consequences loom for the future. One of my close older coworkers, whom I trusted, told me, "Your days are numbered. It is now clear." He knew of my consideration to get out, and agreed with it and warned me, "Don't take a gun with you, because if you get caught, it would be deemed as armed aggression against the state."

Nazdar Jime,

Posílám Ti obrázky památníku obětem komunismu. Tam jsou uvedena data o která jsi projevil zájem. Památník je, myslím, velmi zdařilý, ukazuje na postupné ničení osobnosti v době vlády komunistické strany. Památník je pod Petřínem v ulici Na újezdě.

Tak se měj hezky!

Vlastík Obereigner

A present day sculpture showing the ravages of communism and the destruction of the individual. It was unveiled in May 2002, twelve years after the fall of Communism. It is the work of Czech sculptor Olbram Zoubek and architects Jan Kerel and Zdeněk Holzel.

Chapter 14

Preparations

Sometime in the early spring of 1948, Stan, Joe, and I began planning our escape. This was in close cooperation with Arnost, who lived about twelve kilometers (about seven miles) inland from the Czech and German border. He offered his house in the town of Nyrsko as a springboard to head out.

Commuting home on weekends, Arnost had learned that the border region, a belt about 10 km wide was accessible by special pass only and was heavily patrolled by the police and army. Our path was to go by train to Nyrsko. His town was to be the last stop in the free zone where we'd go to his house and then walk through the solid forest to Germany.

We also learned that because the border was heavily guarded people were getting captured and some were even killed. Our meetings were often held at Joe Taluzek's parent's home, who lived on the outskirts of town, where they raised some chickens. They spent a few of their prior years in America but had to come back for some sort of family consideration, which they regretted. The father spoke good English and became our teacher. He also informed us about life in America. We bought a book called "Basic English" which consisted of the most basic conversations in everyday life.

New concerns and worries began to be part of our daily experience. At work we became careful to not challenge anyone at all anymore so as not to provoke any suspicion. Because of my background on a small farm, I started to worry about my parents and about not being able to help them in the future like I had always done before. With spring time advancing, there would be the hay which needed to be cut and harvested. I really wanted to help, so planned my escape to take place after a good portion of the work would be finished even taking time off at work to help.

About twenty two years later when coming home to visit, my younger sister remembered that there was one more meadow to cut, not quite ripe yet and that my folks didn't want to do it too soon. She said, "I tried every method of persuasion to no avail." The folks were really surprised and did not understand my urgency which was not normal. I never did cut that last meadow.

In the meantime, I wanted to say good-bye to all of my friends, without really saying it. A good opportunity came at a dance in the adjoining village one Sunday. Sometime at the beginning of June, we all came together, the boys and the girls. The band was my favorite, playing the songs that I really liked and we danced. One song played that I will never forget. It was a tango called, "Blue Pavilion", a German song and had been played internationally. It was so touching and beautiful, so dear and knowing that I was hearing it for the last time, it was deeply moving.

The walk home from the dance hall was sentimental with the nice dance melodies turning in my mind with a touch of sadness in my heart. I felt that I was leaving my boyhood along with my friends behind; knowing that I wouldn't see them for a long time, perhaps forever.

After a restless night and my mother's breakfast, I said my goodbyes trying hard to look normal, I left as usual going to work. Only my three friends, one of the older coworkers and one woman in the office knew of my plans. She was one of the original workers with

Mr. Voboril; head of the office, and still in charge. She knew of my plans, gave me some money, wished me good luck, and asked me to write when able.

Many of our previous evenings had been spent at the Taluzek's house while we finalized our plans. We agreed that it would be best if I went first, sort of blazing the trail, cross over and if there were no news of my capture, my two friends would follow me in about one week, all staying overnight at Arnost's house in Nyrsko If they did not cross within that time, I would come back to lead them across.

My departure was to be June 12, 1948, a Saturday, to Arnost's house, then head out for Germany on June 13, a Sunday when most people would be sleeping in and hopefully also the police.

As a part of preparation for the crossing I bought a pocket size detailed map of the border region and a special compass by which a direction can be set in coordination with a map. I said my goodbye to my parents and sisters by letter sent from Plzen. I felt sorry to leave my family and everything behind but my determination was strong and irreversible.

The map I used in June 1948.

Being young I could not have imagined the full impact especially on my mother seeing her son go into such uncertainty through real danger. Many years later, upon my visit at home, the full account was revealed to me by my sister, which was emotional to hear. I could then imagine as a father what my parents had gone through. This would have been extremely hard for our parents to take especially considering the newspaper accounts of people being captured and even shot at the border, designed to discourage anyone with similar intentions.

My father, who had also left home at a young age, had been drafted to fight in the First World War in the Italian Alps. At that time it was part of the Austrian empire. He returned home with a badly wounded leg. By explaining this, my father helped my mother somewhat putting everything in perspective including the probable danger of my persecution if I stayed at home. He knew of my rebellious nature, ethics, and otherwise.

I was warmly received by Arnost at his house in Nyrsko, upon my arrival by train from Plzen. We had a lot to talk about, mainly my route sneaking out of town into the forest. Arnost showed me the way out of town by going to a nearby village, "Hadrava" which is not far from the big forest reaching to the German border. The distance was approximately ten miles. For my food supply we purchased a big roll of dry salami and some buns.

He revealed to me for the first time that he will also leave in the near future to go to Israel. His home in Nyrsko was a big two story villa with a store front below in the main town square. It was most likely the furniture store of his folks, which he was notified by the authorities was to soon be shared with two families. This was part of the communist thieves' efforts to steal any prime property.

I remember sharing Arnost's good feeling of finally being among his people and getting away from the corruption of this society. Also we decided to use an address under the name of "Oulik" in Chicago once I was settled in the camps as a refugee because there may be no mail service there. We had a good evening meal and retired for the night knowing that I had to get up at the crack of dawn.

After somewhat of a restless night, I had no trouble awakening, quickly got dressed and gobbled up a light breakfast. I grabbed my leather oversize briefcase and was ready to go. I thanked Arnost and we said our farewells. Both of us were deeply moved realizing that we might not meet again (it was also still an unknown whether or not our other two friends would be able to escape as well).

I stepped out into a bright early day and headed out, carrying my oversized leather briefcase. Of some concern was my big roll of salami, which stuck out at each end. I thought well, I will look like I am going camping and should just act easy like. Fortunately, I did not meet a soul all the way through Hardrava, for about two and a half miles and made it to the edge of the forest.

So far so good: Making sure no one was around, I took out my border region map and found my approximate location with the aid of the compass.

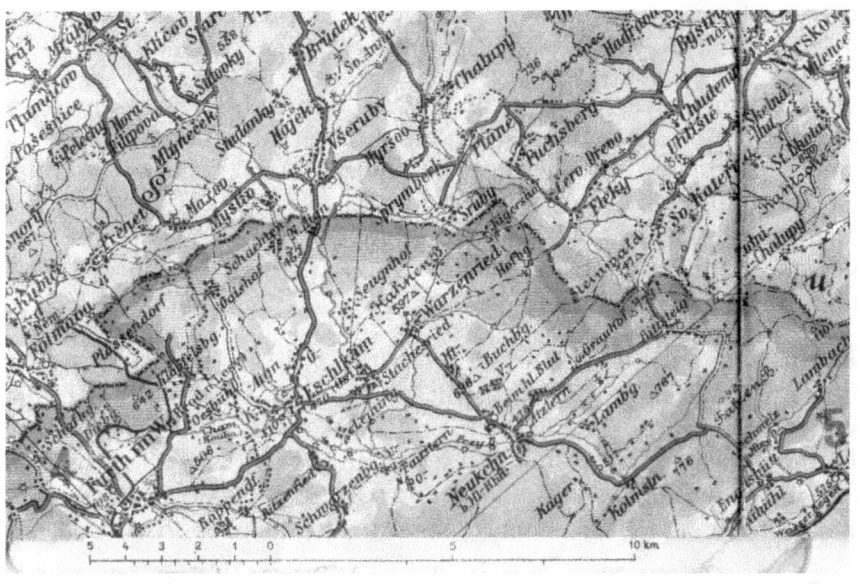

Part of the original map that I used in 1948.

I established my direction due west. I planned to cross in a region where the borderline juts in due east like a big triangle, which should save some miles if I was able to follow my bearing, not so easy to do in the middle of the forest. Making it into the woods felt good, and secure; not as easily to be seen.

I soon came upon nice trails heading my way but remembered Arnost's and other friend's warnings that these were also used exclusively by the border patrols. These now consisted of three people, one the old time border guard, one national policeman, and one soldier. The two selected for their loyalty, were heavily armed, and sometimes had a dog with them, a smart German Shepherd, trained at tracking.

One coworker, an older friend, warned me about this and advised me with a defense: If attacked by this big dog, to wrap my coat around my left arm to form a cushion and then bend down and extend the left arm forward. Let the dog launch at it and then stab him with a knife into his belly. I had about a four inch pocket knife, any longer would have been a weapon if apprehended.

I knew the dogs were trained to scent someone's steps and track, so I tried to jump over or at best only use limited contact with these trails. I stayed clear of the trails and the going was pretty rough through the thicket. The sun was the saving grace since it was still morning. Being in the east, I could navigate due west, slightly south, in order to come to the protruding jagged area which is sort of a triangular protrusion of the border.

About mid-morning, while I was in an area of fairly dense growth, all of a sudden there were real loud steps ahead of me, sort of running fast, noisily through the brush. Quickly recovering from the surprise, I dropped to my knees and waited. Almost immediately I heard the noise going away from me. Still I waited. I realized it was most likely a big deer. After calming down my heart settled down and I cautiously continued.

In an hour or so later, still in the fairly thick growth, another scare happened. Ahead of me there was another noise, sounding like a group of birds taking off. With care I came closer and there was a small cottage.

It was completely abandoned with no doors or windows and brush growing in. It was sort of a quaint little house like in the fairytales. Since there were no roads leading to it now, it was most likely the home of the "Sudeten Germans".

The Czechs had evicted these people under the "Benes Decree" (the President) with full approval of the then major powers. I disliked what I saw. What possible harm or disloyalty could these people represent? How unjust it was to these people living a simple life. I learned that this had been a revengeful act on the part of the Czechs, being led by their incompetent President.

After about three to four hours of walking, I took another reading on the map and re-established the walking direction. Even though the direction angle led through the denser growth I followed it faithfully. As I continued, the forest thinned out somewhat alternating with trees and some clearing. I carefully stuck to the edges of the clearing so as not to be in full view and exposed.

With the terrain being easier to walk on, I sensed that maybe the worst was over. Also it was much lighter in the western direction. Probably past noon now, I became very thirsty. It was about six hours since I had left Arnost's. Food was no problem due to the dry salami but it was also quite salty which added to my thirst. How I wished I had some apples to munch on.

Skirting a good sized clearing all of a sudden there was a well traveled path. I sensed that the border must be near but so dangerous because the guards must have used it. I quickly ducked into the trees out of sight and listened.

Nothing moved so I carefully snuck across going fast. Then probably after about three hundred yards, there was the border marker. It was a square hunk of granite about three feet above ground. The eastern face was engraved with "CSR" and the western side was engraved with "Deutche Bayern". Finally, I felt a big sigh of relief and freedom. I hurried out of there into an open meadow. Fortunately, it was down hill so I knew that I'd be out of sight from the guards.

I finally felt free and extremely elated, shedding all the fear of being pursued. The country opened up and I looked far at some distant hills on a horizon with all the emotion of being free at last! It was like walking into a promised land, escaping the bonds of slavery.

Soon, I came upon a group of houses. One of them was a pub, a German "Gasthaus". Almost dying from thirst, that's where I headed. There were about half a dozen men. They greeted me in a friendly manner with, "Gros Got." I acknowledged the greeting and asked, "Ich bin in Deutschland?" (Am I in Germany?) They said almost in unison, "Ja, du bist in Deutschland." Then they ordered me a mug of beer, which was a God send.

We talked briefly about the situation in Czechoslovakia. I told them how happy I was to be here and then they advised me to go to the border outpost to register. I then thanked them and headed down hill to the station.

Chapter 15

Border Crossings, Part 1

About half way down the hill I met a uniformed fellow, short and skinny with a friendly demeanor who introduced himself as the "Grenz police" (Border patrol guard). As we walked down he told me his history during the war. He said he was in the "Kriegsmarine" (German Navy) in the "undersea boot" (submarine service). I thought to myself, I wonder how many ships you have helped to sink? But, he was friendly and seemed sympathetic to my situation.

The two border guards in the station were something else. Uniformed, and unmistakably German, they behaved like police interrogators. I hadn't carried any personal documents which they didn't approve of. They proceeded to type my data using one finger, which seemed endless. I cooperated at first but became rather impatient, being treated almost like a criminal suspect.

Then, a young lady came in with a young man, and a very young boy. We introduced ourselves. She was Marta Antochova and her accent clearly showed that she was from Prague.

The man who was with her was her cousin, Jara. He was a farmer whose family (father and brother) lived near the border in the Sumava region. The little boy was Zdenek, Marta's son (whose father died of cancer). He was about four years old and appeared very curious about all of his surroundings.

Marta & Little Zdenek

Marta was also happy to have made it over the border but tired as she told me how it was quite difficult traveling with her little Zdenek who couldn't walk such a long distance and had to be helped along the way. She spoke perfect German to the liking of the officials. After translating some of my story it all ended and they called the American army to come and pick us up to be taken to a refugee-collecting type of camp.

In the meantime, another fellow came in. He was a young man who said that he was a student in Prague. After his official processing, two American army jeeps arrived. The soldiers were easy going and quite friendly and it felt so good to be in their presence. Marta, Little Zdenek and her cousin took the first jeep. I went with the student in the second one.

It was a wild ride at high speed in an open jeep. It took about one half to three fourths of an hour to reach a small town called "Furth im Wald". It had a refugee camp setup with some make shift barracks, which housed some of the remnants of the Sudeten Germans. These were a portion of the two and a half million Germans and other nationalities who had been expelled from our country in 1945 at the war's end. These people were not friendly toward us Czechs, even though our situation now was similar to theirs.

We were received by an official, a nice guy who spoke perfect Czech. It was early evening after supper but he managed to give me a piece of dark bread and some thin soup, which didn't taste very good. There were no sleeping accommodations, so he gave me a mattress and told me to find a place wherever I could.

I came into one hall already filled to capacity and found a place to bed down on the floor. As the day was coming to a close at dusk while wandering, two girls came out of nowhere and approached me acting very friendly and nice. Speaking in German, they asked me to go out with them. One was a strikingly beautiful girl of gypsy origin.

I was perplexed about their unusual friendly manner and immediately became suspicious and wondered who they were. I was unresponsive, indifferent and just as quickly as they appeared, they lost interest with me and approached another young man who was walking by. Then I knew they were prostitutes. After an uncomfortable night, the camp leader came and advised us that we will be taken to Regensburg to a Czech refugee camp.

After a ride of about one hour, we arrived at a nice building called the "Goethe Schule". This had previously been a college and was named after the famous German poet "Goethe".

We were received at the entrance by all Czech people who were very friendly.

Goethe Schule

They took our ID data; names, etc. and assigned a room to live in. As part of the registering procedure, we were submitted to an interrogation by the US intelligent service, then called the CIC, now called the CIA (then it was counter intelligence corps). The officer spoke Czech and asked pointed questions regarding things like address, date of birth, employment status, family history, political party affiliation, and the reason for escaping. My answers came quickly, positively and I felt that he was satisfied.

Later on, for two years we were questioned again periodically, learning that if the answers were different or muddled up we would be deemed suspicious making it more difficult to immigrate, particularly to the US.

The assigned room was a big classroom which could hold about thirty men with sleeping cots on the floor. There were all sorts of people, some looking good and trustworthy and some shifty characters. One of my neighbors was one of the latter kind. His name was Cyril with whom I will describe in more detail in future experiences. A few of us went to town. We saw a beautiful gothic cathedral a major landmark, untouched by the war's bombing. Though there was still much devastation remaining in many areas of Germany.

In relation to this period of WW II, in 2004 while visiting again in the Czech Republic, I met a crew member of a US bombing squad, Raymond Noury, and two of his relatives, George and John Torrison. There was so much joy and we became lifelong buddies. I had the honor of being an interpreter at the region wide commemorative event honoring the ten fallen Americans.

On February 22, 1944, Raymond's group bombed Regensburg, as they aimed for the huge airplane factory. Raymond's bomber was damaged and crashed close to my home (about four and a half miles). He was the lone survivor of eleven crew members.

The "Leaning obelisk" in the photo above is a monument in the region of Nepomuk, which was created by Vaclav Fiala, to honor ten fallen American soldiers whose B-24 "Liberator" bomber crashed there.

During his speech to the thousands of people he was like a "rock star", a hero, and loved by all. I met him again in 2009 there and finally again in 2010 in Rhode Island, USA, his present home.

Back in 1948, most of this area in Germany was still recovering from the war. There was the ever present U.S. Army with squirreling jeeps everywhere, with well dressed soldiers.

One area that will never leave my mind was the street of free exchange, a market. This was a fascinating place where just about everything could be bought or sold, or exchanged, mainly currency and cigarettes, with cameras being a close second.

Raymond and I in Nepomuk.

The traders were mostly Jewish. Some dressed in black wearing black flat hats and had long beards with side burns. They conversed in German, and a mixture of Polish, Czech, Russian and some English.

A few days after my arrival there in West Germany, their currency was devalued by about three to one. Everyone's money got diminished three times, not having much left except those who were operating at the exchange street.

I remember when we went there one day after the event and those traders had wads of new money in their hands. With the banks exchanging only so much each day step by step it was incredible how much they had. Even though everything felt chaotic in appearance they showed unbelievable skill.

USAF

Note: During this time the "cold war" began. The Soviet Union created a currency crisis in Germany and imposed the Berlin blockade in June 1948 until May 1949. In response, the western allies organized the Berlin airlift to carry food and supplies to the people of West Berlin.

For the first time in my life, I experienced real hunger; really understanding what starvation meant. The food in this camp was poor. With about 700 to 800 people in this camp, there was no definite status, regarding our existence. No one seemed to know what to do with us. In those days the Germans were suffering and had been starving themselves; not yet recovered fully and the life giving American Marshall Plan of aid was not in full effect. Though helping the people in Berlin, the aid had not yet reached the people in all of the refugee camps.

I also remember that we did not have normal utensils or dishes to eat with. We used discarded food cans to drink the thin soup and morning coffee out of. The portion of dark bread was rock hard; taking considerable time to consume. Perhaps a saving grace was to not think of hunger while trying to eat it. The devaluation of the currency greatly diminished our meager amount of money to exchange on the black market to buy food.

One day when I saw Marta again, it was apparent that she was also suffering and worrying particularly about little Zdenek's diet even though they gave the children somewhat better treatment. Her main concern was the lack of clothing for both of them, with no possibility to buy any.

An additional problem involved her cousin Jara, who was thinking about going back to Czechoslovakia. This was a tough problem because if he were to go back openly through normal avenues, it could have meant jail time and a possible betrayal of everything about Marta and me. So what to do?

As the days passed by, I became more and more determined to go back to lead my friends Stan and Joe across the border. There were numerous news accounts of people being captured and even killed while trying to come across. I felt responsible for their safety and was compelled to go. So, when Marta told me that her cousin needed to go back and would be grateful if he could go with me, I gladly agreed to do it.

We set the time to leave. Marta gave me her mother's and sister's requests for items of clothing among other things. I assured her that I would bring back all she needed and that it would probably take about a week. She expressed her concern for our safety and said it would be a gift from heaven to have all the much needed clothing for her and especially for little Zdenek.

Several young boys had also asked me to go to their parents and inform them of their conditions and that they were o.k.. They gave me about four to five addresses, which I gladly agreed to do since there was no reliable mail into CSR. One man, the shifty one next to me also asked me to go to his wife. Always willing to help, I also agreed.

In retrospect it was really extremely dangerous but I had a mission to accomplish and that was that. Many years later, as I grew older and with children of my own I can hardly imagine how all of our parents must have worried seeing us going into such danger while keeping them in the dark whether we made it or not.

Despite the risks, one day we said our goodbyes and were wished good luck. Before departing Marta looked at me with her big blue beautiful eyes, portraying so much hope and happiness for my success. I knew then that she was very special to me and promised to return.

We bought train tickets from Regensburg to Furth im Wald. We both packed some food, expecting the whole trip to take at least a day and a half. Jara made me worry. He had a simple country nature and didn't seem to realize the risks we were about to undertake. I coached him not to say much in the presence of people, which he promised he would not. But I worried sensing his naive nature that he would not even be aware of the situation.

We arrived in Furth im Wald before evening. We found the refugee camp and prepared to spend a night; planning to head out early in the morning before dawn. I went out to the east part of town, bumped into some old timer and asked if he knew a good way to start going to CSR across the border. He looked at me as if I were crazy and told me so and said it was very dangerous. But he pointed to an area in the near woods to enter. He was a good natured older man and showed his concern and said, "Gruess Gott" (go with God).

Staying in the camp was no problem, which was still disorganized with the refugees so we blended right in. Waking early after an uncomfortable night, I woke up Jara and we got going. It was raining real steady and we were dressed rather light. We soon got soaked. But since it was after the 20th of June the weather was not cold even while being wet. We entered the woods, which were well taken care of with no underbrush, only tall trees. After about two to three hundred yards we walked upon a pathway, which seemed well used, crossed it and headed fast up a hill and through the continuous woods.

After probably another 300 yards we stopped to rest, looked down and spotted a border patrol of three people and a dog walking.

Seeing that they were armed made my heart start to pound. Fortunately they walked easy like to my quick relief. I quickly became aware of the dog who also walked steady on a leash. It occurred to me that the steady rain saved us, diminishing scents and the dog's sense of smell.

Knowing now, how close to danger we were, if the dog had shown any discomfort, they probably would have started a search. We were not that far from them and they could have gotten us. We crouched down and waited for a few minutes and then continued slowly up the hill.

I didn't know upon starting at the bottom that this was the hill of Cerchov, one of the most dominant in this region. At the top it had a huge monument, with a statue of Kozina and his dog, looking into a broad valley below. Erected in 1895, it is the biggest landmark in this part of the border area. Kozina was a martyr, hanged in Plzen in 1695 for being a leader of the rebellious "Chodové people".

[Image from: Ondrej Konicek at the English Language Wikipedia – cc]

Jan Sladky Kozina

The entire country consisting of Bohemia and Moravia, now the Czech Republic, was then under the rule of the Austro-Hungarian empire monarchy headed by the Emperor Ferdinand II, direct descendant of the past Bohemian kings, who was now totally influenced by the Catholic Church, mainly the Jesuit order.

Their main and supreme purpose was to completely dominate these people; many of whom were adhering to a protestant faith. An obvious reason was the absolute power of Rome; ruling most of Europe with uncompromising might and influencing all ways of life. The absolute power of the priests who lived excessively, often immorally, turned the people to better alternatives, which the simple Bible dominated Protestant faith offered.

One of the most tragic events leading to loss of freedom of these people was the loss of a major battle at the White Mountain in 1620. The Czech armies, who were predominately Protestant, fought and had been victorious against the Holy Roman Crusaders since about 1450.

These were big armies, mostly south German and Austrian, totally dominated by Rome. They were also huge in number; financed by the rich church. The Czech armies, smaller in numbers and probably exhausted by fighting many battles for over 175 years, were defeated not by battle but by stealth. The victorious Emperor Ferdinand II took revenge against the defeated people, unprecedented in its history.

This rage culminated shortly by trial and convictions by its main leaders most of whom were of noble status; holders of large properties. A total of twenty seven were executed very publicly at the main Old Town Square in Prague. The method of execution was governed by the degree of guilt resulting in hanging, beheading, and the cutting out of the tongue of Dr. Jesenik, a doctor and rector of the University of Prague.

This barbaric event, witnessed by the new rulers, was designed to completely humiliate and subjugate the nation to return back to the mother church. Because of this and other absolute cruelties, a fair amount of people never adhered to the catholic faith, which persisted for an incredible 300 years of this ruling monarchy.

Despite its utmost efforts, the dissent and split of the church with the people never healed. To complete the degree of the nation's subjugation, the emperor in 1620 took away all properties belonging to the Czech long time noble men, for even a minor disobedience to the church.

This resulted in a confiscation of huge plots of farm land, forest land and castles, which then became properties of the new "Deservants" of the monarchy. These were predominately German, some Spanish and Italian in origin. Even some outstanding mercenaries of the Holy Roman crusader's army were rewarded with large properties.

Above: A view of *Karlstein castle*. *It was the most fortified castle and never conquered. It held the treasure of the Bohemian Empire. It was built on a stone mountain around 1350 to 1400 by King Charles IV. By its historic significance and unsurpassed beauty, it is the most dominant in the country.*

The serfs had to work six days a week for their master. It is recorded that during May and harvest season, the people worked each sunrise to sunset. Most of them were given a small plot of land, which they cared for by hand and only at night, or Sunday after going to church.

Most of the landlords were foreigners; mostly German, so all official language was German, which was a compulsory subject in schools. If the master was greedy, as in most cases, or unjust or cruel, the people sometimes rebelled, so the lords had some executed to restore the slave like order.

I am not sure how the people were paid for their hard work, probably with small amounts of money, and perhaps mainly with grain and other foods for subsistence to maintain strong bodies. I have read that some lords, unable to pay whatever little they owed, gave their serfs additional small plots of land as compensation.

Jindrich Baar   pd

On my visit in 2010, I reflected on an inscription by Jindrich Baar, a Catholic priest and poet; the most loved writer of this religious history. He says: "All the strings in my heart have broken. Only one, only one remains. Dear God, if you love me, allow me to play my last song of love to this hard and rocky land." He composed this shortly before his death. He is so revered, almost everyone in this region owns some of his books, and knows this proclamation by heart.

Back in 1948, during my escape, as I passed by Kozina's beautiful monument, I felt a sense of gratitude and freedom. I touched the base stone and remember saying, "So sorry Kozina, sneaking by you like this, unable to show more respect." The feeling I had right then was similar to when I later saw our great Statue of Liberty, the beautiful lady of hope and freedom.

Descending with Jara downhill through the countryside to the town of Domazlice was probably about six miles. Sneaking into the side streets, close to the railroad station, we entered the building. Fortunately, there was no one there. It was fairly early in the morning, and after walking through rain for so long we looked like wet chickens.

I took Jara with me walking into a rest room, straightening our coats and hair, and walked to the ticket window and ordered two tickets to Plzen. To pay, I reached into my pocket and rolled out a hand full of coins, which were dripping wet. The ticket girl looked sort of puzzled as she counted the money, and I realized that I must look confident and self assured, which I managed. The girl had no comment, and gave us our tickets.

It had also quickly occurred to me that this was the forbidden section of border area within the ten Km. and that there may be some controls. My worry faded when the train arrived and we got in. There were people all around. I was aware of the danger of my situation but tried to portray a happy care free appearance. It didn't take long for Jara to become a problem. He was not sophisticated enough to know how to keep his voice down and he said something which almost took my breath away.

Knowing there was an army officer nearby, I quickly started to talk latching onto what he said, and muddled it up. This was a close call. I motioned to Jara not to speak. He clamed up, no one being the wiser. I watched Jara like a hawk and he remained quiet. We arrived in Plzen by eleven a.m., which was good timing. Most people who I could have bumped into were at work out of sight. I helped with the train ticket for Jara to get to his hometown and as quickly as I could said good-bye and disappeared from the station into the city.

In Plzen

Chapter 16

Borders, Part 2

I discretely waited in the city for the rest of the day until the departure of the last train. It was late in the evening when I purchased a ticket at the last few minutes and ran up to the platform, taking the last car. Not very many people I knew had taken this late of a train but I took no chances. After about an hour, I got off at my usual train stop, waited, and then proceeded when no one was around to head for home.

I used mostly the side roads, even going though fields. After the slow going of almost four miles, I came around my village the back way using the nice path way through the fields and meadows.

Within sight of our house probably about three hundred yards, a big surprise awaited me. Judging by the noise it sounded like someone was running toward me.

Then my dog Haryk jumped on me. Overjoyed, I turned and knelt down to embrace him. He was completely frantic with happiness. He did not bark but made happy sounds that dogs typically do but this worried me in the quiet of the late evening.

Quietly I slipped to our door and knocked discretely and the door opened. My parents stood in shock and complete disbelief that I appeared. I quickly explained that I came back for my two friends and not to worry. My mother and father couldn't get over it for quite a while.

Then my sisters got up and we all rejoiced in semi darkness so as not to raise suspicion with our windows being so close to the road.

Many years later, my sister Drahus told me she was asleep before I arrived, and thought that she must still be dreaming when she saw me there. That night, I slept in my own bed in close company of my dog, who was always only a few feet away.

In the morning after locking the front door, I talked with my sisters. My three sisters remained at home, Drahus, Lidus, and Anna. I had a lot to explain about the life in Germany, my escape and all that had happened since my leaving home. I explained my present plans about seeing several families and bringing messages from their sons. I also told them about Marta whom I had met and that I would be going to her mother to bring Marta some clothing. I showed them a picture of Marta that she had given me and they all approved.

We decided that I would stay in the attic during the day, to avoid any chance of someone coming in and seeing me. Customarily, neighbors come in for whatever reason. One problem was the use of our outhouse, which was outside in the back yard. Of course night was no problem but during the day it was another matter.

I planned to go to Prague by the first early train to Plzen and then transfer trains. Again there were people taking this early train to work, so I would again walk on the side road. Morning came and our mother made breakfast in semi-darkness and then it was time to say goodbye.

I never realized how difficult and emotional it would be after hugging each other. My mother was close to crying and expressed concern about all the dangers. As a final goodbye she touched my forehead and sort of engraved a cross and said, "S Bohem." This is Czech for "Go with God". She said she would pray for my safety. Finally, saying good bye to my dog proved to also be very difficult. He just wouldn't leave me. My sister had to put him in the side room and as I walked out, I could hear him cry.

I walked for four and a half miles to the Nepomuk station. This station was a little farther but had less of a chance of meeting anyone that could recognize me. I discretely purchased a ticket to Prague and staying away from everybody I took the last car and sat in the corner compartment covering my face with a coat as if I were sleeping. After about an hour I transferred to a train heading for Prague. I then found a place to wait out of sight while waiting for the train.

A Czech CD 242 Class Electric locomotive built by Skoda.

After about two hours the train arrived in Prague, the Wilson station. Stepping out, I felt good being in somewhat of a faraway place with many people milling around. First big surprise: As I walked alongside of the train I spotted someone looking out of the window. Within a few more steps I knew who that person was. He was one of my coworkers whose name was Hajny.

Quickly I realized that I must not react if he notices me. Sure enough, the next moment he hollered, "Frank, what are you doing here?" I was lucky to have seen him first. I didn't react in any way, and just kept walking straight ahead, like a complete stranger. I knew him well though. He was sort of a low key and mild mannered boy, who probably would not have given me away. Hopefully, he'd assume that he had just made a mistake, and think that he was just seeing someone else. It appeared to work out that way.

Another surprise came up and this one was potentially more serious. As the crowd of people walked out of the station just before the exit, everyone formed a single line. There was a man in civilian clothes intently looking at everyone as they passed by. It immediately struck me that he was probably a secret policeman.

The line slowed in moving single file so I had time to plan what to do. I realized that I must look really carefree and not show any fear or strain. To my relief, this also worked. I passed by not having him give me a second look. I looked and found the number of the streetcar to the Prague section of town where I would go to my stepsister, Marie.

Upon my arrival she greeted me with kindness and was so nice as always but really concerned about my safety. I had a lot to explain after a good hearty meal. When her husband came from work, he also greeted me with kindness and said that he admired my courage. Later on Marie drew me a bath in their private bathroom. This was luxurious. I will never forget how pleasant it felt and couldn't remember when I had the last one. Probably while swimming with Marta in the Danube river in Regensburg.

In the early evening I wanted to go to Marta's mother's home and found the right street car to get to that section of town. When I arrived there I introduced myself as a friend and currier on Marta's behalf. Marta's mother, Mrs. Smidova, and her sister, Zdena looked at me with suspicion and disbelief, not surprising given the times.

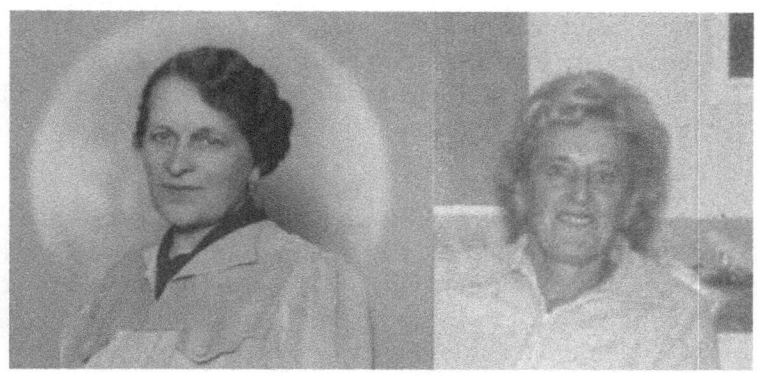

Marta's mother Mrs. Marie Smidova and her sister Zdena.

When I finally gave them Marta's letter and showed them her picture, I was joyfully accepted. I explained what the meager existence in the camp in Germany was like and would like to bring back whatever Marta had asked for. I was given Czech money to also purchase cigarettes which were easily exchangeable for German currency.

After having something to eat, it was decided that I would come back in a few days so they could put everything together. I went back to my stepsister's home for the night and made plans to see about three other families in Prague to give them the information about their sons. The next day, I started out but was not prepared for the receptions.

I was greeted like a messenger from heaven. Some of their boys had been gone for over a month. Not knowing anything about them they were overjoyed for some news. They gave me letters and money. One mother who was so grateful insisted on giving me some special baked preserve filled buns that her son loved. I did my best to explain that I couldn't possibly take it across the border, having already too much to take, but she couldn't be swayed. So, I took the bundle and was sent away with much gratitude.

The last visit was quite a ways away in a town called Sumperk in the Moravia region and was a train ride that took several hours to get there. This was for the one guy with shifty eyes, Cyril. I arrived in Sumperk station and walked about a mile to the address he had given me. It was a good size farm establishment. The woman who received me was very kind. However, another lady, about thirty years old, became very hostile when I introduced myself and told her about her husband back at the camp. In a raised voice she said that he had left her there on the farm alone with three children to take care of.

And then she said, "You dare tell me he is well. I wouldn't care if he was dead." Nothing that I could say to make her feel better worked. She ended our conversation saying, "You better leave him to go to hell" (or something like that). She seemed threatening and made me very uneasy so I hurried out of there.

The train wasn't due for two more hours. I was getting accustomed to sneaking around and did not go into the station but kept out of sight in case the police came. It finally showed up in two hours, which felt too long.

Arriving in Prague, I stopped at Marta's mother's apartment, just long enough to pick up her bags of clothing and left for Plzen. I switched trains to go to Old Plzen to try to catch up with two friends, Joe and Stan.

Mrs. Smidova's apt.

Upon my arrival at the Taluzek's home, Joe's parents told me that the boys had already left for Nyrsko the previous day. I was too late. This was serious because there was no way to reach them by phone in Nyrsko.

So, how could I reach them? It became a real concern that they would start out on their own. I felt very responsible for their safety. It was early evening and I thought of an idea. My plan was to communicate through the railroad wires. I went to the stationmaster. My demeanor was to look very sad and concerned.

I begged the stationmaster, asking him if he could call or send the telegraph to a certain address in Nyrsko, where my two friends were and whom I was supposed to meet to go camping. An emergency occurred, I explained. One of my friend's mother died suddenly and he must come home ASAP and that the camping trip was canceled.

I was so convincing that he believed me and promised to send a wire to the station in Nyrsko and request that they send a station attendant to walk over to deliver the message. I sincerely thanked him and sure enough, it worked. Upon my arrival, the next day I learned that the railroad station orderly came and they knew enough to stay put.

Another surprise awaited me. My two friends brought another boy with them, saying that he wanted to go and that they thought he could tag along (like going to a Sunday picnic). The kid was about sixteen years old and really immature looking and I didn't like it. What to do? Sending him home may have been more risky than coming along so I agreed.

We enjoyed Arnost's hospitality all day and retired early with a plan to head out early in the morning. We all got up early, had some breakfast; said our goodbyes and left. Because it was still June and in an early light, we decided to split up.

We walked two and two. Those behind would follow at a certain distance, so not to appear like a gang getting out. We all made it to Hadrave about three kilometers, not meeting a soul and headed into the woods.

The woods provided good cover and I took the lead, again avoiding all pathways and forest roads. This time, I did not have my compass with me and went by dead reckoning, again having the morning sun at our backs heading slightly south of a westerly course.

I instructed the boys to be quiet, to not step on twigs and to avoid any noise possible. The young kid was a problem, so naïve regardless of my lecturing. We trekked for about three hours. We started up a small hill and then all of a sudden there was a man walking on a pathway at the top. We must have spotted him first. We jumped down the nearest depression and kept low.

The man came closer since the pathway led him that way. We now had a good look at him from about fifteen feet away. He was a border guard armed with a submachine gun.

I thought that he must have seen us but never even looked our way and kept looking ahead completely ignoring our presence. He was an older man, which immediately triggered my memory about the communists not trusting them. He must have been walking home, off duty, since he was alone.

Another frightening moment happened just as the guard was approaching. Joe pulled out a pistol to use, if needed. It must have been our good fortune that the guard did not see it, because if any fireworks had started, we would have been doomed so close to the border. We waited for a few minutes after the guard passed and the coast was clear. We very cautiously advanced west.

We walked in segments. Every few hundred feet or so, we stopped and listened and then proceeded on. The terrain sloped down westward, and I knew that we were right next to the border. Sure enough, we saw one of the granite stones with the country's inscription. How glorious! We made it, all of us!

We walked at a fast pace and the woods receded into an open meadow. I remembered this meadow and knew for sure that this was Germany. This belief proved itself when we met a German border guard. He was the same skinny short submariner whom I bumped into on my first crossing. He recognized me, and was real surprised that I was crossing again. He became suspicious.

The reception at the border station was again quite stiff. The two uniformed guards upon learning that I was there before, and probably remembering my disrespect the last time acted like, "Aha, now we've got you." They started their interrogation, typing with one finger.

After giving them all of our names, I again became annoyed with all of their official nonsense, especially as they began looking into the bags I had brought for Marta. They were looking for contraband. After a while I told them that I will not answer anymore of their questions and want to cooperate with the Americans only.

They wrapped it up and called for the American army officers to bring their jeep to pick us up. They came rather quickly and again there was a very friendly guy with them. We all piled in and went for a joy ride to Regensburg.

Upon our arrival, I was taken for an interrogation to the CIC. As before, there was a Czech speaking officer. He asked me why I went back, etc. I pointed to my buddies and explained that I needed to lead them across. He was quite satisfied. However, he requested that Marta come to certify that I was who I said I was and that she knew me. She came, and was overjoyed to see me. We hugged, and the officer did not have more questions after that.

When we got back to the camp at Regensburg, I told Marta all that she wanted to know, mainly about her mother and sister. She was happy having all the needed clothing for her and little Zdenek.

Sometime later, we found out that Marta's mother had included a letter in the bags of clothes, which she never found. Someone, perhaps the border guard, took it out, especially since there must have been some money with the letter. Marta wondered how could there not be a letter, but I had no knowledge about it.

For the next week to ten days, we had a sort of care free time. The boys went for walks in the city. I spent some time with Marta swimming in the Danube River.

Regensburg, the Danube River, and St. Peter's Cathedral

I remember Marta also washed some of my clothing when she saw that it needed to be done. Laundromats did not exist, only the bathroom sinks were available for use. I appreciated this because I had never washed any clothes before, and really enjoyed being clean.

Despite our situation, especially the lack of food, little Zdenek usually looked happy and had a sparkle in his eyes. But, as the days passed by slowly, we all became aware of hunger, due to poor nutrition. It was not persistent, but came on and off. The people even staged a protest against the kitchen workers. That soon died down because it was obvious they had next to nothing to cook from. One segment of protest that I remember involved one of the cooks. This fellow was a professional cook, and had a huge oversized belly. When anyone saw him, they would wonder how he could possibly get that way.

One man, who was an artist, drew caricatures which were posted on the bulletin board. The best one was depicting this cook, hauling his big belly on the whole cart, spilling all over it, while there were people around him looking like concentration camp victims. When the word got around that he came in that condition, and had always looked that way, people's anger subsided.

Many people had some foreign currency to buy some food, but we had none. Marta was always worried about little Zdenek. I think she received some help from one family on her floor.

If I remember correctly, the man's name was Dr. Feldman. Both he and his wife were concentration camp survivors. They had anticipated this kind of hardship at the camp and had somewhat prepared for it. He was a doctor in the same town, close to Marta's mother's family, which was quite well known, and he knew them. They became close like neighbors and I am sure they helped Marta.

In addition to the hunger situation, another problem surfaced. The young boy who had come along with my two friends was really unhappy and wanted to go home. He was the only child of a well to do family, and never had experienced any hardship.

It was obvious that he wanted to go, no matter what. We knew again that he could go through the official channels, probably with the Red Cross, but that would have been disastrous for our families, mainly Arnost who gave us so much help to get out.

Considering the bleak conditions, with no better outlook for the future in sight, I began considering going back again, taking the boy back, and bringing something back so we could exist better.

The plan formed quickly regardless of the concerns for our safety. I believed that there was really no choice, and no other option, and that I could help so much. Marta gave me a letter for her mother. We said our goodbyes and I promised to come back as soon as possible.

We left for Furth im Wald, the town at the border. I instructed the boy how to behave, so as not to give ourselves away. But, because he was so child like, I couldn't help worrying. This time I did not inform my roommates about my plans, so I didn't have to see anyone over there.

We passed through the camp in Furth Im Wald and started for the border early in the morning. The weather was o.k. but dry, which was of some concern when it would be time to cross the well traveled trail in the woods, knowing it was used by the border guards.

Chapter 17

Last Border Crossing

When we reached the trail, with a good running start, we jumped over it, and headed through the woods up the hill toward the Kozina monument. So far so good, the trip from there to Domazlice was uneventful, not meeting anyone, even though it was now well into the morning. Even though the area is sparsely populated, people do walk around, so we were lucky again.

Domazlice, Czech Republic in 2009.

The train station was empty and we had to wait for the train for over an hour. Fortunately, there was no control (observer) upon boarding, so off we went on to Plzen. I chose a secluded spot, reducing any chance of the boy's saying the wrong thing around any of the other passengers.

I bought a communist newspaper at the railroad station. It was an oversized big format, so it could be assumed that whoever would be reading it would be a communist, a good camouflage. Upon arrival in Plzen, it was already close to noon.

There would not be much of a chance for running into anyone. Most people traveled in the morning and evening, but I did meet a boy, who recognized me. He was from an adjacent village, and our field bordered theirs. He was from good stock, unaware that I had left and I certainly didn't tell him. We had a friendly chat and parted company.

I really preached to the boy who was staying behind, not to reveal anything to anyone about his escape. Many people hopefully didn't know about his attempt, because it was only about three weeks since he had left. I asked him to keep a low profile for a few days so I could get back safely. He promised faithfully, bought a train ticket to Stary Plzenec, thanked me, and we went our own separate ways.

I spent the next several long hours waiting, to be able to go home by late evening. Now looking back, it was really a bad idea going home, with risk of exposure while traveling and exposing also my entire family, causing them real worry and concern about my safety. I could have gone directly to Prague, where very few people knew me, do what was needed and head back. But, I was drawn to see my family again. Their concern did not enter my mind.

I again took the last train at the last minute and the last car. The trip to Nepomuk was quite normal. Upon arrival I again waited as long as possible, but never saw anyone. I set off walking in the dark for home, again by the back way. When I arrived, I was greeted by the family with complete disbelief, and pure shock, that I appeared again.

Even though, I explained in detail what my mission was, it did not diminish our mother's worry. I think now, they felt that nothing was worth risking my life this way. For the first time, seeing the alarm that was caused by my arrival I realized it was probably a mistake that should have been avoided.

Nepomuk, Czech Republic in 2009

By seeing the sincere concern by everyone, I myself became much more concerned about the risks that I was facing. After spending a restless night (with the beginning of related nightmares), I spent the next day with my sisters, talking, playing games, and resting. By early morning, after an emotional good bye, I left for the train station.

Walking to the Nepomuk railroad station and the train ride to Prague was uneventful, not meeting anyone who could recognize me. Arriving at Marta's mother's was quite a surprise without any forewarning notice. Mrs. Smidova did not understand why there had been no response to her previous letter, (even the Red Cross could not have helped because the letter never reached Marta) in which she had asked something of real importance.

She was quite sad to hear about the poor conditions in the refugee camp in Germany, which I described. I also explained my plan to purchase a lot of cigarettes, which could be exchanged for a good value and used to substantially improve Marta's and little Zdenek's existence. She immediately offered whatever money was needed to help.

Later, I understood Mrs. Smidova better from Marta's descriptions and explanations. I realized more about the traumas she had gone through. She had already survived many real tragedies in her life, before and after the war, as well as becoming a widow, when Marta was only four years old. Now, seeing her daughter leave with her grandson brought more fear for their survival, not knowing if they were being deprived, facing hunger, danger, and an unknown future.

So, I was really a messenger of not joyful news, but of real stark reality. She asked me to spend a night because she needed time to write another letter to Marta, and to also gather whatever cash was needed. After a quiet evening in this warm friendly home, I spent a peaceful and comfortable night, the first in quite some time. By morning, I was ready to head back.

After a good breakfast, having real coffee, and money in my pocket, I thanked her, and promised to deliver everything. I tried to console her and asked her to not be consumed with worry, and told her that we will be careful. We said our goodbyes, and with two suit cases given by Mrs. Smidova I made my way to the vicinity of the railroad station.

I looked for a store to buy a good knap sack and the cigarettes. I knew there were special stores that sold tobacco products. But, by buying such a large quantity could arouse suspicion, so I only bought about a third of what I had planned and finished buying more at different stores. Being loaded like a mule, around a railroad station was no problem, since other people traveled this way, but probably not so loaded like I was, so I had to be cautious. The train trip to Plzen was again without problems, only the connection to Nyrsko involved a good portion of time.

With the load I had I couldn't wait normally in the station waiting room, for fear of being seen so I walked elsewhere, keeping my suit cases in sight. I also bought dark glasses, and rearranged my hair a little to fool someone, if seen at first glance.

Plzen, Czech Republic Main Train Station in 2009.

While waiting, many things went through my head. One, issue was that I was hoping they did not change the border boundary position any closer, once being about ten kilometers, which they would not have announced. That would have been a major disaster, especially because I carried no I.D. papers – very foolish and reckless. Luckily, all went well, and I arrived in Nyrsko.

My friend Arnost was a little surprised to see me, but received me warmly, as usual. He also showed some concern about my luggage. I had my full load of two medium suitcases and a knap sack. He was such a dear friend and being in his company was very special. Our mutual and main concern was about my border crossing, and being so loaded. If I left his house going part way through town then about two and a half miles to the village near the woods, all on open roads, it would be very risky. So, we decided that I should go at night after most people are settled down and staying indoors.

After a days rest, I waited until the next evening, and after a good hearty supper, I waited till about ll p.m. We said our last goodbyes, promising to exchange letters through the Chicago address. This time, we both knew we would not be seeing each other again.

It was sad for me, to see him standing there, being so alone, with no family or real friends. Even while facing a big challenge, I looked forward to be among my friends in freedom. Arnost reminded me that he too will be among friends again when he goes to Israel. I left feeling happy for my dear friend that he also would find new freedom and be in a much better living environment, which he so fully deserved.

Heading out into the night, my guardian angel was with me, not seeing a living soul, during about an hour of walking to Hadrava, near the woods. I now realized how lucky I was, never before giving much thought to the obvious exposure and especially now, with all of this luggage, going west.

It felt good to slip into the forest again, back in safe surroundings. Never having had experienced night travel cutting through the dark forest was quite different from the previous times, and felt much, much more difficult.

I could not see the pathways, and wasn't able to cross fully, without leaving foot prints behind, plus, the many dry branches on the ground, made lots of noise, when stepped on. While resting to catch my breath, I noticed that the area back of me was lighter. Then it dawned on me, that it must be the moon that had come up, after I entered the forest.

This was a wonderful stroke of luck, to be able to better establish my direction. Again, I had not considered this as a God sent aid, but now looking back, after so many years, I can't imagine how I would have made it without it. Having had this new sense of direction, it gave me more confidence struggling across. As I remember, the ground sloped steadily uphill, which after about three hours, was fairly exhausting, causing heavy perspiration. I was totally drenched in sweat. This was another problem, not having had any water (In those days, there were no plastic bottles and glass was too heavy).

I just plowed my way across despite it all, knowing that I was closing in on the border. Then a big shock came! I heard dogs barking behind me. It sounding like there was more than one. Their barks resonated with aggressiveness, echoing loudly through the woods. That was frightening and my heart began pounding like a sledge hammer. I briefly stopped to compose myself. Many things flashed in my mind, in fast succession.

First I remembered my older coworker telling me what the best defense would be, if attacked by a dog. I did have a dagger approximately 6 inches long this time. But I dismissed the idea, knowing there was more than one dog.

I also remembered that they used good sized German Shepherds. Judging by the strong barking sounds that I could now hear, there was no doubt left about that. I considered dropping my load right there and making a run for it.

From photo by Ellen Levy Finch - cc
German Sheppard

Perhaps the border was near. I dismissed the idea of dropping my load because it would have been a big disappointment to everyone, and besides I could never outrun the dogs anyway. I decided to walk as fast as I could, half running carrying all I had.

Now, I dropped all caution, being noisy, stepping on all sorts of twigs and limbs, only to keep going. After about fifteen minutes, I briefly stopped to catch my breath again, listening and a small ray of hope emerged. The barking seemed more distant, and I realized that the guards must not have turned the dogs loose, and chose to hang on to them, walking on difficult terrain as I was.

I must have increased the distance between us having given it all that I had. I gave a big sigh of relief, and thanked my dear guardian angel who again came to my aid. Now, it was getting lighter, a new dawn was approaching. As I continued I could see a wide clearing about 300 to 400 feet across.

I wondered if I should run across it or walk around the perimeter, which would have been safer, but would take a lot more time. Knowing the dogs were still out there, I decided to take a chance and run. While running, I knew I was a perfect target, so I hoped my luck would still hold. I made it, and came into a small growth of trees, when suddenly there was a well traveled path.

I knew right then it was the main route used by the guards and that I must get out of there real fast, but stopped briefly and listened. All was quiet and I dashed across like a shot. In another two hundred feet or so, there was the border marker. Just glancing at it I kept going as fast as I could. Now, I was on the German side in the clearing going downhill, anxious to increase the distance between me and the border. It was known that people were captured, even shot across the line. I knew they were capable of this and so I gave it my last few ounces of energy.

In a few minutes I looked back behind me and saw that I was down hill enough, with the hill cresting behind me, and the woods, along with its border, were out of sight. Now I was free, I made it! As before, pausing, and looking into the distant hills across a big valley, I came out of bondage, into a promised land. It would be hard to describe my exhilaration! This time, I knew that I had received a special blessing and for that, I will always be thankful.

I sensed that I was in a familiar area and that I had been in this very place before, which would have been incredible, going through the forest at night. Suddenly, I saw a border guard walking down my way, so it was confirmed. This was the same spot. The guard came closer and I couldn't believe that it was the same submariner again. He was also surprised to see me and said something in German, like, "Oh, it is you again?"

I could hardly speak, being so dehydrated, and totally drenched in perspiration. We walked into the same border outpost. Facing the same strict uniformed officials, who also remembered me. After they gave me a glass of water, they couldn't hide their official might, since this time they caught me red handed. They smugly began applying all the rules in full measure, most likely remembering my previous disrespect for them.

So the process started like this, in German: "So, lets see what we have here?" They took the two suitcases and backpack, and started to empty it on the big round table. It was quite a heap, with packs of cigarettes falling off. They then started to count the packages and began typing, again with one finger. It was so sad for me, sitting there exhausted, now realizing that it may all have been for nothing. Being on the defensive, I did not object for quite some time. They appeared to be satisfied with their important official duty, and called the Americans to come and get me. What happened next, I will never forget, and will fondly describe.

An American soldier came who had to duck his head through the door. He was a big powerful looking man and was packing a big gun at his hip, cowboy style. He walked sort of easy like not saying a word. Both guards jumped up and clicked their heals saying something, but he never even looked at them. As I watched him intently, I assumed he was a sergeant with stripes on his shoulder.

Having previously read quite a few real western stories, I felt that I was now meeting a real westerner in person. He looked around and saw the heap of cigarettes, and then looked at me and said something that I didn't understand. (I imagined that he was a Texan by his appearance.) Sensing his sympathy though, I got up and started my plea, to reclaim my treasure. I was able to say in English: "We are hungry in the camp." I pointed to the cigarettes and said, "Food." Without any hesitation he pointed to the bigger suitcase, which I then handed to him, and he walked to the table with it. The suitcase looked like big jaws. Immediately, the guards realized what his next move would be. They jumped up and briskly said, "Nein, nein." and waved their arms in displeasure and disagreement.

He ignored them and swung his big arm into the heap, filling up the suitcase to the brim. Those guards now really objected. I understood them as they explained that it had all been counted and officially recorded. Regardless of that, I helped the American close the suitcase and he motioned that we should go. He said something peppery as we left.

I was so grateful to be in his company and had received back almost half of my load, but I couldn't explain my gratitude clearly enough. He only grinned with approval, and understanding, in his casual and easy like manner. This was such an enormous and merciful act and was engraved forever in my mind. Even over 60 years later, now at home in the US whenever I meet a Texan it is always a special honor and if possible, I will tell them this story, which they really enjoy. There is always a good feeling of closeness I have for these people.

Sitting up front with the driver, it was a really wild and thrilling ride being in an American military jeep.

After covering some distance we came to a big bridge, over the Danube River. There was a potentially serious incident that happened here.

USAR

U.S. Army jeep

As we were on the bridge, a huge truck traveling the same direction on our left began encroaching into our lane more and more, until we were right next to the guardrail. I remember looking down, way down into the river and then looking at the big tire on our left. Unable to go any further, we stopped. Then, the truck stopped also. In a second the Texan sprang into action and jumped to his feet and standing so tall, he pulled out his big gun and aimed it right at the other driver and said something in a very raised voice.

The driver must have understood because he started to back up immediately. We could have been pushed easily into the river, through the flimsy railing but it did not happen. Perhaps the German driver acted on his grudge, which many Germans no doubt had. He may have been satisfied with just showing the American the potential of power, left in their hands. I also remember that I was never scared during this time feeling the invincible power of the American's company. If the beginning of our trip seemed good and pleasant, now it was triumphant. The rest of the way was without incident to Regensburg and the Goethe Schule.

After stopping and unloading my belongings, it was time to again show my gratitude to this good man. It was so painful, l was not able to express myself clearly, except with a simple thank you. He looked at me and smiled. He seemed to understand my difficulty with speaking and just nodded his head and said, (if I remember correctly) "Good luck to you buddy." Then he took off and was gone.

My next and final act was to go to the CIC office to be interrogated again and hopefully be accepted back as a refugee. The officer on duty again understood the Czech language very well and began on a fairly serious note. He read something, which showed my last crossing over.

When he asked me why I did it, I sincerely explained about our dire situation here, and especially with regards to my friend Marta, and her little boy's plight, not having enough to eat. I explained to him that my trip was not for profit, only a good deed to help others.

Marta

He softened up and began speaking in more humane terms. He said, "You were extremely lucky so far, to have survived the extreme dangers, but don't do it anymore. Your luck will eventually run out. Stay here, and with patience, your future will be brighter." This sounded like fatherly advice coming from him, and I received it with respect. Then he asked for an aide to bring Marta in. She hurriedly came and was so happy to see me. We hugged and kissed and she told the officer that I was indeed Vaclav Frank. He smiled and we said our goodbyes and walked over to the camp.

We had so much to talk about again, especially about her mother and sister. Every word I said, she accepted with so much gratitude, and was so anxious to hear it, so that certain things I repeated knowing how precious it was for her to hear. I began to understand more about the depth of Marta's feelings, and her sincere happiness of my return, being a messenger of her mother's love.

Even if I had come back with nothing but news from her mother, that kind of love was like bringing part of her home to her. This was part of everything dear to her, and truly made her heart overflow with joy. I do believe that this event more than any other had a profound influence on her own feeling of well being and knowledge which brought with it a new contentment with a brighter vision of hope.

Czechoslovakian Victims of Communism, 1948 to 1989

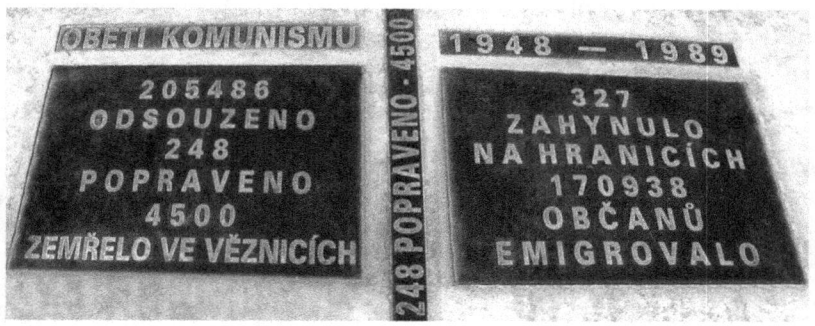

205,486 were falsely convicted, 248 were executed, and 4,500 died in prison, mainly in "Jachymov" the uranium mines, where Mr. Voboril also died.

327 perished crossing the border. 170,938 citizens emigrated.

Chapter 18

A Plague, DDT and Potatoes

After returning with my supply of cigarettes from Czechoslovakia, our lives improved somewhat, being able to barter for food. I, with Joe and Stan roamed around town to pass the time of day. I also checked up on Marta to see how she and little Zdenek were doing and enjoyed spending time with them. Our time spent swimming in the Danube was cut short after the start of a plague, an epidemic nearby. The American commanders isolated the town and forbid all swimming in the river. No movement in or out of town lasted for about a week or so. When there was no sign of the epidemic spreading, the curfew was lifted.

Once toward evening while walking with Marta along the river, we spotted a boat, and heard music coming from it. We thought that it would be fun to check it out, so we went aboard, crossing on a rickety cat walk type of bridge from the bank. This boat was offering some musical entertainment, with dancing and a three to four piece band. We liked it, bought some soda pop and went dancing.

It was nothing like what we had been used to, but was adequate. I still remember one song they played over and over, which in German was: "Sing Me Dein Lied Noch Ainmal" (Sing Me Your Song Again). There were probably ten couples dancing on the floor and because we were all making the same steps, the boat was sort of rocking with the rhythm, which made it more fun than the music itself. Civilian life in Germany was slowly awakening.

Within about a month after my final return, we were told that we will be shipped to southern Germany to a different camp near the town of Schwabisch Gmund. It was an artillery camp, well built, with two story brick buildings. The trip lasted about three to four hours. We were transported in the big US Army trucks. They had wood benches on each side and space in the middle for our suitcases and our meager possessions. Our anticipation was soon diminished.

When we got in we found that everything was really dirty. Most of the rooms had bunches of straw all over the floor almost like the cow stables that I remembered from my past at home. After we unloaded in this camp, we had to go through a detox or delousing treatment. They used generous amounts of DDT a white powder, dumping it all over our bodies. I can still remember the taste of it. I am sure, the harmful health effect of this agent was then not known. Even if it were, it was just too useful.

Note: It took about twenty years of DDT use, which resulted in harm to birds and small animals, and eradication of entire bird populations, before it was realized and finally abolished. A famous naturalist, Rachael Carlson, in the US wrote about this in her book "The Silent Spring".

But, back in our camp, after sweeping the straw out and off all of the floors, a generous amount of DDT was used again, and left to sit for a few hours to be fully effective, before the final clean up. With the primitive brooms I am sure there was a lot left for us to breathe. The poor young children in our population did not receive any better consideration. We were told that this kind of clean up was necessary because of some European people who had previously lived in this camp and had left it in such a bad condition.

This camp had adequate sanitary facilities and showers, even warm water on occasion. The facilities functioned well to our liking, and were a great contrast to the Goethe School Camp in Regensburg, which had been a teaching institution and had no need for these facilities when first built.

Our hopes for better food rations were quashed, not receiving anything better, maybe slightly even worse than before. The greenish soup had some evidence of some green vegetation, probably from the nearby wild growing field. There were some meager rations of real dark bread, which probably kept us barely alive. At one time, we received a humanitarian shipment from the Red Cross and the people almost mobbed in anticipation.

We soon discovered it contained only sanitary items, mostly tooth brushing powder, and tooth brushes. All the camp artists had a field day displaying on the bulletin board images of the concentration of the camp people barely standing or crawling but all displaying their shining white teeth. Though I don't remember all of the foot notes and slogans exactly, they basically stated things such as: "A civilized way to die." or "Death with dignity." I saw young boys dusting their dark bread with this stuff, because it was sweet. It probably stopped when they developed bad abdominal cramps and bloating, or when they ran out of this powder.

The situation here was also made more difficult for people to go to town to buy anything because it was about five to six km away. There were about six hundred people and they all were becoming more restless and rebellious because of hunger. It culminated one day at lunch time outside, with people gathering and shouting in front of the administration offices. The gathering became very intense when they broke inside and dragged the supply officials out. They were behaving like a lynch mob.

One older man, I believe he was Polish, was accused of stealing our food. Someone held him by the neck, and shook him out of his senses, which made him completely horrified, until some of our other men came forward. Showing strength and dignity, they calmed the hot heads down and told them this was not the way civilized people solve problems. They suggested that we select three of our trusted members who would then demand seeing all records of supplies coming in, and the daily use of these in the kitchen.

The crowd dispersed when these three men went into the offices. In better than a day, it was learned that there really was not enough coming in and that no one was stealing. The three also insisted on strict supervision of the kitchen. Psychologically, this all helped, but not the real problem, the hunger.

Photo courtesy of USDA NRCS

In late August, someone noticed a nice potato field close by. Without any suggestions, some of us found the immediate answer to our situation.

One evening after dark, I went with Marta crouching low into the field, pulled out a plant and digging with our bare hands found some nice potatoes. I am reluctant to use the word stealing because it was a matter of survival for us.

Time passed very slowly with nothing to do. I spent some time with my friends Stan and Joe, but mostly I was with Marta. In probably about three weeks to a month, I received some very shocking news from Stan and Joe. They informed me that they considered joining the French Foreign Legion in order to escape their stagnant life.

I was quite alarmed, and knew that it would be a nine or ten year commitment with absolutely no way out, unless dead. I tried hard to persuade them to reconsider, explaining that perhaps our lives would improve once we achieved some status, beyond this state of just being held with no one knowing what to do with us. All of my efforts proved to be futile. One day their time had come and we said our goodbyes.

For all of us it was so heart breaking to part company, including for Marta, since we had seen each other on a daily basis. I was possibly the saddest since I had functioned as a leader among us from the beginning, and worried that I had deserted them after joining Marta. They knew that we had become inseparable and understood. They always liked Marta and wished us the best.

After their departure, I learned that their recruiting French agent gave them some money to start out with and made a lot of promises. I knew they were facing a real hard life ahead in the toughest military outfit (of those days) in the world. This army took in all sorts of criminals as well, even known war criminals, and generally men whose life was at the lower end of the scale.

France had colonies in Africa, and mainly in the Far East, controlling the French Indochina, now known as Viet Nam. This colony was infiltrated heavily by communists, and became rebellious and the Foreign Legion army, who had big bases of operation there, started to fight them. This erupted into a war with France and the US provided military equipment, including aircraft.

This war erupted by late 1949. The French fought hard, but due to a large number of Vietnamese, who really fought a fight for their independence, the war was lost. Later, in about 1951, as I was beginning my life in the United States, and able to write home, I learned for the first time that my friend Josef Taluzek had been killed in battle.

It was sad knowledge for me. Josef had been so far away in a strange country, and I would never be able to pay my final respects, or to console his family who had moved away from Old Plzen. Marta later told me she was sure that if I had not met her that I would have also become a "Legionnaire Estrange". She knew how close we were and I think she was right. Now Marta and I were left to ourselves, and we became even closer, feeling bonded forever, we made plans for our marriage.

Some encouraging news filtered through the camp. In early September 1948, we were to be shipped to Italy, to another camp. This was really exciting to us, knowing that Italy was a much warmer country generally, and our light clothing would be much better suited there than in the cold winter of Germany.

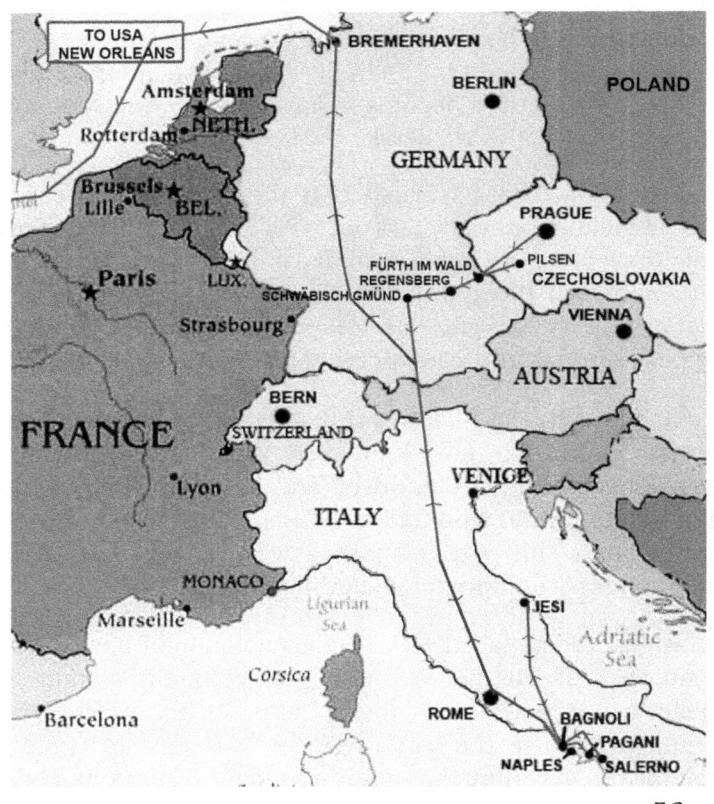

Route of our refugee camp life, 1948 to 1950.

It was announced in a few days that it would become a reality. They gave us about a week to get ready. This was such a big event and gave us new hope for a brighter horizon. Perhaps only later, going to the USA would take first place. We could have been ready in a few hours. The time came and with our three suitcases packed we were taken by the US military trucks to a railroad station. Our train consisted of freight boxcars, with crude benches and no windows.

We surely didn't mind, and just wanted to hurry up and get going. I remember little Zdenek and how happy and excited he was. Paradoxically, I believe these were some of the same boxcars left over from the war, with those horrible histories of hauling entire families to concentration camps. Now, with an entirely different mission and purpose, we started off sometime in the late morning heading into Austria, through the Tyrol country, and the foot hills of the Alp Mountains.

Photo by: Natale Carioni - *cc*
Mount Cervino (Matterhorn) from the South in the Alp Mountains.

This is one of the most beautiful spots in all of Europe. We were able to get a glimpse of this beauty through the side door, which could be forced to open unless it got too cold to do so. There was also a door at each end with a little platform that we took turns at for some sightseeing. It was exhilarating for everyone to be moving toward Italy.

Unfortunately, no one gave us any food or water, not even the children, like Zdenek, who didn't complain and was still so excited and happy to be traveling. I believe that we stopped once toward the end of the day while still in Austria to use the sanitary facilities, but still no food was available.

As evening approached, we came to the Italian border, and stopped to switch to an Italian train engine and its crew. There was a notable event during this stop. A freight train with CSR marking on all of it's cars, was surely destined to Czechoslovakia. Many people got out and wrote derogatory messages in Czech on its sides, even drawing funny anti-communist caricatures.

I can't imagine where all the white chalk came from since who would think of using any, but a lot of it was used. It really made everyone happy to see those pointed messages. We hoped that when they reached their destination that there would not be any water or brooms handy for removal of the messages, and would then be a nice way of exposing some contrary opinions.

It is said that Italians are crazy drivers, and to that it should include also the train's engineers. As soon as they hooked onto our boxcars, we felt that we were in a race. What a difference up till now, which had been a leisurely and fairly reasonable drive. Now the cars swayed from side to side and were quite noisy.

The ride became crazier when we passed the Brenner Pass; the continental divide. It was really scary, especially with all the screeching at the curves. It felt like we were riding on two wheels. Marta was scared too, but not little Zdenek, who probably thought that it was a fun ride. After about an hour of this, all downhill, the country leveled off on the Italian plain.

We finally relaxed and tried to get some sleep. It was the middle of the night. When morning came up, we still felt a little drowsy, and were hungry. The saving grace were the few potatoes that Marta had managed to bring. She was always concerned about the lack of food. We never forgot the value of these potatoes, with thanks to the old German farmer.

By 8 am, we eased into Rome. How glorious! I never dreamed to ever see or be in this eternal city. This was a real memorable and festive entry for us refugees. I distinctly remember that I had a feeling that we were entering a majestic domain, even when only just seeing the railroad yard's landscape.

USAR

Rome, Italy in 1944

Also there was a particularly strong sweet aroma, like ripe fruit in the air. Even over sixty years later, I still clearly recall the strong scent. With everything we had been through so far, we felt that this was surely the best entry anyone could have arriving in such a warm and pleasant country. Some people offering aid came from car to car and served us some warm liquid, a mixture of soup or coffee, according to one's taste and imagination.

I took some and swallowed it, without tasting it much, and it warmed me up. Marta tasted it and couldn't drink it, despite my pleading (This inability to tolerate unpleasant food was probably due to her upbringing in Prague. This was a trait that I learned to respect). I felt sorry for her condition of hunger. Fortunately, they also gave us some white wine grapes, from the nice Italian tradition and I gave Marta my portion which was a food that she loved. I remember hoping that little Zdenek didn't see the previous look of repulsion for the warm liquid on his mother's face.

After a couple of hours when everyone's immediate needs were satisfied and the meager food eaten, we left Roma and entered slowly into the rest of Bella Italia. I stood on the platform and watched all that I could. Everything was quite different here compared to the rest of Europe. Perhaps because I had always liked trains, I was amazed at how advanced theirs were. All electrified, the cars were really sleek.

What our outfit looked like to them must have been a shock. There was a distinct puzzlement in their expressions when we met, we probably, looked primitive, maybe something like cave men. In my later years in the US, I read and saw movies about the "Okies moving to California", which seemed similar to this situation (People from Oklahoma, leaving their farm, due to a bad recession of the 30's and the severe draught).

The train took us south to Naples, about a two hour ride, where we were met by the same kind of army trucks as we had been transported by previously. They took us for another ride, this time to Bagnoli, in the outskirts of Naples, to a huge camp on a hill. Our impression was a mixture of apprehension, and perhaps some fear of being swallowed up by this huge impersonal looking army style city.

It was built by the dictator Mussolini as a fascist military showplace, sometime before the 1940s. As we proceeded to unload in the central square of this huge complex, we were in for a big shock. We were received by very crude, coarse looking camp personnel, who were unpleasant toward us, even hostile.

NATO

These buildings in Bagnoli were used as a Displaced Person Camp between 1946 and 1951. In 1953 they became the headquarters for Allied Forces South, AFSOUTH.

We had never seen people like these ever before and soon learned that they were from Croatia. That was part of Yugoslavia then, and all of them had sided with the Germans, fighting the Serbians, who were loyal to their king. Their history was very bloody. Some were criminals of war with cruelty inscribed on their faces. Even though it was almost four years after the war it looked like they never forgot it and were still living within those terrible times.

Again, the first order at reception was the dusting (hand pump applied) by the DDT. It was done in an unpleasant way, as if they were handling cattle. I remember feeling upset at being treated that way, and thinking it seemed to be a normal procedure for them. We gave our names and were led to our sleeping cubicles. Marta, with Zdenek were put in the women's barracks, and I was put with the men.

At the evening meal time I met with Marta and we assessed our situation. Both of us agreed that this place seemed like a giant prison. It was completely surrounded by rolled barbed wire. We thought, well, at least the sun was pleasantly warm, which was somewhat special to us, here in the southern hemisphere.

Note: In its November 21, 1949 issue, the newspaper "Stars and Stripes" reported that "Pneumonia and stomach disorders have killed eight refugee babies during the past eight weeks at the Bagnoli refugee camp near Naples." "IRO officials said the deaths followed an epidemic of measles at Bagnoli which filled the camp hospitals to overflowing."

Chapter 19

Bagnoli and Jesi

In this camp in Bagnoli, along with those of us who were refugees, there were may displaced people. They were the remnants of all sorts of war time segments of the European nations, who had been forcibly removed from their homes. These included Russian, Ukrainian, and Polish prisoners of war, who refused to go back to their home countries after all the hostilities, primarily because these countries became communist.

Camp leadership was British and American which was a relief to us. The population numbered about 5,500 hoards of people. Food was cooked and served in one building. The distribution was done with the use of I.D. distribution cards. which were punched upon receipt of food, again by one of those rough looking characters. The population was split into two groups. Each line was over 2,000 people long, and it took at least an hour of slow moving to be served.

A nice thing happened during this monotonous waiting and that was that the camp amplified music, which was broadcast through giant speakers through the camp. They played Italian music only. The Santa Lucia, was beautifully sung and the La Paloma, (originally Spanish) were well known, and we really enjoyed it. We both felt what a nice soft touch this music was in this prison like place.

The song La Paloma was very popular in those post war years, and was typically played at dances as a tango. This graceful, sensuous, South American dance, always so dreamy, transformed our minds, if only for a little while, away from the camp's reality. It remained so dear to us from this time, that later for many years in America while attending dances, we requested this tango. Back in Bagnoli it was like a sound coming from heaven, when we stood there in that long line of 2,000 hungry people.

Considering how undernourished we were, receiving any amount of food should have been somewhat of a pleasant occasion, but even that was compromised, due to the coarse people who served it. A rough looking fellow stood at the window, resting his big club like stick, or cane, against the wall, punching the camp cards. Some people said that he was an illiterate sheepherder. He had some difficulty recognizing each card, which was top or bottom. Later on, I saw some of our guys grabbing his card out of his hands, and turning it the right way up for him. They called him an illiterate idiot, which resulted in a lot of shouting and probably a good release of tension for everyone in the line.

The menu hardly ever changed. Typically, it consisted of some thin fish soup, a piece of cooked fish, soft as a dish rag, and a piece of white Italian bread, which was delicious, but unfortunately, always in short supply and small amounts. Marta couldn't eat the soup or the fish, so she traded for my piece of bread. Little Zdenek had it easier, since they had a special kitchen for children.

A normal day started with breakfast, beginning again with the long line of people, we received imitation coffee with milk and a piece of white bread. The news for the day was announced over the loud speakers, in multiple languages, starting with Italian, then Serbo-Croatian, German and English. These broadcasts were repeated during the day, which gave us a good opportunity to listen to and learn languages.

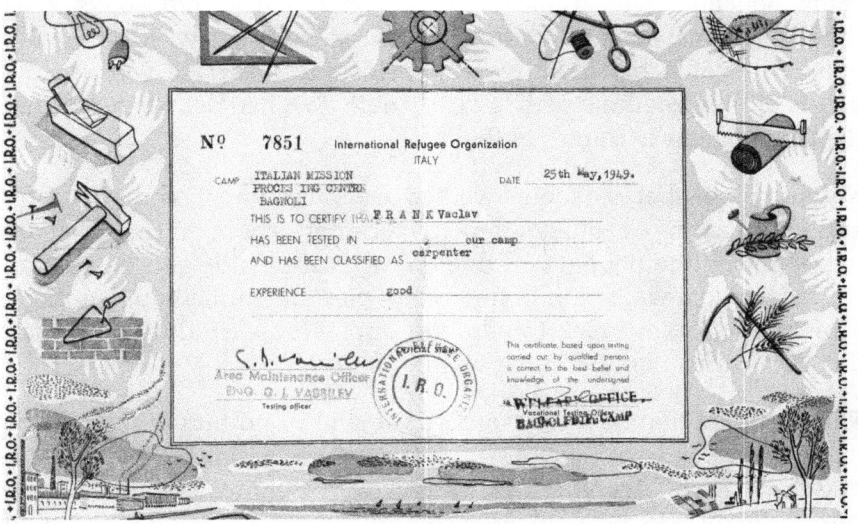

My IRO work certificate.

In about two days, we were given the camp I.D. cards that registered our name with the "Camp IRO" status, the International Refugee Organization. With these I.D.s we could go out of the camp.

Passing through the guard gate, we entered Bagnoli, a Naples suburb. We immediately walked into a crowded street, teaming with all sorts of peddlers selling and buying everything under the sun. They all called out "Vendere, vendere". We noticed that people were mostly selling pieces of clothing, and purchasing food and fruit at the next street down the hill. This was all fascinating to us. People were everywhere. The venders were shouting, and sometimes arguing.

Marta liked grapes, so we bought some. The next street was used for the fish market with many varieties of fish, even a small octopus, which they kept alive in water. When a sale was made, they threw it into boiling oil to cook it on the spot. Some of those fellows held the octopus up high in their hands, for all to see, with all those tentacles hanging down, looking so ugly. We walked away from that.

I noticed all the fishermen were suntanned and rugged looking and were barefooted, standing on the wet ground. This was all so fascinating to watch and we passed the biggest part of the day there.

After about a week of this existence, I inquired about a job in the camp which had positions such as: camp police, and cooks, plus there was a carpenter's shop. I soon realized that with this many people it would be a long wait. Besides all positions were in the hands of the Croatians who favored their own people. So, forgetting the camp I went to Naples to find work.

Not knowing where to look, I walked around town, till mid afternoon and found a dingy cabinet shop. It was a dark room off the sidewalk with about three people working on furniture inside and outside on the sidewalk. I walked in to find the owner and immediately noticed a picture of Saint Mary (Madonna) and Mussolini, the late Italian dictator, with a light illuminating it.

The burly looking boss approached me and I told him in my halting Italian that I was a refugee (profugo in Italian) and needed work. He asked me first: "Are you a communist? Are you a fascist?" I said resoundingly, "No, no, I am not a communist. I am a refugee escaping from communism."

He then showed me the primitive place and asked, if I could do what we were looking at. I said that I could, and would like to be paid for what I was worth. He said, "Benne", and told me to come in the morning. I came as early as they let us out of the camp, and went to work pitching in with all I had. He gave me some hand polishing work to do which was easy and he liked what I did. The work lasted for about two weeks when we could not leave the camp, only with a special permit, which I could not get.

By about the third week, we inquired at the camp director's office about the possibility of Marta and I getting married, so we could live normally together. There were no objections from the director's office, but it would have to be held in Naples at the municipal office, and we would need an interpreter.

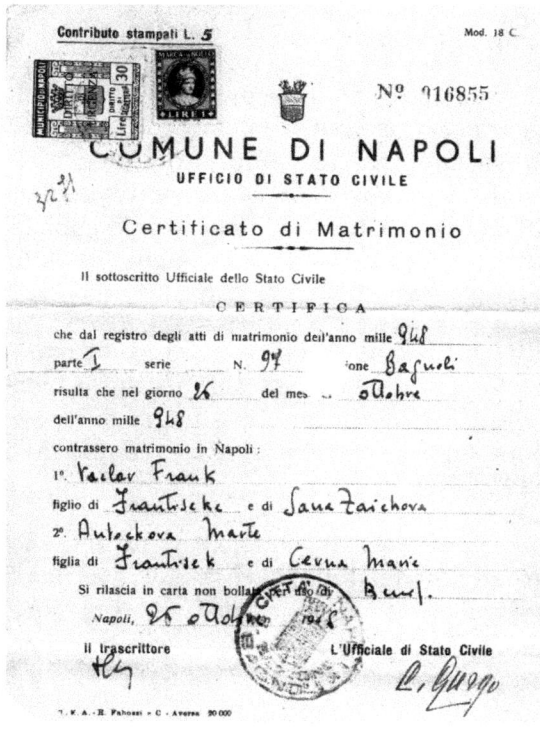

On October 26, 1948, we went with the Yugoslav interpreter to Naples to the "Officio Matrimonio".

The Yugoslav interpreter explained to each of us what our responsibilities were to be. I was to always go to work, provide money for the family, and give money to my wife to manage the household. Marta's role was to be a good wife, homemaker, cook, clean, and do whatever was necessary.

They gave us a Certificate of Marriage.

It gave us a very special feeling to be married here in Napoli (Naples), which was known in Europe, to be the most beautiful place in the world, with its curved bay and Mount Vesuvius, a dominating volcano, in the background.

Naples, Italy and Mount Vesuvius

We got back to the camp, hurried up to catch the dinner distribution, but arrived too late and the door was shut. Luckily, we still had enough time to look up the accommodation officer to assign us a family quarter, which he did. We moved to a different building (Bloco Q), which contained families. Our new home was a cubicle about eight by ten feet, with cardboard walls about eight feet tall, one of many in a huge hall.

We were so happy to finally be living as a family. It was a lot more pleasant in so many ways. Now, we were also able to share food easier, wash our clothes collectively and even do some of our own home cooking. This was done on an electric hot plate, the one that Marta brought from Germany.

Because there were no electric outlets, I managed to extend the wires, from the hot plate, and hooked them to some overhead exposed wires being about twelve feet up. The insulation on these wires had to be scratched off, so as to make good contact from wire to wire.

The few groceries that we needed were very reasonable, like potatoes, cream of wheat and other basics. Many families caught on in doing the same thing, until the electric circuit got overloaded and the fuses blew. The camp maintenance man did not want to keep replacing the fuses, knowing the real problem. Once, when the building remained dark, we all knew they were not going to fix it. Someone came up with a solution of using a p.c. of heavy wire as a fuse. They did it and it worked, the wire was red hot, but it held. This was of course was very dangerous and could have caused shock, electrocution, or a fire due to burning wires. We were lucky.

By about mid November, we received some old G.I. clothing and shoes. The clothing was no problem, and we sold some items to the fishermen, but the shoes proved more difficult. The guy that distributed the shoes, handed me a pair that was a size 16, despite my objections. But, since my shoes were still pretty good, I went out to sell the big ones. I walked all day, without any success. Most people laughed when they saw such large shoes. Some people even stuck their feet in with their shoes still on, and showed that they could still rattle their feet around.

The next day I went to Naples to a big market place called, "Piazza Garibaldi". This was the biggest open free market in the whole region. Still, I had the same problem, with the big shoes. When I came to one wise guy, who again tried them on while laughing, finally said, as he pointed up to the tall statue of Garibaldi, who stood on a high pedestal, "You go and sell them to him. They will surely fit." I don't know how I ever sold them, if ever.

We also had some nice surprises on occasion. One was a visit by the U.S. Navy, the 7th fleet, about twelve to fourteen war ships of all kinds. We were all elated about their arrival, and went to Naples to see it. It was so beautiful to see this huge might of ships in the spectacular Naples harbor.

USN

Modern Naples Harbor, Italy

Adding to the beauty of this spectacle was that the ships appeared to be shining white in the sunlight, probably because they were painted light grey.

It gave us an enormous feeling of security, coming from these good and powerful friends. Italy, like most of Europe was living in a democracy, but racked by communist inspired strikes. Some were so large, and were challenging the governments in power, which were not so sound. Usually these strikes contained mixtures of coalitions, which included the socialists, and communists.

Being aware of this at times shaky situation, we refugees from communist controlled countries feared that if the communists gained full power that we would be very unwelcome guests and could be sent back to where we came from. That is why we were so encouraged, and our sense of security so enhanced by the US Navy's visit.

While walking in Naples, we couldn't believe the enormous numbers of US sailors who were everywhere. They all looked so immaculate in their well pressed white uniforms. They were also so happy looking, and always well received by the local population, who over night set up all sorts of stands everywhere, selling just about everything imaginable.

It was so fascinating to see, and hear the venders shouting, and asking for the boys to buy their goods. They shouted, "Americans, vieni qua" (Americans, come here.)! In a few days these sailors came to our camp, to play baseball. We filled this camp sport's area only about a quarter full. We must have disappointed them with such a low turnout. For many of us, it was the first time that we had seen this sport, and knew nothing about it.

I remember times when there was probably a home run, and the visiting sailors really applauded, but our camp people just sat there unresponsive. During their stay, which lasted for about two weeks, the sailors came to play baseball at least two times. Soccer would have been a different matter. The whole of Europe was dedicated to soccer games, with baseball nonexistent. We had our camp soccer teams, which were played to a large audience, and with Italian teams. But, it always ended up in a big brawl, requiring a good number of police to restore order. Obviously, built up frustrations of the people in the camp found a release of tensions this way.

We were also told that the US Navy had come during some national elections, to make a show of force and support for the conservatives favor. It must have helped, because the communists did not achieve a substantial stance of power. I believe that the period of our stay, was about the peak of the conservatives glory, declining ever since.

When the time for the departure of the fleet came, we went to watch. It was so magnificent to see these gleaming beautiful ships lined up, heading out to sea slowly, and so majestically. It was a farewell, never to be forgotten. Most of us who were present were saddened by the departure of these dear friends, but also knew that they would also be there if called upon.

Even though these memories go back over sixty years, I still remember the reassuring support that we received, and knew that this enormous fleet was only a part of the strength of the US, whose power was the biggest in the world, advocating democracy and freedom to all nations.

Wintertime was passing, ever so slowly, with its grey skies, rainy and windy weather. I don't remember having had any frost, but our cardboard cubicles became uncomfortably cool. The huge concrete halls had no heat. We had no winter clothing, so in our cubicles, we wrapped ourselves with the bed blankets. Marta always worried about little Zdenek, who liked to be outside, but he never complained about the cold. We knew he loved playing and exploring the grounds.

One way that Marta and I found to escape the cold was to attend the camp's movie theater. This building also did not have any heat but was concrete without any windows, so not so cold. Taking a blanket along, we watched American movies. These shows were mostly westerns and war episodes dubbed in Italian.

It turned out to be another good way to learn more of the Italian language (in addition to the daily public address system). Later in the US after I had learned the English language, I really appreciated watching and hearing John Wayne, Henry Fonda and others, in the original English versions.

January 15th gave us news over the public system. Along with 150 others, we would be moved to a camp in Jesi in northern Italy. We had no idea where this place was, or what to expect. Considering our boring life here in Bagnoli, it brought a spark of adventure, at least for a change, and with some hope for a better existence.

On the appointed day, the standard military trucks came to take us to the rail station. It was late afternoon, still wintertime, with the evening darkness prevailing when we got into the train. We sat on a wooden bench and huddled together in almost total darkness. I vividly remember the mysterious feeling hearing the noise of the speeding train, being in a dark space, as we rushed into the unknown. The unheated car prevented us from sleeping, except for little Zdenek, who found comfort in his mother's lap. Considering that we were enveloped by semi darkness, the night seemed to be without end. We arrived at Ancona at daybreak.

Army trucks similar to the ones shown in the photo below picked us up to travel to the Jesi camp. This region of the north was cold. The trucks had canvass tops and were quite drafty. We were not accustomed or dressed for this weather, so we huddled together.

USAR

My first impression was that the brutal starkness, with tall blue mountains in the background seemed to add to the cold. The camp had previously been a military base, and this was what was left over from the war. There were rows after rows of Quonset huts. These barracks were silver huts in the shape of long half barrels and made of metal. Each building was about twenty feet wide by forty feet long.

They put us into one, which was divided into four parts. We had about a ten foot long by twenty foot length of floor space. The partitions were made of corrugated brown paper with two wood stoves. Each hut was divided into two units at each end and shared a wood stove in a cut out opening in the partition.

This arrangement was our first lucky break because the unit close to our own was occupied and they had the stove real hot. Despite the lack of any furnishings with the exception of the bed, this was heavenly to us, coming from the cold night into a near freezing morning and at last to finally be able to warm up.

After soaking up all the heat, we began to feel real hunger. Upon arrival we were told the camp rules and of what times the meals would be served. It was close to breakfast time so I ran into the mess hall.

After some problem of not being registered yet, they gave me some utensils, coffee and bread and some porridge, which I carried to Marta and Zdenek. Having our first breakfast here by the warmth of the wood stove was so comforting, and we soon met our neighbors indirectly through the opening around the stove.

They were two Russian men, very big, burly, healthy looking and seemed friendly enough, so we communicated with a mixture of languages. Since the wood stove was also used to cook on, these fellows made a pot of tea after breakfast, quite normal, but while boiling hot, they put in a big spoonful of white lard, making it a grayish concoction. The sight and smell soon made Marta turn away in disgust.

Despite that minor disappointment, we appreciated their kindness, as they kept the fire going. Even when I volunteered to bring in wood, they said, "Nenada charasho" (in Russian: Not necessary. All is fine).

My next concern was to find something to sit on. The only warm spot in the room was by the stove, but standing for long periods was tiresome. I searched and found some discarded wood crates by the kitchen, which were quite comfortable to sit on.

It is hard to imagine exactly what we did with all the time on our hands, being unable to go out into the cold for lack of warm clothing, and to so often sit in the semi dark room with nothing to do or read even, but we managed gratefully, and looked for better times ahead.

Meanwhile, little Zdenek was industrious with finding pieces of wood, and cardboard. With a lot of creative imagination he passed the long hours as well. As I look back over the years now, I think this was probably the beginning of a trend in his ability to find ways to entertain himself without store bought toys. And I remember how, in years later, when in the US he was always making things to play with and sharing it generously with his younger brothers who loved it, never being bored in his company.

This camp had a communal hall called the "Cantina" for the purpose of people to get together, but it was frequented by some rough characters, drinking wine and being rowdy. I went there to see just once, never to return. The lunch time meal was something to look forward to, typically made with noodles, but very spicy.

The chef was Hungarian. Marta had a problem with this distinctly over spiced meal, so she'd swap a portion of it for my Italian bread, which was a good trade. We made it through the rest of January, with the weather turning a little warmer and even the wash facility had flowing water.

As time went on, we found a way to simply cope with it all, even having the benefit of some partly sunny days. We began to notice the surrounding country and it's beauty.

In about three weeks into our stay, Marta began to have some difficulty eating the breakfasts. Considering the quality, it was not really surprising, but it kept going on. Then one morning, Marta told me that she was pregnant, having gone through a period of morning sickness.

This was big news to me and I became concerned about her health and general well being even more than before. The camp's meals were what they were with no possibility of changing anything like it or not. The best I could do was to share a portion of my meals that she liked, hoping to get by. She really craved fruit like grapes, but there wasn't any place to buy any. Again, Marta managed to endure this difficult period, being strong willed and always hoping for a better tomorrow.

A better tomorrow did come. The morning sickness subsided. And, best of all, we heard that by early spring which was only a few weeks away, we would be going back to Bagnoli. We were to start the immigration process with big hopes for a new future.

So, it finally happened one day. We were given two days to pack and get ready to start the journey back to Bagnoli. All of the people were in an upbeat mood about the beginning of the immigration process, and even the train trip back was hardly thought of.

Chapter 20

Back to Camp Bagnoli and on to Camp Pagani

Back in Bagnoli, we settled in building "M" which housed families only. It also contained cardboard partitioned cubicles about eight feet high. We still had our electric hot plate, and managed to hook it up again to the wires that were up twelve feet above us, high at the ceiling. And, as soon as possible, I cooked a small meal for Marta. She had considerable difficulty eating the camp meals, primarily due to usage of some cheap cooking oil, and the changes associated with her pregnancy.

Like we did before, I managed to sell whatever we could, such as pieces of clothing outside the camp's gate to the Italian traders. I obtained a little money to buy some cream of wheat and a little butter and sugar. Within a short time, the process for immigration started with the camp loud speakers calling out many names to report fast for political screening, manned by the CIC (now called the CIA). The questions asked were sort of touchy and provocative, which were meant to trip anyone, who might be hiding something in their background. We passed without any problem.

Next came the medical exams. These were quite thorough, and included chest x-rays. They were also screening for tuberculosis. We learned that TB was indeed a problem, especially among the young men, who smoked, drank, and often lived a loose life. This was a contagious disease which was running rampant.

In a relatively short time, we heard that an investigation by the US would soon be coming in regards to the food supply. This was triggered by many people's letters to their relatives in America, who eventually revealed it all to the US senate. Enough senators listened and became very alarmed, especially after seeing the high incidents of TB cases. I recall two senators that came to our camp to see for themselves. One was Senator of Nevada, who had a reputation of being quite crusty and tough and hated corruption.

We all knew that the food supply was allocated by the UN International Refugee Organization, which always fell short of arriving. I don't recall any real improvement, except that there were bulletins displayed, which listed the calorie counts of each meal served. I am quite sure that the senators had good intentions but could not penetrate the tangled web of transporting this large quantity of food through the ports, and railroads (Some of which were dominated by the mafia).

One positive step taken was the immediate separation of all TB infected people who were taken to a different camp. There they could finally have access to medical treatment, plus in these special camps they would have abundant food.

The options for us to get out of the Italian refugee camps were limited at that time. The choices included Australia, South American countries and Canada. We, like most people, wanted to get out of the refugee camps, and Australia looked like the best choice. Australia took in hundreds of thousands of people. The immigrants would populate the land, but were also given conditions, such as being required to give two years of labor where ever it was needed. This could mean the separation of families for long periods of time.

I passed the medical exam o.k. except for some concern about a heart murmur, which was probably the result of my early boyhood scarlet fever sickness. Marta did not do so well. She was about four months pregnant, which would have made the trip to Australia potentially serious for her. This was a reality, especially when considering the old troop transport ships that were being used.

Most ships would depart from Naples, and then go through the Suez Canal, across the Red Sea to the south. The ship had to pass across the equator, with temperatures of about 120 plus, and without any air conditioning. We had heard that some people died on the way.

We were disappointed about being stranded in the camp, and we tried to accept it as a part of our fate, but still hoped for an appeal of the decision by the chief immigration officer. After some difficulty, I met the officer face to face and asked for reconsideration, for our family to be admitted to Australia. He was a very pleasant English gentleman, impeccably dressed, and smoked a pipe.

He introduced himself as a British diplomat and explained that he was familiar with most countries that were open for immigration. He looked at our file and asked: "Why do you want to go there so badly?" I replied that we like most other people in camp wanted to leave this environment and explained that we were fearful of the Italian political situation. He then said that he could not advise going to Australia, even if we were able to go. Number one, the medical condition of my wife prevented the arduous trip across the ocean. And number two, he explained, "You as Europeans would never be happy there."

He went on to say, "I know firsthand. I was there. You have a good chance to go to America, where you will be happy. It will probably take more than another year, but it is worth waiting for. Because of your wife's condition, I can assign you to a much better camp, where your life would be easier. The camp's name is Pagani, and it is about thirty kilometers southeast of Naples." Everything he said was said with sincerity, down to earth, and I knew it was for the good of our family. I respectfully thanked him. We shook hands and he said, "Good luck."

I gave Marta the good news, and she was happy to hear it, especially because of the concern that was shown for her health and well being by the officer. We both considered that it was an act of kindness that was indeed affecting our future. It was also the first time during our eight to nine months of living in these camps that anyone of authority had shown us such a kind face and consideration. We were happy to depart for Pagani.

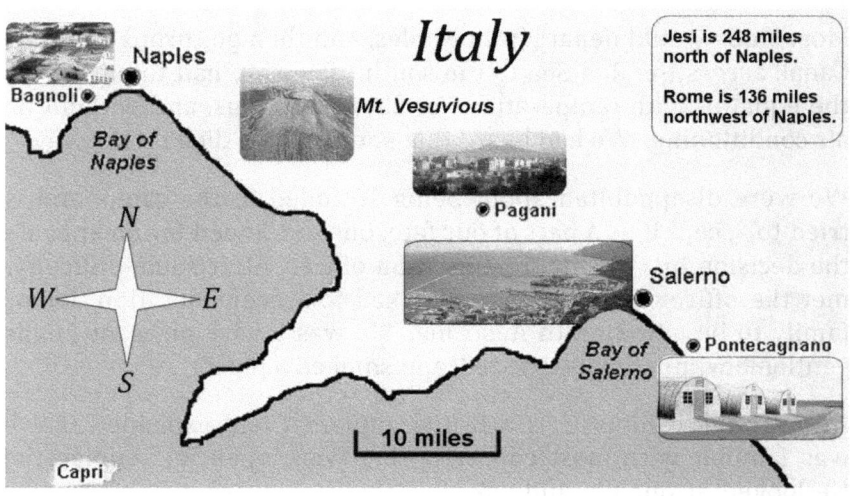

Note: Camp Salerno was by the sea near Pontecagnano.

Upon our arrival, we were in for a pleasant surprise. We moved into a masonry house, and were assigned a nice room in one corner, with a door that had a lock, and a window that over looked an orange grove. The contrast of all of this to where we had been before was incredible. For the first time we were genuinely happy.

In no time, little Zdenek was outside, marveling about the oranges on the trees, and picked some to bring in. We soon found out that there was a small school classroom in this camp, so we signed him up. He was enthusiastic to go and learn everything possible.

Our good fortune did not end with the new living quarters, and little school room, I also found a job within a few days in the camp kitchen, cooking for young mothers and children. My bosses were two women. One was Slovenian and the other was Serbian. I could communicate easily with them in Serbo-Croatian and we got along very well.

One of my tasks was to stir the huge oil fired kettles with a big wooden paddle. What became difficult was the hot temperature in this small room, which was only about six feet by eight feet, and half of that space was taken up by the cook stove. The heat was unbearable over 60 Celsius, 140 Fahrenheit. Within only a few minutes, my clothes would become totally wet, while perspiring profusely. My coworkers and I took turns of ten minutes each enduring the heat. We went out to hose off and drink water and then returned back to work in ten minutes.

One of the benefits from this job was that I could always bring home some extra food that Marta liked, which she really appreciated. With her pregnancy advancing, she finally liked what was being served. We the cooks were forbidden to eat our own cooking, and were restricted to eat food only from the big camp kitchen.

Our head boss and supervisor was an Italian, "Senior Angelli". He was very strict about cleanliness, especially when it came to the tiled floor. He had eyes like a hawk and was always looking to find something to complain about. The two ladies called him names in Serbian, slang that was so original and peppery and that I had never heard before.

In about six weeks, I was transferred to the big camp kitchen, which I also liked, because all cooks and the chef were Czechs. The chef "Pokorny" was previously a chef in a famous Prague restaurant. He had a very good reputation, and could even do wonders with whatever supplies we had in the camp. We all had a good time and horsed around at times, passing the time between meals.

Marta wanted to walk every evening after supper, as part of her strict pregnancy regiment. The weather was very nice from May through June, so it was a pleasant walk into town, where we joined in at a main street promenade, full of local people. The custom here was that all businesses closed by approximately 1 to 2 p.m. for a break which lasted for one or two hours and then they'd open up again lasting into the night. I found that the coolness of the evening was enticing, particularly with the occasional glass of wine.

My kitchen job gave enough income for us to buy a few special things, such as grapes for Marta which she craved, along with other kinds of fruit. To supplement our meager finances, Marta sometimes received some support from her uncle who lived in America. He sent her twenty dollars a few times. This was a big help to us, especially when the dollar traded at its highest value to the Italian lira. Marta also spent her time outside in the orange grove, with little Zdenek, while I worked six day weeks. After about a month, Zdenek left the refugee camp's school and started school in Pagani at the public school, attending with the local town's children.

Pagani Elementary School

He walked by himself from the camp into town. He was known by his teachers as the "profugo figlio" (refugee boy). He soon blended right in, making new friends, and learned the language along with the other students.

Marta and I with a friend visiting Zdenek's school in Pagani in 2000

My cook job had some light moments, mainly when I was ordered to serve food to the people. Typically, I faced the long line assembled outside the serving window. As I dished up the food, I would sometimes hear complaints coming from some of the folks, in all kinds of languages. I learned to understand much of what they had to say. Unfortunately, the comments often were meant as insults, such as: "This food is not fit for pigs to eat.", or even worse kind of statements.

One time, one of my coworkers was serving the food, when an unhappy recipient accused him of cooking for pigs. My server friend then answered, "Well, from the looks of you, you are not far from being one." This ignited the hot temper of the recipient who threw the entire liquid content at the server's face. The server then furious, dropped his ladle and bolted outside after the accuser, to settle the score. My other coworkers and I took over after enjoying a good laugh.

After about two months in the big kitchen, I was transferred again to cook in a special and smaller kitchen, which prepared food for people with tuberculosis. As mentioned before, many of those infected with TB were young people, mostly young men, about twenty five to thirty years of age, They were housed in special barracks, but were not kept isolated from the rest of the camp's population, which was strange considering how contagious this disease was.

The diet the cooks followed was very rich, using a lot of butter, eggs and all the high protein food sources at our disposal. It was thought that this would be beneficial and helpful for those infected. I served the meals many times to them through an opening in a window. I remember how some of them appeared gray in the face and hollow looking.

The space between us was about three feet, which means that I could have easily gotten infected. Luckily, I did not. No one ever raised the issue, or seemed to worry about it. These poor young people were sent to this camp, after being rejected by all countries for immigration. Eventually, Norway took them all, and placed them in special TB sanitariums in their northern country.

This was a most humane act that I so admired and still never fail to praise Norway, especially to any Norwegians that I come in contact with. Seeing the many sad gray faces, without a future, unwanted and rejected, then some noble country gives a helping hand, restoring a little hope. What an act of humanity.

The summer months passed by and Marta and I became aware that the day was coming for the birth of our child. I now know how brave she was, facing it all, in an unfamiliar foreign country, without any family except myself, and little Zdenek. It is amazing that Marta never expressed any concern, or worries.

We found that there was a medical facility not too far from our camp. It gave us some comfort when we learned that it was owned and operated by one doctor who was called, "Il Professore", whose good record was well known in the area. We felt prepared, and had been receiving fairly good care in the camp. Marta was regularly assisted and advised by a skilled nurse, mainly regarding the need for physical activity, as a precondition for a healthy birth process.

The time for delivery came by about the first of September, announcing itself with the beginning of Marta's abdominal pain. I contacted the camp first aid station for admission to the clinic. It was managed quickly and we walked over there, with the assistance of the nurse. Each of us held Marta by the arms, and helped her as she walked up the long flight of stairs to the second floor of the clinic.

The "Il Professore" was a little aged man, rather pleasant and received us warmly. He introduced us to his nurse, the only one there, who was an older and pleasant lady (she was also the housekeeper). She appeared to be down to earth, and very experienced, which made Marta feel more at ease. This was especially noticed when the nurse showed concern and kindness during the painful contractions Marta was having.

I was told to go home, which I didn't like, but Marta was worried about little Zdenek, who was home alone. She asked me to come back in the evening, which I promised to do. I remember the room was pretty big in size, with lots of windows, which Marta paced back and forth by.

Upon arrival the next morning, I learned that the doctor had left for a two days vacation to the island of Capri, west of Naples. Marta said that he had determined upon examination that the birth will not happen during that time, and told her not to worry. We were both concerned and fearful. Poor Marta, being with those periodic times of pain, and having to face at least two more days. Another problem was the food, which was strictly Italian, and cooked with olive oil which Marta disliked. I always brought her grapes.

The days dragged on until finally the "Senior Il Professore" returned and was ready to assume his duties. Obviously, he was quite skilled, and he knew by the increased frequency of the contractions that the time was approaching. The birth happened during my absence after I had been sent home, late in the evening of September 3rd, 1949. We had a baby son, "uno bambino figlio" (baby boy), a real big baby, eleven plus pounds.

When I returned in early morning the elderly nurse showed me the baby, as she held him in her arms. He was quite developed with already nice features, and lots of dark hair. She called him "bello bambino grosso" (beautiful big baby).

Marta with Little Pavel

Seeing Marta laying there in bed, was unforgettable, so peaceful, a picture of happiness, looking so beautiful, and just half awake and resting. She told me that it had been a difficult delivery because the baby was so big. The lady attendant cradled our new son, except for nursing time when she gave him to Marta who otherwise needed complete rest. I also held him whenever possible and spent a lot of time there, taking an absence from my kitchen job and taking care of little Zdenek, who was so happy to have a little brother.

Zdenek was often left unattended much of this time and was very well behaved, understanding the situation. He was doing well in school (first grade). Thinking way back, I find it so amazing for a young six year old boy, to walk alone to school in a foreign country, being scarcely familiar with it's language, and sit in class without a hint of any problems. We never heard of any trouble and remember that he participated with everyone there very well.

Marta was released in about a week, and returned home to our quaint little room which I had cleaned thoroughly, like a little bird's nest. I also brought something special for her from the kitchen. Of all of the happy occasions in our lives, this time of Marta's coming home with a baby, being reunited again within our own neat little nest, was a paramount of happiness. We were totally devoted to each other, and shared feelings of great contentment with each of our roles.

Typically, one of my chores was to bring home flour, sugar, and butter to make an omelet on our hot plate, which Marta and Zdenek loved. So many years have passed but I still remember this peaceful transformation of complete happiness. This was so obvious in Marta's beautiful face. We were so happy and glad to have our family. Someone gave us a baby buggy, which made it possible for Marta to go on walks outside, strolling our baby, so pleasant in the balmy weather and surrounded by the orange grove.

At one of the routine checkups at the camp infirmary, the nurse noticed a bump on the lower area of our baby's abdomen. Suspecting a hernia (lower membrane rupture), she told us that this usually happens when the baby cries excessively. We suspected this may have occurred after birth, when the nurse took him away, so that Marta could have the needed rest after the hardship of her labor.

We were sent back to the same clinic for an evaluation. The professor told us that it should be operated on as soon as possible because new born baby's nerves and sensory systems are not fully developed until after three weeks. It would be performed without anesthesia, which is risky for infants. We were convinced and agreed. Within a few days we walked over to have it done.

I carried our baby to the clinic, and laid him down on a small operation table. Then, to my surprise I was told that I could stay and watch. It was so painful to see our baby son's struggle. He was strapped down and really crying hard. It only took about fifteen minutes or less. After a small incision and then the internal stitching was completed, the cut was sewn together and the operation was over.

We were instructed about how to care for the wound, I picked him up, and passed him to Marta down stairs. He really clung to her and calmed down somewhat. The healing was without complications, and made remarkable progress. Now, it was time to think about baptism.

Although, there were no churches in this camp, we were visited by various high ranking priests of Czech descent from the Vatican in Rome. One of the highest ranking was Monsignor Jaroslav Machula, who readily agreed to perform the ceremony in the local catholic basilica "Santo Lorenzo". We walked over with a witness, one I believe to have been Desensky, a past Czech government congressman.

The basilica was majestic, dedicated to a local saint, dating back to around the 14th century. We gave our baby the name of "Pavel" (Paul) with Joseph as his middle name. The monsignor performed the Holy Baptism and graciously, after saying our prayers, he gave Pavel some money, which is normally done by the witness, but being all poor refugees, he compensated. Our lives continued on happily into the winter months.

At about the end of September, I was transferred to the TB kitchen as a cook, as I mentioned before, and Marta had special kitchen privileges for young mothers and so did Zdenek. Marta liked their cooking, which was cooked by Czech women. Zdenek after only a few months became fluent in Italian. It was fun listening to him speak it.

Sometime in the fall months we were visited by an American delegation pertaining to our food and nutrition. When little Pavel was examined, they determined that he was too fat, and should be put on a diet. Marta felt that was ridiculous and that he was a good healthy baby.

Chapter 21

Family life in Camp Pagani and on to Camp Salerno

As time advanced through the fall and approaching winter months, the weather turned into occasional showers. This made it a little harder for Marta to spend time outside, strolling with our baby son. She loved this so much, always finding some time to be out. On the social level, we did not really associate with many others in our barrack. Most folks were of different nationalities, and everyone more or less kept to themselves.

We settled into a routine of family life. Marta was busy with little Pavel, household chores, and wrote letters to her relatives. I worked in the kitchen, probably seven days a week now, and came home after lunch for about an hour, after serving lunch to the people. The evening meal and cleanup ended about 6 pm. In addition to my schedule, I was given a position to be in charge of our barrack, mainly overseeing the upkeep of the rest rooms and washroom.

At times, I had my hands full with some unruly people, probably due to drunkenness. The toilets were quite primitive, a hollowed out depression with a hole in the concrete floor, a hose for flushing. There were about thirty people living in this barrack so one needed patience at times to use the facilities.

One encounter, I remember took place in a wash room with a big proud man, a Montenegro, who came from what is now a part of Yugoslavia. I was washing some clothing in the sink when this guy came in majestic like, and looked at me in amazement as he asked in a scolding manner, "What are you doing?"

"I am washing clothes as you can see," I replied. He then said, "Where is your woman?" I said, "My wife is sick, and cannot do it." He said in a forceful manner, "A woman is never sick." Clenching his fist, he turned around and spat on the floor in disgust and slowly walked away.

I also had to quell some noisy arguments within some families, upon complaints by their neighbors. Some of the people of southern countries became quite violent during their family arguments. I being younger than most of them, had to use some pointed psychology to quiet them with the hope of not also becoming the recipient of their anger. I sensed that being of a different nationality possibility helped with influencing them to be less hostile, and take some pride in their nationality's good traits. A big plus was that I had learned to speak many of their languages, except Albanian and Hungarian.

Our job in the main kitchen was not at all dreary work, since most of the cooks, except for one, an Albanian, were Czechs, pulling pranks on each other, doing all sorts of funny things in our slack time between meals.

One episode I remember was where my name "Frank" was used for such a purpose. Because my name is the same as that of a notorious Nazi, during the war, who was an Assisting Governor of "Bohmen Und Mahren" (Czechoslovakia), was suspected of giving Hitler the idea to raze the town of Lidice and kill most people within it. His name was Karl Herman Frank, who was tried and hung, after the liberation.

So my fellow cooks conducted a mock trial asking me pertinent questions, etc. Considering the gravest crimes that this man among others, had committed, should hardly lend itself for entertainment, but it did. Perhaps, because it had only been four to five years since the war, with all of its horrors, some people were rendered insensitive to it.

This camp had some health care facilities which I never needed, perhaps Marta did though with respect to little Pavel's needs. I did visit a dental office once, having a toothache. I don't recall any dental treatment given.

The toothache most likely diminished itself after the shock of seeing the "doctor". I remember he was Hungarian, rather short, pudgy, with pink colored skin, almost bald headed and most prominent he wore a soiled white coat, with blood on it. I recall excusing myself as I quickly backed out.

Economically, our situation improved markedly, due to my steady employment. Plus, we did not have to spend very much money, except for some fresh fruit for Marta and Zdenek.

Soon the Christmas season came, our second in Italy. We used an orange tree branch as a Christmas tree, and decorated it with colored papers and fruit. Marta cooked something special on our hot plate, in addition to the fairly festive camp's meal.

Mostly we huddled together in our little room, reminiscing about our loved ones back home. Marta always talked lovingly about her mother, whom she missed so much. I fully understood, knowing what a wonderful and loving mother she was. We counted our blessings this special day. Little Pavel was content and Zdenek played happily with some toys previously received from Marta's uncle from America.

Zdenek with toy airplane.

The winter months passed slowly, and into early March, we heard rumors that we would be moving again, to another camp further south when warmer weather arrives. And it did indeed happen by the end of March, we heard that we would be going to Salerno. We of course knew nothing about this new camp, except that it was right on the beach of the Mediterranean sea. Built there by the US Army who landed and fought there.

We loved Pagani and had made wonderful memories there, but being on the beach was also appealing. Besides, because of the previous moves, we were sort of becoming nomads, eliminating any trauma of moving.

One appointed day, we simply hopped into the canvas covered US Army trucks, and headed south to Salerno, approximately fifty kilometers southeast of Naples. Marta covered small Pavel very well, against the draft. Fortunately, southern Italy is much warmer than our northerly latitude, which we had been used to. We arrived within about two hours to our new "Campo Salerno". It was very similar to Camp Jesi, with many round Quonset huts, except that the entire area along the sea, quite the way inland was totally barren.

There was not one tree in sight, except some low scrub brush. The saving grace was the sparkling blue Mediterranean, very inviting and a real Joy to look at. Our hut was divided again into four quarters, separated by ropes holding a cloth or blankets.

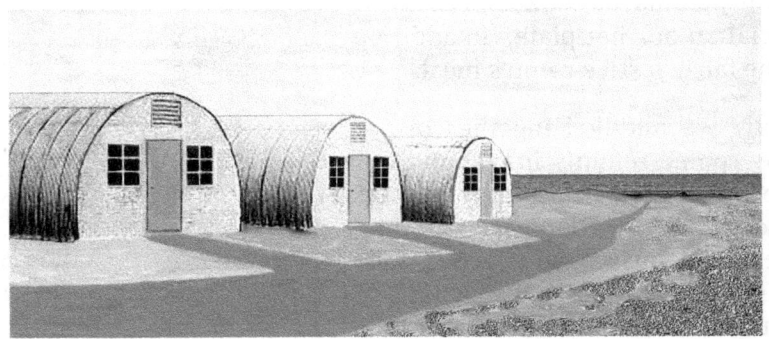

z.a.

Our immediate neighbors were Polish, the Romanofs, husband and wife, and very friendly. Mrs. Romanof adored little Pavel and wanted to hold him, and walk with him. On the other side were a couple of Slovenians.

Their names were Illjaseich Giacomimo, also very friendly, and good people. In the opposite corner was a Croatian lady, Katicia, with a young son. She was very robust, full of life and quite loud when she spoke, but tolerable.

After accommodating our few belongings we went for a walk to the edge of the water. We loved what we saw, just small waves, splashing on the beach. The sand was light grey and very clean and a pleasure to walk on. The weather was sunny, and comfortable for light attire. We found the mess hall, and had our first meal, Italian, with everything red, macaroni, olive oil, and delicious Italian bread.

Little Pavel with me.

Marta and Zdenek had their special kitchen, and so did little Pavel. Marta had to try hard to get used to it, of course I loved it, especially the abundant cheese in everything. In a few days, we got acquainted with many of the Czech people to socialize and swap stories. Our camp director was "Senior Rossi" with only one arm. Again from the diplomatic service, speaking several languages, he seemed to be sort of an unassuming and nice fellow.

After a few days, I went to the camp administrative office to inquire about a job. They promised that there might be an opening in the woodworking shop as a helper since the prime positions were already taken by Czechs from Russia. My new boss was about middle aged and not very skilled with a big loud mouth.

I found a way to get along with him. Most of the work was quite crude camp furniture repair. A real big break came for me when the director's wooden sail boat got damaged in a storm, and was brought in for repair. The director himself came in to oversee the work.

My boss started to loud mouth about what to do and how to do it. Mr. Rossi after listening to him awhile turned to me and asked if I could do it. Ignoring my boss totally, who eased his way out, after being told that I would be doing it on my own.

I had never worked on a fine wooden sail boat, nor even looked at one close up before this, but I figured out that I would simply copy the damaged side to the good one. I really enjoyed making the curved ribs, all different, slowly rebuilding the boat's skeleton. In about two weeks I installed the planking enveloping the body.

After varnishing, Mr. Rossi came, and said that he liked it and gave me a high compliment and a good bonus. We then took the boat into the sea and submerged it, so that all of the wood would swell and tighten up to avoid leaks. It came out with flying colors.

From that point on, I was my own boss, coexisting with my old boss. Unfortunately, there is one incident that I will never forget what he did. There was a gypsy family in the camp and the young man played violin, which was well known to be synonymous with many gypsies. This man brought in his violin, a real fine instrument, with a detached neck, the part holding the strings, glued to the violin case.

I started to tell my boss that it had to be cleaned, fitted and properly glued, applying pressure, to be real firm. He brushed me aside, saying that he knew what to do, so I let him be. What he did was criminal. He put a steel wood screw through the neck into the violin case, totally ruining it.

When the gypsy came for it, he burst out crying, "How could you ruin something that has been in my family for generations?" I really felt sorry for him. The crude Russian just brushed it off, like he'd made a fuss over nothing. From then on, I was really my own boss, for another month or so, until our work ran out.

I was then assigned to the camp police for the night watch. It was very boring pacing between barracks from 6 p.m. till 2 a.m. with only a stick in my hand. Among other things, I focused on the stars in heaven, trying to remember all of the constellations from my limited knowledge at school, the Big Dipper and Orion, which I loved because it was always in the morning sky when I walked to the train during the time of my apprenticeship training.

As the weather warmed up later on in the spring, we went swimming. Surprisingly the water was warm and we really loved the gentle waves, lifting us up and down not breaking, only gently at the edge of the beach.

Babysitting for Pavel was no problem. The ladies of the two families loved to watch over him.

Zdenek in the sea.

Zdenek loved learning how to swim. Swimming almost every day, we became experts, or so we thought, even going out into the stormy sea. Once we did that and it was a real thrill to be tossed up and down and at times out of sight. Marta gave up in a while when she was thrown into the sand. I stayed with it for quite a while, probably being too brave and foolish, which was dangerous with no one else around, considering the extreme roughness of the waves.

Gulf of Salerno   cc

We also went swimming in the evening when the normal breeze subsided and the water was so smooth like oil, only gently lifting up and down. One day while the water was really smooth, we decided to swim out to sea for some distance. Marta had good sense turning back in about three to four hundred feet, but I loving it, kept going.

I just kept heading out further and further until I looked back to shore and it seemed far away, so I also turned around. Then, I kicked something under water perhaps a fish? I really became scared and swam as fast as I could to shore to get out of there. At that distance, it was very foolish, almost crazy. Perhaps my guardian angel again was with me.

With the advance of early summer, the sun became warmer, giving us all beautiful suntans but making our round tin hut quite hot, almost uncomfortable at times. We had to keep all windows and doors open to get some air through. Fortunately, the evenings cooled down, so we could sleep.

Again, we got accustomed to this life style, but knew that sooner or later we would be called back to the Bagnoli camp to start the immigration process for our exit to America. With this in mind another problem came to the surface.

Previously, I had developed an abdominal hernia, it was not a problem, unless I stood on my feet for any length of time and then it bulged out, being slightly painful. I could hide this condition, and knew how to avoid its exposure at all the previous medical exams, except for one, when a rough doctor found it. It was then on my record being a handicap for immigration.

We heard that any future sponsor which was the norm for entry to the US would have had to put up a good deal of money as a guarantee. My best option was to have it operated on and to be whole again. The camp office put me on a waiting list for surgery at the Bagnoli camp hospital, scheduled for about two to three weeks away.

In the meantime there was an excursion planned to go to Rome and of course the Vatican city. This year 1950, was declared a Holy year by the Pope Pius XI. I wanted to go, and wanted Marta to go as well, but she urged me to go without her because little Pavel was only nine months old. I felt somewhat selfish, but Marta was really happy there among friends, and so was not alone.

It was a little difficult to leave if only for about four to five days, but one early morning we boarded our usual army trucks, and rolled and tied the canvas forward and left via Roma. It was a wild ride, so typical of these Italian drivers, without consideration for their human cargo.

We even got into an accident when our truck got too close to another truck which was going in the opposite direction; badly mangling a young lady's hand, which she had been resting on the outside of the truck railing enclosure. After first aid she was brave, but her husband became uncontrollable. Seeing this injury really put us all into a sober mood, until we arrived.

Chapter 22

Rome

One interesting item I remember as we approached Rome, about ten to twelve kilometers out, we traveled on a highway called "Via Appia". It was built by the Romans over two thousand years ago, was absolutely straight, dead level, and is in good service still.

We also passed the stone aqua ducts, huge arched structures, high above ground spanning whole valleys for long distances, which carried water to ancient Rome. How great were those engineers and builders in those times. We were accommodated at a Catholic convent dormitory. It was a basic and sparse quarters but luxurious for us, compared to our homes at the camps

Three of us went sightseeing in the city. First we went to St. Peters Basilica, and then the Vatican. We were totally stunned by the enormous size and beauty and detail of everything in view. The inlaid marble floors, the highly decorated ceilings, marble statues everywhere. As if to greet its visitors, close to the entry, there was Michelangelo's white marble statue of "La Pieta", the most magnificent work of art ever, being the lifelike image of Saint Mary cradling the lifeless body of Jesus, after the crucifixion (below).

Observers are surrounded by hundreds of statues all masterfully executed. This is a divine miracle transformed by human mind and hands.

It, along with the paintings of the Sistine Chapel by Michelangelo, who painted this high arched ceiling, which is probably one hundred feet across and seventy five feet high, has a myriad of scenes, including "Genesis", God's creation of the world.

tfi

Michelangelo's La Pieta

All of the images were created bigger in scale in order to appear normal from the floor. He often worked while lying on his back on top of the scaffold. It is incomprehensible how this God gifted sculptor, painter and architect could create all of his great works of art in his lifetime.

We also went to the catacombs under the Vatican, a vast network of caves, used by early Christians for hiding to avoid persecution. It is considered to be a Holy ground where confessions are held. Upon urging by the nuns at our convent, we also went having learned that it was a Holy Year in addition to being on Holy grounds, even the gravest sins are forgotten.

Catacombs

I do not recall what language I used to confess. If it was Italian, I wonder if I had enough knowledge to describe my sins. The priest gave me absolution and I felt good about it. Another memorable attraction was the famous "Fountain Di Trevi", where people toss coins, making a wish, which comes true. We did not have money to throw away, so we missed the opportunity.

Also, one monument of significance is the "Vittorio Emanuele", monument at Piaza Venezia (Venetian Square). It is an enormous building in a semi circle, beautiful architecture, so endearing, and gratifying to look at. On the front there is a huge statue in bronze of King Vittorio Emanuele II sitting on a horse, so huge that twelve people could fit into its body.

USAR

Vittorio Emanuele Square, Rome

This king unified all of Italy into one big nation. The people showed their gratitude with the beauty and size of this monument. It really speaks well of the enormous respect for this great ruler.

One of the last great attractions in Rome that I really wanted to see because of our son's name was the Saint Paul Basilica, which is at the outskirts of the city. It gave me a lasting impression, and was somewhat humble in its architecture, yet it has its own beauty, if subdued, perhaps depicting the life of Saint Paul himself, who was martyred as a true Christian by the Romans on the same spot. High above the main entry, there is a large painting of Paul as a soldier, being converted to Christianity, as one of Jesus' disciples.

Upon conclusion in relation to this cathedral, after this visit and with a strong bond in my heart, I sincerely wished and hoped that Marta with the rest of our family, especially Paul, could come and share all the glories of Rome.

My wishes were fulfilled more than a half a century later when in 2003, Marta and I were joined with Paul's family visiting Rome, Naples, and Pagani, Paul's place of birth. I enjoyed sharing my knowledge of many years ago, being particularly glad that Paul could see the glorious memorial of his patron saint.

Here we are in 2003, enjoying the sites in Italy.

Back in 1950, while traveling within the city of Rome, we used the public transportation, street cars and busses. Not having any small change to spare, we simply hopped on, squeezing in among the local people, being fortunate that the conductors could not get around and check. Until one time, a man came and asked for his "biglieti". I told him in the distinct Napoleon dialect, that we were from Naples, and were new in town, "Siamo Napolitani." He then said "Sete Napolitani, alora scendette" (So you are Napalitanos, ah? Then, get out). And, we gladly did.

At the appointed time, we thanked our hosts, the sisters, and piled into our trucks and left for home,. It was so joyous to come back to my family, finding them all happy and nicely suntanned, especially Marta who looked so beautiful. Our baby Pavel was full of life, and starting to crawl around and exploring his world.

It was helpful for Marta, with little Zdenek guarding Pavel. Our neighbors, the ladies absolutely adored him, especially the Slovenian lady, who often begged to take care of him. I remember she called him Paolo or Paolino (in Italian). But as expected, not long after my return, there was an announcement, giving us a time frame regarding our departure back to Bagnoli for the immigration process, which would be in early April of 1950.

We knew it was an inevitable part of our refugee life to move on again, even though we loved it here. It presented a problem for me, regarding my physical handicap, having a hernia. If left uncorrected, it would dim our chances severely to pass the medical exam and qualify to be accepted by any country. Wanting to face the problem head on I inquired in the camp infirmary to apply for some corrective surgery. They took my name and acted somewhat vague about the time and place that this could be done.

Not being satisfied, in view of our overall situation I went to the camp director "Senior Rossi". He knew me, was sympathetic and totally understanding. He called the camp hospital in Bagnoli, and asked for a time schedule for the procedure. I think it was within two days that they had an opening, a short notice, but a good solution to my problem. I sadly informed Marta, who understood assuring me that she will be alright. It was to be about a week to ten days until my return.

My young family came with me to the truck and then I departed. Bagnoli camp had its hospital on a third floor building, and was run by one doctor and staff. I learned that his name was Kuharik a typical Czech name, but he was a German, who had served in the German army as an Assistant Surgeon General, a high position. He was known for his great surgical skills. He wanted to go to America, but the American high command, knowing the dire need of so many refugees imposed a condition that he serve for a certain period of time before being released to go.

The next day after my arrival, I was examined by him. I was immediately aware that this was to be a strictly military type of procedure. He was a big powerful looking man a burly, no nonsense guy. I was fully confident that he knew his business. The following day, after a starvation diet, I was to have my surgery. With assistance of a nurse, I was laid on a table, and strapped down.

The doctor came in ready, and asked me in German, how was I? Then a Serbian assistant held a cloth up about mid section and said in Serbian that I would not want to see this, and that I may become a little frightened because I was not being put to sleep first. Everything moved rapidly. I saw the doctor holding a big syringe and then the pain happened, while I was being poked in a sensitive area several times.

I squirmed, straining the leather straps, but it didn't last long. In about twelve minutes, he started to operate. I felt nothing, except some motions. It was over in about fifteen minutes, the Serb put the cloth down and the doctor said "Fertig" (finished). The nurse unstrapped me and I waited to be removed off of the table for a few moments, but then the doctor said, "Ouf Stehen" (Get up.), in a military like command.

I found it a little incredible, but I knew that was the order. Crawling off and being bent over I was assisted by a nurse to my room. After about an hour or so, I started to have severe pain in my lower abdomen. This went on all night and well into the next day.

By the middle of the second morning the doctor came marching in, with about four pretty Italian nurses, and ripped my blanket off to look me over. I was completely naked from the waist down and I was embarrassed in front of that sort of audience. He looked me over, satisfied, and then said in German, "Auf stehen" (Get up.), and told me to walk down the hallway. Suppressing the pain, and bent over, I crawled out and walked for about five minutes. He also said that I must walk every morning as much as possible, which I did.

About the third or fourth day, I met the doctor in the hallway. When he saw me, he stopped and said in German, "This is no way a soldier should walk" (bent down). He came to me and put his big arm behind my lower back and one on my upper chest and bent me straight up. The pain in the wound was excruciating, like being stabbed by a knife.

I let out a loud holler and he just laughed like the devil and walked away. Except for the pain, it did not hurt me, the pain subsided and I was beginning to look forward to getting out of there. I also learned that our family had been moved from the Salerno camp and was now also in Bagnoli; a good news report for me, knowing that I will be able to walk home soon.

One item of interest: My neighbor at the adjacent bed was a Croatian college professor, whom I conversed with in his language. He didn't know that I was of Czech origin. When he found out, he was amazed at how well I could speak, thinking that I was a "Slavonic" (Slovenian). I thought it was a compliment, owing to the exposure to all various nationals, with the Yugoslavs being the most prominent.

My time finally came to be checked out. After thanking the doctor I was released. I had a considerable amount of difficulty in the camp offices when I tried to find out where my family had been moved to. It would have been simple if Marta could have come for a visit to see me in the hospital, but that wasn't possible because babies were not permitted to enter and no one was available to take care of him. Finally finding our new address I ever so slowly came home. It was joyful to be back with my happy family.

And because I was still stitched up I found out that there were certain privileges within the camp, mainly not having to wait in the long lines for food. I simply walked up ahead and told the camp guard, "Dopo operacione" (After operation.), and was allowed to go first. Marta and the children had the special kitchen, being spared waiting among the two thousand people.

During this early stay in this camp, we were to undergo all the intricate processes for immigration; having applied for America as number one and Canada as number two choice. In about two weeks I felt almost normal again and began to inquire about a job in the camp. Because of my convalescent status, I was qualified for a desk job, which was something entirely new in my life. Soon an office position emerged, as an assistant in the camp director's office.

I spruced up and went to apply to the camp director's secretary's office. I was introduced to her. She appeared to be a very nice and pleasant English lady and her assistant husband an Italian named Di Lorenzo (Di means that there is a lineage of nobility). He was a happy and flamboyant official, and the one in charge of hiring. I felt tense though, because this job was published as a position that required fluency in English and Italian.

He started off speaking in Italian, saying, "Parlate inglese?" (Speak English?) And, I replied, "Si" (Yes). He said, "Wa Bene." (Good.) Then he asked if I could type on the typewriter. And again I said, "Si, Si." (Yes, yes.) Praying that he won't ask me to show him, having one in front of him, he said, "Wa Bene." (You are hired.) I could not believe my good luck since not one word was said in English.

I was then shown my desk in a small room, in front of the director's office. I was the first person to see for any refugee complaining of any injustice to them, listening and evaluating its merits. If serious I would send them to the secretary, if trivial I was to send them away, with the help of the camp guard if needed. Only a very few people came in, mostly with trivial complaints.

One I recall, was a Serbian, whom I dismissed as not having any valid reason to complain who got quite upset telling me, "You cannot go anywhere in this camp, where there are no Czechs in charge." The camp guard escorted him out. Another one of my duties was to say good morning to all of the V.I.P.s especially the director, an English man, "Lord Cowden", who was the highest-ranking official of all the UN camps in Italy.

I previously and erroneously assumed that this was the Bagnoli Camp Director, who was at a different location. This very reserved aristocrat walked by simply nodding his head to my good morning greetings, only once giving me an order, which I did not understand to my horror. Fortunately the secretary (the English lady), had heard it, and came in and told me in Italian which saved my day.

Another nice thing happened at this job, which would affect our family's future. Sir Cowden had another secretary, an American girl from Chicago, Miss Vasilewski, strikingly beautiful, and friendly, who once asked me about what our hoped for destination was to be in America. At that point in time, we were already in the process of selecting offers of various sponsors.

So far as I knew at that time, we had three offers, which I explained to her. Number one was to go to New York City, number two was to farm in Wisconsin and the last choice was Oregon. She immediately said, "You must go to Oregon, because it is one of the most beautiful states, having big shipyards with plenty of jobs, and most of all it is known as 'God's country'." She was so positive, and well meaning that after I discussed this with Marta, Oregon became our first choice.

Of course, as many Europeans we only knew about the existence of New York and Chicago in the US, and never heard of Oregon. Having later come to live in Oregon, I at times think of this girl, wishing I could show my gratitude. For lack of knowledge, we would have probably chosen New York.

Summer months came along and so did the warm temperatures. Our little living cubicle was on the third floor, and was warmer from the roof tile. It was usually o.k. until about 3 pm, getting warmer and staying so through the evening. So as not to be fried inside, like most people, we went outside and into town for a walk, returning when all windows were open, and it was more tolerable.

pd

View of Bagnoli, camp is in the center above city.

Our past nomadic life style: moving from one camp to another deprived our little Zdenek of school. There simply was none in Salerno, or Bagnoli. We had not thought much about it knowing that we were in transition, and that eventually there will be some catching up to do. Our immigration process started first with the political screening, with the reviewing of files and summary of all of the previous interrogations.

We had been singled out, not together as a family. I had an Italian officer who after reviewing my file, again asked some pertinent questions, mainly in concern of our background, like have I ever been a Nazi, or a communist, etc. Some of the questions were sort of tricky, but having a clear conscience, it was easy to answer. America was very strict in this manner, as compared to other countries.

Although knowing our probable good outcome, we didn't know how we passed, until sometime later, being called to proceed with the medical exam, which was a signal that so far, it was o.k. The chest x-ray was most likely the key since they knew that there was TB in the camp.

Then came the heart exam and other routine tests, but not the blood tests, probably too expensive. The doctor kept going over my heart and heard a murmur, which I knew was the mark from the scarlet fever left from my early years. I did pass, so did Marta with the children. Finally it was time for the administrative procedure, mainly tying down our sponsor, requiring our photos and exchange of letters, since we now knew our sponsor. It was the "American Czech Ladies Society of Oregon".

We were now on very solid footing, knowing we will make it out, but not knowing the time. There was some concern in those days about certain quotas, that the US accepted certain numbers of people per year being different for every nation.

During the summer, my office job was eliminated, probably because it was unnecessary. I actually did not mind, being bored to the limit, only giving polite greetings to my superiors, and having endless conversations with the camp guard, whose life stories I knew by heart.

There was an opening for a cabinet maker, which I took. It had a very good man in charge, a Serbian engineer, who lived in the US before the war and got stuck in Yugoslavia the entire war time, and was now trying to go back. I liked him. We did mostly repair of wooden furniture. A nice bi-product of working there was that I could make a ship chest for our family out of scrap wood, which we needed now.

I assembled the trunk parts in our cubicle, which also served as a table. About the beginning of July this camp underwent a big transformation. It was split into two parts. The first was the processing center, which included us and the second was the embarkation center, which collected thousands of people from all of the camps in Europe, & processed them to go to Australia.

Our camp was the final assembly center, before being transported to the port in Naples, to board ships for Australia. This area was separated by tall wire fences, to keep the people from mingling. Still there were many smart slickers trading money for valuables.

Many unfortunate people not being processed for embarkation were moved to make room for the thousands of these people in transit. This camp had a big central plaza, which was like a giant ant hill one day, and the next day all cleared for the new group.

NATO

*Note the central plaza of the Bagnoli DP Camp.
Photo taken after it became AFSOUTH headquarters.*

It was incredible how anyone could make sense of these hordes of people, grouping up, and sending them half way across the world. As the summer drew to a close, we grew more anxious, knowing that our time must be coming up, so we could leave.

In the meantime Marta and I studied English from the books that we brought with us. Little Zdenek did fairly well with the Italian language. Despite the fact that he had missed quite a lot of school (since Pagani), he must have been very self reliant and well disciplined with so much waiting time on his hands. Little Pavel did very well, and was growing like a weed. He was very active and full of life. I remember when we went into the town in the evening I carried him, since we had no stroller any more. And, after an hour or so he got to be pretty heavy. He was growing fast.

With summer slowly turning into fall, we grew more and more anxious, feeling at times, that it will never happen. Although knowing that it must come. Finally by the beginning of October our name appeared on the bulletin board, giving our departure time, about a week out, going to Bremen in northern Germany, to board a ship to go to the USA.

Boy, this was incredible. We could shout with joy, hoping that it was all for real and it will indeed happen. Marta, was typically cautious and concerned about all of us being dressed warmly. We knew that going way north, the weather would not be like that in southern Italy to which we were now accustomed.

We scrounged around for some money and bought something warm for little Zdenek and Pavel. I was o.k. but Marta also needed a warmer coat. Somehow we managed, owing to my meager job pay and money received for another ship trunk that I made and sold to our neighbors. Now, we were ready.

Chapter 23

Bremerhaven and the Liberty Ship

The time came about October 7th, and we said good bye to our few acquaintances, rather emotional for them, seeing us leave to head for America, while they stayed behind. We climbed into the trucks and were taken to the train station to board the train.

The assigned compartment was private, even with beds that folded up, so luxurious; we wondered if it were really happening to us, after riding the bumpy army trucks? When the train started to roll, we knew that it was real. The trip was beautiful, going through Rome, north to the mountains. Now being evening, we'd be waking up on the other side of the Alps in the Austrian Tyrol region, considered the most beautiful in Europe.

We remembered that we could not have seen it over two years ago, when heading south, being in the box car unable to see. Adding to all the natural beauty, there was fresh snow, such a romantic fairy tale. This beauty never did fade from our memories.

Marta, always so caring, must have taken some food along and some water. These long range trains usually have some food on board, but I don't remember receiving any. After about three hours, we passed through a beautiful region, into more normal country in northern Austria, and through Germany. We arrived in Bremen in the afternoon and were transferred temporarily to a military camp.

USAR

Bremen

Here we were split apart, Marta with our baby and I with Zdenek. After I learned where Marta was we joined her and went to the mess hall for a meal. I remember that the food was unmistakably German, very close to our Czech cooking, with a lot of cabbage sauerkraut and even dumplings on occasion. Everything was neat, clean and well organized. We slept on military style cots. We liked it and were told that we would be staying for about two weeks while waiting for our ship.

Being separated was not easy, especially being away from little Pavel. We prolonged our time at the mess hall at each meal, walked into town, weather permitting, wrote some letters, and waited for the next meal get together. Most of our evenings were spent at Marta's dorm, in the hall way, walking around, until little Pavel started to fall asleep, then I joined Zdenek to retire for the night.

About the second week, we had our hands full taking care of Pavel, owing to his discomfort from teething. If he cried for any length of time, the other women there would get disturbed, and poor Marta had to carry him out into the hall way. When I found out, seeing how tired Marta was, I stayed after supper and helped her carrying our little Pavel, until he fell asleep, knowing from previous nights that he will wake again after awhile. I took over the baby sitting, so Marta could sleep for a few hours, undisturbed at least until midnight, when I left to join Zdenek.

We were also assigned work, like cutting firewood for the heating and the kitchen. So I, with about three other Czechs started to cut wood, with a bow saw. It was supervised by an elderly German, who kept urging us to keep cutting. The three other guys were sort of wise guys moving like snails to the dislike of the supervisor.

Then one of them told him in German, "You stupid Germans are always about work. All you live for is work." The supervisor then said, "You wait, if you get to America, you will find out what work is all about." He said that he knew first hand, being a prisoner in the US, and knew the American way of life. And indeed, I remembered later how I worked very hard, with hardly any time off.

Watching the bulletin intently until one lucky day our name appeared, advising us of the final medical exam before boarding the ship in a few days. Good news, except little Zdenek developed a sore throat and tonsillitis. Boy, what were we to do? Going to the camp infirmary was not an option, since it would be a giveaway of a condition not suitable for long travel. Knowing from home remedies, we knew that lemon juice is helpful for the condition. So I bought some lemons, cut them into halves, and asked Zdenek to try to suck up all of the juice even though it was extremely sour.

On the day of the exam, I thought of a plan. Zdenek's condition improved somewhat, but he still had swelling, if we could be one of the last people for the doctor to see, after seeing the throats of fourteen to fifteen hundred people, he may be a little careless. It worked, we passed. Zdenek continued his lemon treatment, and he was much better.

We were being transported by trucks again to the port of Bremerhaven and there was our ship, looming so big at the dock. It was an army troop transport, named "General Harry Taylor"; a Liberty ship. This ship was built in California in 1943 and converted to a transport ship in Vancouver Washington in 1944.

Everything happened with military precision. We walked on a wide plank to the ship, where we were separated again, Marta with our baby to one side, and I with Zdenek on the other, going down stairs to a huge space with sleeping bunks, metal and canvas, two side by side, and three high.

Remembering our bunk numbers we went up on the deck to watch the ship leave. In hardly anytime a man came, part of the ship's crew and pointed his finger at me and three other people and said, "You, you, you, and you, come with me." So we followed down, way below the decks to the ship's galley, where he introduced us to the cook in charge. We learned that we were rounded up by an escort officer, Mr. Hunt, who assigned all of the necessary work and chores to us the non-paying passengers.

We were to report to the chef in the early morning, cook breakfast and lunch. As we looked around the place, we spotted a big pan on the bench, full of red gravy and a lot of meat. Not having seen so much good food in over two years, we asked if we could have some of it. He laughingly said, "Eat all that you want." He gave us some utensils, so we ate, and ate, even though it was cold, and then went up to our bunks.

By now, it was turning into evening and the ship was underway. Our first night was somewhat uneasy, getting used to the uncomfortable bunks and the ships rocking. Early in the morning I was wakened for duty in the galley. Right away, I became sick especially smelling the odors of fried bacon and eggs. I knew, that having the big meal the previous day was a mistake.

Coffee helped, but I couldn't eat anything, until it became so intense that I headed for the rest room, and vomited, after which I felt a little better. The entire day I was still nauseated, and spent time on the deck, feeling better in the fresh air. Zdenek also had a similar problem, but not too bad.

Somehow, he already found where Marta and Pavel were, and took me there. I was not prepared for what I saw. My poor Marta was in a room seasick, and miserable and trying to take care of Pavel. There was another woman there with three small children, crawling all over the floor, and quite unkempt. She was also a picture of misery being seasick as well.

I was so sorry to see Marta going through this, and the best that I could do was take her, after bundling up little Pavel, up to the deck, making her feel a little better. She was so brave, facing all of these difficult situations. She was also relieved when she saw Zdenek, who snapped out of his brief sea discomfort. Amazingly little Pavel, did quite well, being completely unaffected by the ships rocking, except for his ongoing teething problem.

White Cliffs of Dover

About the second day out, while we were on deck, a very nice thing happened to us. While our ship was leaving the English channel, going west to open sea we could see the southern tip of England, and soon, the most beautiful white Cliffs of Dover. The sun peaked out briefly, and it was like the white veil of Europe, waving it's farewell to us. We were both deeply moved, leaving our home, our loved ones, facing our distant and new future. We both knew about the romance of the White Cliffs of Dover, from the American movies, even songs, being composed about them.

We were now in the open sea, of the north Atlantic, noticing the waves being much bigger, rocking our ship. Marta now felt a little better, but still had a hard time eating solid food, so I shared my portion of whatever she liked. Taking our baby to the special children's dining room, was difficult for her, so I took Pavel myself.

Upon approaching the entry, there was a Serbian guard there, who stopped me and forbid entry, because I was a man, and only mothers with babies could come in. He said, "You must bring your woman." I replied, "My woman is sick and can not come." I pushed him aside, making him even more irritated, and this created a disturbance.

The British escort officer came by and asked what was going on. After my explanation, he very sympathetically said, "By all means come right in." So, I did, and managed quite well with feeding Pavel. Marta recovered sufficiently to function, even though the conditions in her room remained bad.

Another big problem arose, which was the crew chipping away old paint from the steel super-structure, which was right above Marta's quarters. They used pneumatic hammers which were incredibly loud, and resonated below, sounding like machine gunfire. Anyone enduring this would go insane in no time. It went on for several days, though not during the nights. I was quite upset about this.

After a few days of terrible weather, we were being tossed around by the stormy seas. We were still permitted to go out on deck, only limited to the center of the ship, with the bow and aft being off limits. One could see looking forward the tremendous power of the rough seas, lifting the entire front of the ship way up into the air, then see it crashing down, into the water, with all of its huge weight, splashing the water widely.

pd

Mountainous seas, viewed from the ship.

The forces were incredible, and hard to believe, making me wonder how much punishment and how long can we take it. My apprehension was correct having later learned that these Liberty ships did have a history of breaking in half in extremely rough seas. This made it necessary to weld thick steel plates, as a band on each side reinforcing its middle against possible break up.

As any rules are made there will always be someone to break them, as was the case here, with the off limits signs. One young man a Yugoslavian national crossed the chain and sign, and went up front to the tip of the bow, and got tossed around. He fell and injured his head, fatally. It was announced on the ships loud speakers and also gave the time for his burial at sea. After this incident all decks were closed and we were like sardines in a tin can, being tossed around.

The burial at sea ceremony was performed one calm morning, so we were allowed on the deck. There was a long shute (wood platform, about 25 X 3 feet) attached to the ship's railing with the dead person at the upper end draped with a US flag.

One of the uniformed ship's officers gave a speech in English that probably few understood and then saluted. The shute was tipped at a steeper angle, and the body, wrapped in a white cloth, went sliding down and splashed into the eternal sea. It was a sad, sober ceremony and performed quickly.

Now, being in continuous storms and cooped up inside, I was becoming somewhat unhappy with my cooking job. Unfortunately, this was due mainly to the strong odor of many pounds of fried bacon in two big (about thirty six inches wide) kettles, plus the typical two thousand four hundred eggs. They were poured in and then stirred with a big wooden paddle, until scrambled in form. About one and a half eggs per person. It would take well over two hours to cook.

Ship Galley USN

Yet, very few people ate it, because of the rampant sea sickness, and their weak stomachs. The allocated supply was there and probably orders to serve it were mandatory. All of the fish in our vicinity never had it so good.

At the end of one day's shift, I confronted our escort officer about the possibility of changing jobs. He understood my discomfort and promised to have another job by the next day. Arriving at the appointed place, he gave me a small sack of sawdust, a bucket, a short broom, and a dust pan with a wooden (thirty six inches long) handle. He then took me to the areas that were frequented by the people and showed me spots where people had vomited.

He asked me to sprinkle some sawdust on it and then sweep and put it in the bucket. Of course I could see many people were seasick, but was unaware that some people would use any area for disposal. The problem got a lot worse, not to have the deck with its railings to go to as well. I went around being more disgusted by the minute.

Within about an hour, I went to Mr. Hunt the escort officer and asked for my kitchen job back. He grinned and probably anticipated my reaction, and readily agreed. The bacon and eggs did not really smell so bad after all. Part of our breakfast preparation which started by 4 a.m., was to break all the eggs, all two thousand, four hundred of them. I don't recall how many garbage cans we filled up. There were about five of us, sitting on wooden crates, breaking the eggs one by one, into the cans. We all got fairly fast at it, being almost routine, until one morning.

The storm raged so badly and the floor tipped so steeply that we went sliding across in the eggs and all, hitting the opposite wall. With eggs breaking, and some garbage cans that were almost full tipping, and splashing, the floor became extremely slick and slippery. It became a total pandemonium as we rode back and forth, most of the people became sick and were vomiting, and were almost totally out of control.

One of the guys, a very large and obese man, with an oversized belly, fell off the foot stool and rolled in the splashing eggs as he tried to crawl on all fours, and was dripping with eggs. I burst out laughing and noticed the chief cook, an American, also laughing so hard and bending over in the door way.

Most people left sicker than dogs, but I felt alright and actually was having fun. So did the chief cook, who brought out some wet burlap sacks, which we placed under us and the containers, and all the sliding stopped. Why did he not do it at the beginning? It was probably worth the fun. That early morning, I was the only one left, to finish the breakfast. I stayed much longer than usual, but finished it all. The next day, I earned some high praise from Mr. Hunt.

Our little Zdenek entertained himself. He went exploring the ship with all of its intricate nooks and crannies, also spending time with Marta and me, mainly at meal times. This continuous storm lasted for about ten days, at times, quite fearful, as one time coming to my bunk about 6 a.m. the whole ship began to vibrate uncontrollably, and was very frightening, and happened several times.

Most people around us were up and some were praying. We later learned that if the ships aft rose out of water, the propellers spin wildly, vibrating the whole ship. The crew must cut them off disengaging until the ship goes down to its normal position. It is dangerous if left unattended. It would do real damage.

We were at sea now, close to two weeks, when the very important American holiday rolled around, Thanksgiving Day, our first ever. Even on this refugee ship, we had a full course turkey dinner, complete with mash potatoes and gravy and some of the trimmings. The chef in our galley took me to the lowest part of the ship, the cold locker, where there was a long row of turkeys hanging on a pole. We took several maybe fifteen, which were so big; I could hardly lift one in one hand. They looked almost as big, as a small hog.

We cooked the turkeys in the huge steam kettles, and when soft, we browned them in the oven. The potatoes were peeled by machine, and we cooked them, another machine did the smashing. It all turned out fairly good, considering the huge quantity. At dinner, I was proud to introduce Marta and Zdenek to my cooking skill. Marta being a somewhat picky eater reserved her comment.

Another experience I would like to mention concerns the feeding of many hundreds of people in the storms, where nothing is stable, always moving, unless tied down. People were served on metal trays, and tables were covered with plastic, so when the ship is tilting, all items slide to one side unless one hangs onto their dish, etc.. Now when thinking about this kind of situation again, it was really a hilarious mess, often with food all over the place. Anyone needing a diet, this was his chance.

By the second week, we sensed that we must be approaching America. The bad storm finally quit and we saw the sun again, with high white clouds. It was a joy to be out on the deck again. For the first time, Marta was happy knowing that we will finally make it. All of a sudden someone spotted land to our left, the Bermuda Island, giving us a great feeling that we are now so close to the USA.

USN

Our transport ship, the General Harry Taylor.

Great crowds gathered on the left deck, pointing and looking intently at this brownish protrusion in the ocean. We were altogether, just looking as if we could not believe our eyes. It was the real new world. Coming out of darkness of the continuous storms and now being greeted by this warm sunny sky, with only a few fluffy white clouds, was like a sincere welcoming smile, accepting us in its arms. We all felt so good!

As we continued on, we were visited by the US Coast Guard, and a doctor. About four people looked us over, and examined us. They were also looking closely at our baggage, including our wooden ship trunk. Upon examination of some of the belongings they announced publically that we should dispose of most of the stuff, because transporting it to our destinations would cost far more than buying the same upon our arrival.

It really caught on and someone started to throw clothing over board, and others happily followed. Pretty soon, the ocean was a blazed in color, trailing behind us. The feeling was that we were shedding all of the remnants of our poor past, now looking forward to accept everything new and better.

The US delegation stayed with us for a while. They were mainly interested in the physical condition of the people. This meant visiting the first aid infirmary, examining charts of any sickness on board. This proved almost tragic for our family, since Marta must have taken little Pavel in at some point, because he had a mild fever.

When she got called in now, the doctor simply told her that if our baby's fever does not subside by embarkation, we will be sent back to Germany, and not be allowed to come on land. Marta was shocked, speechless, after what she had endured so bravely, now it could be all for nothing. All of our hopes and dreams totally shattered. We were stunned.

I so admire Marta to have been able to function; not collapsing or totally giving up. I knew she put all of her hopes to her dear Saint Mary, whom she worshiped dearly. I decided to ask our escort officer, whom I had gotten to know well, if there was any chance for an appeal. He told me that there was none. This was US law, and we, the refugees would have no influence in this matter. I also resolved to pray, and felt that it was our only hope.

Chapter 24

USA

Forty eight stars in 1950   pda

We sailed on to the south west, now close to Florida, out to the Gulf of Mexico, then up north heading to the Mississippi Delta, and finally to the city of New Orleans. The weather was good and there were a lot of reasons to be cheerful, but we were sad, and avoiding thoughts about what could happen to us now. Marta, in the meantime cared intensely about little Pavel. Someone suggested, perhaps the ship's nurse, to give him a small dose of aspirin to break the fever.

By the landscape of the Mississippi Delta I came to see Marta and our little Pavel and she greeted me with a faint grateful smile and told me that the fever had broken and he began to eat again. Praise the lord, our prayers had been heard. I also told Zdenek the good news and that we were pretty soon to get off the ship. He was so happy and excited to hear it all.

The length of the trip up the Mississippi is very long probably over one hundred miles. We just sailed steadily north, as if it had no end. Finally, we inched our way into port. Most people behaved very joyously, and though we were glad to have finally gotten here, we were still subdued from the shock of the previous days.

They organized the exiting of the ship by having the families with children go down the plank first. Marta still had to appear at the infirmary for Pavel's final check up. He was fine, but they just had to make sure.

Finally we stood on American soil, on November 29, 1950, our promised land! Not knowing where to go, we stood to one side of the crowd for a while, waiting for something to happen. Pretty soon a lady appeared, beautiful, and elegantly dressed and called us by name. We acknowledged her and she then led us to her car, a big Cadillac convertible.

She began to ask us questions, and obviously had some of our information, but had to make sure. Her English, of course was excellent, but ours was limited, so it was a slow conversation. She asked if we wanted to fly, which we did not understand, so she waved her arms, like a bird flying and said, "Fly, fly." And we said, "No, no fly."

So, she said, "O.k. then you want to go by train?" But, again we didn't quite understand, so she said, "By choo-choo." She churned both of her arms like the wheels of a train locomotive. We replied, "Yes, yes, choo-choo, o.k., we will go by train." She was so pleasant and smiling and so upbeat that really uplifted our moods. What a beautiful way to welcome confused and tired new comers. She took us to a hotel to wait for the train, and promised to come and pick us up.

While waiting, I went out to a little store to buy some cigarettes, the first after three weeks. An elderly seedy looking old timer with a cow boy hat came in. He saw that I had a hard time with my language and ordered two whiskeys, one for me and one for him. We clicked glasses, and he said something like a welcome to me.

I don't know what kind of moonshine it was, but it took my breath away and felt good. In about two hours the nice lady came back, to pick us up to go to the train station. She already had all of our tickets ready and took us to our private compartment, and gave us some fruit and water. We thanked her most sincerely, as she in her lovely pleasant way wished us good luck and a safe journey.

Now looking around, we couldn't believe the luxury of our compartment. There were soft seats, which folded into a bed and a table and even a small sink. Starting to move, it was so smooth, and quiet, without any motion. We felt so happy, being under way, so comfortable knowing that this is for real, now, and no one could turn us back.

I spent all of my time at the window eagerly looking out at the sights of America. It was quite different from countries we came from rather flat as a pancake with only a few trees here and there, all farmland, and predominately brown after harvest time. With evening rolling along, I went into one special car to buy some food for our family, having been given some money by the nice lady as part of our package.

Our first night was comfortable except for a few interruptions by little Pavel, whom Marta fed, making him happy and content. I have no recollection of how Marta managed to change the baby's diapers. Did she have fresh diapers? The disposable type did not exist. How did she manage to do the washing? The ship probably had some provisions, but now, we were to be on the train for two days and two nights. How could she have managed? How inconsiderate of me not to have taken more of an interest.

By morning in Arkansas now, there was an abrupt change in the landscape. Still being very flat, but with mile after mile of yellowish rusty colored dry grass. We did not know then that it was the prairie. Seeing this monotonous landscape mile after mile, no trees, I kept thinking, surely we'll run into some more interesting country, but it hardly changed all day.

Midwest prairie   FSA

The first stop we made was in Kansas City, and we went out into the train station's restaurant. I remember the entire building was built like a very ornate big palace; the dining room looked like it was fit for royalty. We wondered if they would let us in, but no one objected. Being seated a smiling American waiter came with a menu, that we could hardly understand, but we picked something reasonably priced. It was a good meal, with a nice bonus of a basket of baked buns, boy we couldn't stop eating them, being so hungry. When finished Marta said, "We have a long ways to go, you better put some of these in your pocket for the road." So, I discretely stuffed my pockets full, leaving a few in the basket.

We thought that this was so generous, the American way. Anywhere in Europe, we could have gotten one or two buns and that was it. We still went through mostly dried up prairie, mile after mile, becoming a little uneasy. If this was America, it would be hard to get used to. We rolled into Denver in Colorado, by early morning. It was a noticeable crispy day.

Marta kept thinking about her uncle who lived there and how much she wished that she could contact him, but there wasn't enough time. She looked sad as we pulled out, feeling that she was so close to the brother of her mother, whom she loved so much. Her uncle died within two years after our arrival, but she was able to visit his widow and their children.

Leaving Denver, we were greeted right away by the most spectacular mountains, that we had ever seen. What a big change from all the flat land that we had been through. We sure loved it. One could hardly get over the entire grand spectacle, only to be greeted by much more and an even bigger scene.

A beautiful part of all of this wonder was that we began to see trees, our kind of trees, the pines, birches, and others, all over these mountains. We hadn't seen these now for over two and a half years, and when seeing them being dispersed so beautifully all over, we knew, that this is our country, our home. In this exhilarating mood I asked a porter in the hall way, that I would like to have a beer. Surprisingly, he said that he will bring me one, and did in a moment. Giving it to me he said something like, "Here you are Governor." He was a very pleasant and helpful man, but calling me Governor was sort of puzzling to me.

We were almost sorry with the evening approaching to miss all of the scenery through the night. We woke up early some place in

Wyoming, still beautiful but on a smaller scale, continuing on into and through Idaho. We saw a lot of rolling bare hills.

Not knowing which state we entered, one could almost guess that we had come to Oregon, where the trees began to appear, increasing as we traveled on. In several hours, we came by a very large river, which we seemed to follow. To our right, there was water, the other, our left, mainly tall rocky cliffs, having "our" trees at its base. This was gratifying to see being quite worried through Idaho, that perhaps there wouldn't be any more trees. I also noticed, that there were other trees than pines, taller and deeper green, (Later I learned these were Douglas fir), and a beautiful sprinkling of others, taking on the fall colors.

Columbia River Gorge

As I continued to watch this new country, the river appeared to get bigger and bigger, I thought no river could be that big and it must be some sort of bay, knowing Portland was not far from the ocean. After about six hours from the time I thought we entered Oregon, we turned away from the river, continuing now through a sparsely inhabited area. As we neared Portland, probably by Hood River, it started to rain lightly, the very first time seeing rain, since we left Louisiana. I couldn't help noticing how fresh and lush green this part of country was, as compared to what we had seen elsewhere.

At a much reduced speed we approached our final destination, now going through the city, crossing another good size river, slowly coming to a stop. Finally, we arrived! Making sure that this was really Portland, we repacked our two suitcases and started to descend. The conductor or porter helped Marta down the iron steps, holding her arm, which I thought was very considerate and special.

Assembling ourselves on the platform, a lady approached us, smiling broadly and saying that she was Mrs. Nerad, our sponsor. She was a rather energetic and Czech speaking lady in her thirties.

Answering all sorts of questions as we were walking, we got into her car, a big wooden clad station wagon, and she drove us to her parent's house in SE Portland.

Being welcomed by Mrs. Nerad

It was early evening now when we entered the home. We were introduced to Mrs. Nerad's elderly parents, Mr. and Mrs. Becvar and her three sisters and a son in law, Tom Barber. There were so many questions asked and unanswered it could go on all night, we joined the family for supper a fine Czech meal, and had a beer relaxed, and talked some more. Marta excused herself being a little tired from the trip, caring for little Pavel and everyone understood. First a blessing of all blessings was that we were offered a bath (returning to human again, after so much time).

During the evening we talked about so many things, one of which was my first name, which was Vaclav (in relation to American folklore: "The Good King Wenceslaus" sung at Christmas time). Mr. Becvar, a rather distinguished and very kind appearing gentleman, made a statement. He said that my name Vaclav, was translated into James, here in America. He said it in a very convincing and matter of fact manner, so I became James, right there and then. The name seemed all right to me, and I was willing to go along with my host country, respecting it's tradition. Note: Zdenek became Sidney and Pavel became Paul.

After a good night's sleep and a generous American breakfast, we were told that we will travel to Seaside, a little ocean side town, about eighty five miles away. First, Mrs. Nerad drove me to the east part of town, to show me their new house, in a new subdivision.

It was all made out of wood, which seemed rather strange to me, being used to always see houses of masonry. But it looked comfortable with pleasant colors, and realizing this is how things are done here. I also remember how I admired the lady's driving skills. She drove fast, and effortlessly, like there was nothing to it. We hardly ever saw this in post war Europe, except of course the American tourists in Germany and Italy.

Our trip to Seaside was full of anticipation, going to our new home. A memorable item of the trip was to see the vast areas of burnt forest. It was about thirty miles from Portland, all the way to the sea. This was totally incredible, seeing about a fifty miles long stretch of the vast huge area each side of the highway. It was mostly blackened out, with a myriad of charred blackened poles standing.

FSA

Tillamook Burn

We were told that this was the biggest forest fire in the country. In about 1933, then again in 1937, perhaps in the world, which started due to some loggers carelessness sometime in the month of May, which no one could fight or stop, until November, when it was stopped by the fall rains. Hundreds of thousands of acres of forest burned, so incredibly sad to see.

Later, upon visiting a museum in the Tillamook forest, a display showed the history of this fire, the "Tillamook Burn". They have stories of people directly involved, including the victims of this fire. One victim had said, "I always wondered about what hell looks like, and now I know." This sad, shocking scene slowly recovered after being replanted with trees, often with the help of school children.

Years later even some of our children, Zdenek, Paul, and Jimmy planted some trees while in high school, as a forest restoration project. They were given certificates of achievements, including a map that gave an exact location of their units, where they planted the trees for future reference.

We arrived in Seaside. It was raining hard. We were driven to the most prominent tourist attraction, the promenade turn-around featuring the statues of Lewis and Clark, the early explorers of the West.

Seaside Turn-around FSA

I opened my window for a better look and got a full face of wetness with wind driving rain. That was something to get used to. Not so easy, when it rains for days on end. Later, when I asked some old timers if it always rained like this, they smiled and replied, "Oh yes, even more than this."

We moved in with the Nerad family, in their rented home, which didn't seem adequate, to accommodate all of us. We were given a small room upstairs. The family had two children of their own, a boy and a girl, close to the age of our Zdenek. Considering the wet weather, we knew that we needed to make the best of the fairly limited space inside the home yet, everyone was cheerful and outgoing, and because we felt so renewed and courageous, we were confident that everything would be alright.

We met Mr. Nerad, who was considerably older than his wife, and a reserved gentleman, who spoke only English, but understood some Czech words, those commonly used. Mr. Nerad took me to see his place of business, where he worked, the "Hacker Floor Co." in down town Seaside. Then he drove me to the nearby town of Astoria, to see a floor being installed in a new home with cork tile.

Our original immigration documents showed our sponsor to have been the "Czech American Ladies' Society" and that we were being accommodated and employed by the Nerad family, also a member of this society. The reality was quite different, because there was no work for me now and a slim hope for the immediate future because this little town of Seaside was a summer resort town which closed much of the summer activities for the winter.

This was a disappointment for me. I was eager and ready to go to work, to support my family. Mr. Nerad gave me some hope that something might come along. In a few days, the rain let up and I was given a job restoring the wooden clad ford station wagon (called the "Woody"), which was clad in maple, and had deteriorated by weather on some of its sections. It needed to be re-sanded and re-varnished.

The only problem was, that it had to be done outside in the back yard, with no garage available. I was glad to do the job, and watched the weather, and hoped the cloudy skies would hold off its showers. I was able to work all day, sanding vigorously and varnished the section before evening. The next day it rained so that was the end of that.

Marta in the meantime was busy catching up on all of the household chores, like the clothes washing, etc. She also helped Mrs. Nerad with other house chores. Zdenek was enrolled in school which posed a problem concerning his clothing, especially a rain coat, which he didn't have.

He had to walk to school for about six to seven blocks. He was eager to learn and was brave. He got used to the language and the teaching method, being quite different from that of Pagani, some ten months ago. As most people we met, the teachers were kind and helpful, giving him time in the transition. Not only did he not complain, he was cheerful, bright eyed, and eager to go and learn.

This town had it's own news paper that published our arrival in town. It had our pictures at the station with a nice story. The result was that some of the stores called, and gave us some needed items, like clothing, all for free. Marta really enjoyed that, needing just about everything. She walked in and picked what she needed and also got something for Zdenek, which made them so happy.

Seaside, Oregon   FSA

In addition, we got free passes at the local movie theater. As we became adjusted to our new life, we were in for a few surprises. For example, one item was fresh corn with butter. We had never seen this served to people before. Being assured that it was good, I managed but Marta had a little difficult time with it, and so did Zdenek. I explained to the Nerads that in our homeland, corn was fed only to the farm animals, which brought more reassurance from them that it was alright for us to eat it.

One evening, as a special treat, again a first time experience for us, Mrs. Nerad insisted that we try her pumpkin pie, saying it had turned out so well. She asked me, how I liked it. I replied that it was most delicious, managing a convincing face. Marta sitting right next to me then said that she had had too much to eat, and that I could have her slice also, and pushed it over to me. Maintaining composure, of course I had to eat it (I never again ate any pumpkin pie. I hated it. It tasted like it must have been unseasoned blended mud, and I never understood how so many people could like it).

In about three to four days, some strain was becoming evident between our hosts, and us. This started with a scuffle between our Zdenek and their son, who was sort of pesky, and mischievous. Marta and I knew that Zdenek was not aggressive and would never do such a thing, unless provoked. Mrs. Nerod was really upset, even after all of our assurances that it would not happen again.

Another more damaging situation occurred when she confronted Marta about using too much milk from the kitchen. We used it for our baby Pavel. She was really adamant about its usage and separated our allotment from theirs. This dismayed and upset Marta very much, because it felt like she was picking on our baby. We let it go until the evening when I saw Mr. Nerad coming home with only one egg for the dinner. Then we knew that these people could not afford to care for us.

About the fifth day I was informed by our host, that because things were not working out as expected, we will have to move out to a nearby cottage, already arranged and that she had also called the local Catholic church, informing them about our situation. In parting, I thanked them for all the care that had been done on our behalf.

We gladly departed, scooping up and taking our few belongings to a nearby cottage. Immediately, we felt good being there, even though it was a small summer cottage. It was perfect for us. It had a living room, one bedroom and a small kitchen with an oil fired iron stove used for heat and cooking. There was also a bathroom with a walk in shower. We felt a real sense of freedom and were thrilled to be left to ourselves.

Our landlord came in and introduced himself as Mr. Fred Rinehart, a retired lieutenant, commander of the navy. He was nice to us and promised to do everything that he could for our transition and comfort. He showed us how to turn on the stove, and where all the cooking utensils and dishes were. It was late evening by the time we got settled and we needed to figure out what to cook. There wasn't any food in our new home, so we decided to use the few dollars left (from our train allowance) for some grocery shopping.

After finding a grocery store, I tried to find the things Marta had asked for, but the list was in Czech, which the store clerk couldn't read. Despite that and with some help while looking at the pictures on the items we managed and I brought some groceries home. Marta was happy taking charge and cooked our first meal in our new home.

Marta was a wonderful cook and we enjoyed celebrating the holidays such as this one with our growing family. Above photo shows Jimmy and Davy with us in December, 1961 in Portland.

Chapter 25

Seaside, Oregon

The next afternoon, we had a visitor, who introduced himself as Father Deis, a pastor of Our Lady of Victory Catholic Church. He came to see how we were doing, and if there was anything he could help us with. There was so much goodness about him. He was so sympathetic, and understanding. He promised to do what he could, and would return.

Our Lady of Victory Church

Later on, he came back with two boxes of groceries for us and said that he will be back the next day. Marta was overjoyed and now had everything she needed. Despite our good fortune, the sad circumstances that led us to our new home involved the hardness of the economic times in Seaside.

Father Deis came as promised, and even brought some toys for the children. Then we drove to the town of Astoria to the J.C. Penny store to buy me some shoes and clothing, a complete outfit. This very friendly trip with Father Deis to Astoria, will always be remembered.

Father Deis

There was a glorious spectacle as we approached the town, crossing over Young's Bay with lakes of water on each side for miles, as if being in a boat in the middle of the ocean, with the town on a hill in the distance, shining brightly in the sun and being framed by a veil of white fog. In subsequent years this memorable image always emerges in my mind, when going to Astoria, and always brings me a happy feeling. Father Deis promised to inquire about the possibility of a job for me, through his parish members, which I really appreciated.

Later that afternoon, our landlord, Mr. Reinhart came in and gave me a blue navy coat. It was a warm wool coat, with a high collar. He said that it didn't fit him anymore, and that it was just right for me. He also told me that I should look for a possible job at the navy base at Tongue Point near Astoria.

He promised to give me a letter of recommendation, which coming from a retired navy officer should be helpful. So, the next day I took a bus to Astoria for job hunting. Having arrived, I learned that the navy base was about four miles out of town, so I started walking. It rained steadily, but the navy coat did not get soaked and kept me warm and dry. I arrived, close to noon at the gated guard house, being manned by two or three sailors. I gave them the letter, and explained why I came (in my broken English).

They looked puzzled at the letter and at me and said that positively I could not come in. This was a Navy establishment and entering it was by special permit only. So within a few minutes I turned around and headed back, knowing it was hopeless to try. How naive could Mr. Rinehart be, thinking that a young man, not even speaking English and not even having any I.D. (Some time later we received our Alien I.D. card, showing our name and a date of birth, etc.) could be employed in a military establishment.

I began to worry, knowing we had to pay rent. Although reasonable, it cost about $25 to $30 per month. By the next day our horizons brightened up, when a lady in a very pleasant manner introduced herself to us as Mrs. Frida Walders. She owned a home cleaning service. Upon recommendation by the Catholic Church, she offered me a job, washing windows, cleaning homes, vacuuming and all such chores. I readily accepted, and thanked her. I was grateful for the pay rate of $1.00 per hour.

So, the following day Mrs. Walders picked me up to go to work. She was so pleasant and so helpful, showing me what to do, patiently explaining everything. My first job was cleaning the exterior windows at a Seaside house. It was at the upper story, which required the use of a long ladder. Apparently, I was too thorough as I cleaned. By the end of this job, Mrs. Walders asked me to be a little faster getting done. I was probably too fussy, a part of my nature.

Our cleaning work was not only in Seaside, but also in Astoria, and Cannon Beach, which I remember well, as we came in, we were greeted by some very pleasant people. When they learned that I was new in the country, they were so nice, offering a lot of encouragement and wishing me well. They had a beautiful home, with big windows, all appearing as if sitting on top of the waves. I admired it so much, and thought what a beautiful way to live.

All the people that we met, upon entering their home were always so nice and when they learned of my background, they always proudly told me about their own origin. Most of them remembered the horrors of war, identifying with me as one of the victims. They were more sympathetic and proud that I came here; of course, Mrs. Walders was also very happy and proud to have me working for her.

At some point, she took me to her home to meet her mother, Mrs. McNeal. I will never forget the reception that I received. She was all goodness, and welcomed me, saying how happy she was that I came. I had met many wonderful people in my early life, but this was so exceptional accepting us with so much love, and doing everything to make me feel happy to be among them.

We were slowly understanding and learning that these were the extremely good Americans, the best people ever born, anywhere, being so righteous and generous to all. We knew and never forgot, how blessed we were by our good Lord to have come here. There are times, when I remembered then and still to this day, the Camp Director's secretary from Chicago who told me that Oregon was known as "God's Country". These people must be "God's people".

The Oregon coast view from my home in Manzanita, 2011.

Slowly the Christmas season approached and we began to count our money in preparation. I gladly left it all up to Marta, who knew what the greatest needs were. Surely, she thought of our children, always growing and always needing new clothing especially Zdenek, who was doing well in school. He was really advancing in his English skills, & blending right in with all the other children.

Little Pavel was now over a year old, and walking. He needed everything to a size bigger. He was such a happy baby to come home to. I am also quite sure that Marta got most of the necessary things at the stores that originally offered free clothing for her at a big discount, or often free all together.

I remember that cold month of December. Marta would take Pavel out for a walk with a baby buggy, which she loved to do. She managed to always keep him warm and healthy. My income was enough for us to exist, and I even received a pay increase from Mrs. Walders, who also knew first hand what our needs were.

Only a few days remained till Christmas. I came home one evening and saw there was a decorated Christmas tree, lit up in all of its glory, with a number of festive colored gifts at its base. Being overwhelmed by this great surprise, I knew without asking that it could only be the good Father Deis who gave this to us.

Marta was happy and excited with all of the preparations of the special meals, including some baking of the special Christmas treats, having first figured out how to use the old stove oven.

Years later, our daughter Marta Ellen with Husky.

Mr. Reinhart also came and brought some toys for the children, and wished us a Merry Christmas. He was in real high spirits, not unusual for him, but this was the season. At the appointed time, on Christmas Eve, we had our delicious dinner, which was started with Marta leading us in the prayer of "Our Father".

Later, our children opened their gifts, and happily played with them. Even little Pavel was so excited and crawled all over the floor, chasing some of the toys. I just sat there with Marta being happy as we watched the happiness all around. We felt the blessing of this first memorable Christmas in America in our little home.

We spent the balance of our evening watching the children playing and remembering our dear ones at home, wondering how they were doing, and if they were in good health, and happy as we were. Marta remembered her dear mother whom she loved so much and felt close to her this special evening. The Christmas day was wonderful; Marta was able to cook what she favored which we also liked. The weather was kind, not raining, and so we went out for a walk.

With the passing of the season, we went back to our normal pace of life. I left in the morning, and was gone all day, coming home to a happy family. It was now better for Marta, with Zdenek having the Christmas holiday time off. He spent most of the time at home and they did things together.

By now, we began to get acquainted with people of Czech descent, who had seen the previous news paper article and obtained our address from the Nerads. Many folks had also heard about the hard time regarding Mr. Nerad's loss of business.

We never saw or talked to the Nerads after we left them. However, there was some communication with the Czech Ladies Club in Portland. One of the Czech families that came to us were the Horecnys, who lived in Hamlet, about fifteen miles from Seaside.

They owned a logging business. The Horecnys were extremely friendly to us, and promised to come back to drive us to their home in Hamlet for dinner and a friendly evening. This happened within a few days. We were being picked up by Mr. Horecny, who drove the biggest car that I had ever seen. It was a Lincoln Continental convertible, with a twelve cylinder engine.

We really enjoyed being with them, hearing about their early days from their pioneer beginnings from 1918, being one of the first original inhabitants of their area. Now they were quite well to do, and they really liked us and wanted to help. They immediately gave us some good frozen elk meat, the first ever that we had seen.

We saw them several times, and later on they visited us in Portland, after we moved there. They brought us some Czech language news papers from the east, along with other Czech publications, for Marta to read.

With the January predominately wet and always windy weather, Marta and the children stayed mostly indoors. She was busy taking care of little Pavel, cooking, and doing household chores. About this time an idea was emerging in our minds that we should move to Portland, a much bigger city, where I could probably get a job in my occupation as a cabinetmaker.

Marta, being born and raised in a big city, knew that she would not be so isolated in Portland. I understood her feelings of isolation, even though I had not experienced it very much myself, except for brief periods. Once we decided that we'd try to move, she felt much better and we looked forward to it.

I mentioned this to Father Deis, who fully understood knowing our existence here had limited opportunities. He promised to contact another priest in Portland to search for a job. It was now close to the end of January when I received word that I should come to Portland to apply at the B.P. John Furniture Company. I was given a few days to come in. The company was to let me in through a different door so that I would not have to stand in line with so many other people.

It was hard for me to inform Mrs. Walders about our intentions. She was somewhat heartbroken about it but also knew that our situation was temporary and that I could do better in Portland. Her job was a God Send to our family, always being so supportive. I asked that she somehow carefully tell her mother, Mrs. McNeal, that sweetest of all souls, whom I probably would have been unable to tell myself.

On the specified day I took a Greyhound bus to Portland and arrived by about 11 a.m. The bus stopped somewhere downtown, around

Third Avenue. I checked the address I was given and looked for someone to ask for directions.

A man walked by and I asked him where S.W. Macadam Avenue was. I then realized that he was drunk. He pointed out that it was toward the south. So I headed south going along Barbur Boulevard and when the road turned right knew that next I would have to find Macadam Avenue.

With no stairs and not knowing any other way to reach Macadam Avenue, I simply crawled down the embankment and went weaving through the streets at the west side of Ross Island Bridge. I finally found Macadam Avenue and continued south. I had to walk along the road, dodging cars, since there was no sidewalk.

I found B.P. John Furniture (The area is now known as Johns Landing.), and saw a long line of people standing at one entrance. I passed them and headed for the side door as per instruction. Upon my knocking, it opened and I walked inside to an office.

They already had my name there and told me that I was hired and to come to work in three days. I think the hourly pay was about $1.25 to $1.30, and was fine with me. Having this under my belt, I headed back, arriving home close to evening.

Marta was happy about the job, but apprehensive about being left alone with the children. I assured her that as soon as a reasonable place was found that she could come to Portland also. Getting ready to leave, I went to see Father Deis, to thank him and say goodbye.

He was glad to see me landing a new job, and gave me additional instructions with an address where I would be able to rent a room for a short time. He also gave me a telephone number for Father Czylinski, a Catholic priest in Portland to contact.

I thanked this good priest from the bottom of my heart, saying, "Father, you have done so much for our family, how can I ever repay you or reciprocate for so much?" He said simply, "Jim, don't thank me, but help others, when you are able." I promised that I would. After our good byes, he said, "You must come back in the future. I would like to see how you are doing."

Photo below: Our family 61 years later at the church in Seaside.

It was with considerable difficulty for me to say good-bye to Marta and our children. I left for Portland to report for work the next day. And for my living quarters, as per the address given to me I found a two story house in SW Portland.

Upon entering and introducing myself, I was joyously greeted by an elderly lady. This family was of Italian heritage, so I started talking Italian. The hostess then became so happy that she hugged me, and called me, "Mio figlio." (My son.)

It was also a most happy introduction to a nice clean room. In the morning, after a hearty breakfast, I headed to work. It was a good half hour walk away. It was a big factory which employed about six hundred people. They produced common inexpensive furniture, all high production, and assembled on continually moving belts, an assembly line.

I was not prepared for what I saw there. Pieces of all sorts of furniture being moved about (by walking speed) on these belts and someone at frequent stations, performing their tasks, so that by the time it reached the end of the line, the item of furniture was finished.

My first job was installing triangular blocks in the corners of each cabinet, as it rolled by, using hot glue. First, I was given three blocks to glue in every cabinet, and I had to move real fast to keep up. The foreman came and gave me another block to put in now and again, and I really had to move, but did manage after a while. Our line made six hundred bedroom dressers a day.

To produce six hundred bedroom dressers in an eight hour shift, one has to really move. Having received four blocks to place between my left hand fingers, which was the maximum for a normal five finger hand. I eventually kept up with the pace. The work was incredibly boring, more than anything that I had ever done. Somehow, the monotony of repeated moves makes the time go at a snails pace.

My immediate foreman was Mr. Sitner a nice elderly gentleman. He came to the U.S. from Russia. I learned some of the history of these people, so called the "Volga Deutch". Volga was a major river in Russia, with one of the most fertile lands that was settled by a big German colony around 1860, under the rule of Catherine the Great, also of German descent.

These very prosperous people were set upon by the new communist rulers, who moved them out. Portland had a big settlement, working mostly in woodworking. All of them were very kind to us and in sympathy being refugees like us. They also helped us later, by loaning us money for a down payment on our first house. I really respect and continue to admire these good people.

Left: Marta on the porch of our new house in NE Portland.

Below: Zdenek and Pavel

Chapter 26

Portland, Oregon

Looking east over Portland with Mt. Hood in the background.

My foreman, Mr. Sitner, told me that his son had just graduated from medical school and if our family needed a doctor to call him. We did call his son, who gladly came to our house, and took care of our children. He was a surgeon also, once operating on Pavel. He was our only family doctor until his retirement.

Once while at work, I received a break. The factory owner, Mr. John came in and requested that I go with him to sort out some veneer stock. This was a great honor to pick me out of six hundred. He must have known some of my history from the priest. I could tell that he liked me, even though I couldn't understand all of what he said.

As the chain of events evolved I told Marta in my letters to her of how unhappy I was at my job. She in turn told this to the Horecny's when they visited her, who sent me a letter advising me to go to a certain nice cabinet shop where they made custom furniture.

Mr. Horecny's brother also worked there. The shop was called, "Nicolai Neppach Company", a custom mill and cabinet shop. I wasted no time and excused myself one afternoon to go over to the shop and inquire. I liked the place right off the bat.

It was exactly what I would like to do. I introduced myself in my limited English to the cabinet foreman Mr. Nussbaum, and he seemed pleased with me. There were several old country cabinet makers, i.e., Germans, Swedes, Norwegians, and a Scotch man. All of these people were good craftsmen, and Mr. Nussbaum knew that because I had been apprenticed that I had a good background.

He told me that he might give me a try, and to come back in about a week. Also, if I was hired, I would have to have my own tools. The pay was about $1.60 per hour. I was worried that the cost of the tools would be a stumbling block for me. It was now about ten days since I had come to Portland and had not been able to visit my family, because of the cost of the bus fare (we only wrote letters).

By about that time, I learned that Marta had moved in with Mrs. McNeal, my previous boss, Mrs. Walder's mother. These kind and always caring people saw Marta's isolation in the small cottage and invited her to live with them temporarily, until we could all be together in Portland. Marta enjoyed their pleasant company. At last, my own situation was about to change in Portland. I was informed by Father Czylinski, that an apartment was available.

So, after work I went over to see it. I met Mr. Henry Sheeland, whose family owned a couple of two story rental houses on S.W. Sixth Avenue, close to what is now Portland State University. He was very nice, and commented, "You are a nice looking boy of Czechoslovakia." I wore my navy p-coat, so I probably looked nice and trim, like a sailor, fresh off the ship.

Our new apartment home was near the corner of Sixth Ave. and College Street in S.W. Portland. I sent a letter with the good news asking Marta to come. I also explained in the letter that we had just received our first "Alien" ID cards. We were instructed to have the head of the family report every three months to the Immigration and Naturalization office to update our present situation. (It was five years before we could apply for our US citizenship.)

Working hard all of the time, I once totally forgot to report, until they notified me. The official was sort of stern faced, and raked me over for not reporting. I told him not being very apologetic that I worked all the time and didn't think it was such a big deal. Then, after seeing my disrespect for his office, told me what could happen if I ever forgot again. Upon my dismissal, I felt that he was too strict but correct, regarding my disrespectful attitude. As a European, it was part of our culture to never trust a bureaucrat, since for many hundreds of years, they mainly oppressed people.

Soon I received a message that my family was waiting for me at our new apartment, which was only a short walk away. Wasting no time, I hurried over and there they were. It was a wonderful reunion after about two weeks. It was so good to see everybody so happy. Mrs. Walders was so kind to bring them to Portland. Little Pavel was very active and full of life. Marta told me that everyone where she stayed pampered Pavel because he looked so cute and sweet.

Our Zdenek had to change school again, for the third time, but he was courageous and eager to start again. In a few short months in Seaside, he had caught on to the English language very well. All in little over a year, never having any special care or help of any kind, just going to school like everyone else.

Our apartment was sparsely furnished, and our landlord the Sheelands, helped with many of the basic needs. Marta really liked Mrs. Sheeland, who came from North Dakota, and was so practical and down to earth, helping her so much. Being from a different state, there was some closeness to Marta. With the Sheeland's help, and being devout Catholics, Zdenek was enrolled in the St. Anthony Parochial school. Its teachers were Catholic nuns, who wore their full garb at the time.

In no time we began to feel at home, Marta taking charge of the household. Being settled now I went back to the Nicolai Neppach Co. to see if I had been hired. Happily I was. I had to purchase my tools, a major expense, and join the union, which I was apprehensive about because of my earlier experience with the communists. I had to be sworn in, being called a brother, part of the "Millmen's and Journeymen's Brotherhood Union".

I remember feeling that the sworn in allegiance to the rules and by laws were objectionable, and in about the same spirit, what I had been through before, but hopefully, this was America, and they will be reasonable. This dictatorial power became a problem for me about four and a half years later, when I with a few other workers accepted a certain increased pay consideration, in lieu of a ten minute coffee break from our company. For the most part I was happy here. However, the union came down hard for us breaking its rule against self-negotiation, and assessed each of us a fine which was about $30.00, about half of my weekly wages. They demanded that we sign a statement saying that this money was a voluntary contribution to the pension fund. Evidently, calling it a fine was illegal. I refused to sign any contribution statement. After a few months of pressure, I quit the job, after four and a half years with this company. I began a new job doing custom cabinet work in my garage and basement, being happy doing exactly what I wanted.

One of many picnics with our family and friends.

On the weekends, we were usually picked up by someone sharing their home and hospitality. Being a newly arrived young family, we were quite special to them, wanting to know all about our history, and of course, telling us theirs. We met the Cerny's and Virostek's in the Czech-American club whose sons, tragically, had both died in the war.

I remember the kindness of these mothers, whose loss was still fresh and so hard to bare. They welcomed us to America and gave us encouragement. These meetings greatly enhanced my appreciation of the American's sacrifice. The same can be said about another mother I met years later, Mrs Willey (during a real estate purchase). She also explained that she lost her son in war in the pacific.

Regrettably there was an event, which happened shortly after the arrival of my family to Portland, which could have had very serious consequences. One of the Czech visitors told us that someone had mentioned that it was unfair that American boys were fighting in Korea, while the young new comers, like me, were staying. That message really got to me, affecting my pride and my conviction to stop the communists of North Korea.

Considering it to be my duty to do my part, I went to the Selective Service office, to enlist, to volunteer and see what my present status was. They looked at my alien card, which had me marked as "A-3", not subject for enlistment at that time. Returning home Marta was upset, that I would consider leaving my family for military duty.

I quickly realized how inconsiderate it was toward my family, who were just starting to exist, and the severe hardship that it could have caused. The combination of my experience with the history of communist oppression, whom I hated, temporarily played a role in my action. It was also a wakeup call to appreciate and care for my family first and foremost, being the most important in my life.

The end of March that year, started with beautiful sunny weather every day. Gone were the cold windy rainy days that we knew, ever since we had arrived. We enjoyed walking outdoors. Our landlord, Mr. Sheeland took us out many early evenings for a ride in his car, showing us all of the outstanding parts of the city. We really enjoyed these outings, and being in their pleasant company.

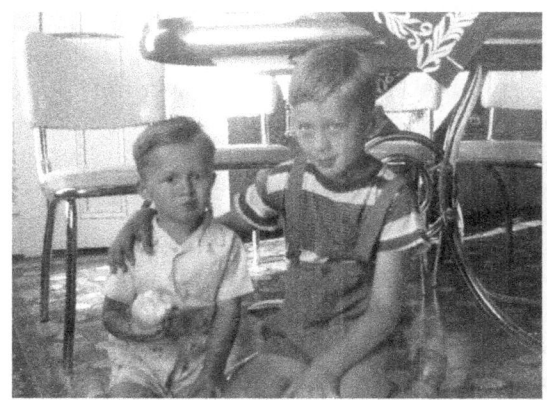

Pavel and Zdenek in our apartment on SW 6th and College Street, Portland 1951

Finally, we were really settling down in our new home, in our new country. Marta and I shared the next sixty plus years, in marriage, raised five children, and developed a successful home construction business. Yet, still while I dwell in moments of quiet reflection and review these times, I find the same emotions return to my mind and heart.

When I reflect on the nearly three years of Marta's and my common journey (June 1948 to March of 1951), it is still as hard today as it was back then, to put into words, the depth of what we felt. We left our homes with all of our loved ones and everything precious to us, entering a world of uncertain future, with only hope and a lot of courage.

Along the way, we received the divine blessings and prayers of our mothers and all of the goodness bestowed upon us by so many, whom we can never repay, or show sufficient gratitude. I am left with knowing only that I will never forget, and hoping that all of these good deeds will be a beacon of guidance for all of our family.

Frank family: Jimmy, Paul, Marta, David, Marta Ellen, and me.

Epilogue

Those of us, who have taken bold steps, often courageous and painful at some important periods of our lives, quite often bring about consequences which affect not only our own future, but influence many other lives as well. For instance, It was with the best of intentions that I strived to find freedom, and improve my well being and search for opportunities to make a solid future.

Climbing the ladder of success to reach my goal was made too difficult in the climate of a totalitarian society. Even at the very beginning of the bold steps I had taken while escaping the communist control of our Czech homeland, there was a vacuum, a void left behind. This effect often appears as if it were a punishment of the defenseless ones dearest to me.

So many times, I was unable to help them with their fears. We each felt equally as powerless, only becoming witnesses, to the lack of humanity the cowards kept imposing on all of us who lived and died in that era.

Before my memoirs are finished, I need to add one more story. The following happened to my mother, father, and sisters, as told to me by my sister, 22 years after I left them in 1948, when I was finally able to visit them there again. They waited all those years feeling that it would be too harsh to tell me any earlier.

This was revealed to me after I had successfully immigrated, became a US citizen, and Marta and I were raising a large family of our own. So, it was with a parent's eyes, and heart that we heard this story from our past.

After about two to three weeks after my final departure, my family was informed by the newly installed communist leaders of my village, that I was shot and killed at the border. It was a cruel shock to all of my family, especially my mother. She became overcome with grief.

Two of my older sisters and my father, were not completely convinced having some questions and sensing a possible revenge or retribution taking place, to get even by those in charge. Upon formally questioning the proper officials, a piece of cloth was produced as proof. It was said to have been taken from the clothes that I had been wearing. This was recognized as indeed the cloth that was from a suit that a tailor in Plzen had made for me a few months before. My family wondered why I would wear my best suit while crossing over, but the fact that it was from my suit was enough to convince them that I had probably been killed.

My sisters told me that then an unspeakable sadness came over my mother. She became inconsolable. Her hands began to tremble and she was unable to do anything. My family grieved for over two weeks, but finally recovered enough, to ask for my body, so it could have a Christian burial in the family plot.

The officials were evasive, and uncooperative, despite the family's grieving pleas. My younger sister Anna came to the rescue. She had been dating an army officer who was a party member and because of his rank and position could penetrate the communist web. They found out that it was all a hoax, an orchestrated event. He even found out that the clothing was from a tailor who had become a communist, and probably did this to save his shop. Apparently the tailor remembered sewing a suit for me, and donated the scrap of material to the officials.

The whole family was relieved, but never able to understand how some people from the same village could cooperate in this monstrous lie. My dear mother suffered the most. Her hair turned completely white, and her hands trembled slightly for many years later. My sister said that it was similar to how the Heidelberg family suffered in 1942. How much could this good and simple soul endure? I was so sorry and still grieve when this memory comes.

For many years, I received letters from my mother and sisters, who never mentioned it, not even with a hint, feeling that I would carry a heavy weight of guilt. They later realized that this would be a fulfillment of the communist's inhumanity, so I was told.

By comparison, this was not a serious crime by the communists, but a psychological revenge, though very damaging with lifelong consequences. It was one of many, many much crueler events which did destroy entire communities, families, and individuals. Mr. Voboril was one of those countless victims, who died in prison in the prime of his life.

Appendix 1: Family and Friends

First row: Father and Mother.
Second row: Three of my sisters, Anna, Lidus, and Drahus.
Below: From the left, my sister Marta, me, Anna, Lidus, & Drahus.

In the old Czech country in 1967. My father is sitting on the far right, next to him is Marta, Jimmy, Dasa, Zdenek, Zdena, Lidus, Drahus and many other family members.

In Portland, Oregon, about 1991, the family gets together for a picnic. From the right is Mundy, Marta holding our granddaughter Alyssa, our granddaughter Anna, Zdenek, Marta Ellen holding our grandson Jimmy Jr., our grandson Brian, and Jose with our granddaughter Aurielle.

In the Czech Republic in 2009: from left to right is Lidus, me, Drahus, and David. The next photo shows Dajka on the left with her son Prokop. Lidus is on the far right next to Pavel (Dajka's husband).

Lenka Simandl

At Jan's piano concert in Plzen where he gave a solo performance. He is an up and coming famous pianist. From the left is Karel Simandl (Jan's grandfather), Jan Simandl (my sister Anna's grandson), Prokop Jiran (my niece Dajka's son), me, and Lenka Simandl (Anna's daughter and Jan's mother). Lenka plays the violin and frequently travels to other contries to give concerts. She is great.

Below: Marta Ellen with Alyssa in the Czech Republic in 2009

Below: Aurielle, Flyer, Alyssa, Jose, and Marta Ellen

left: Ryan and Aurielle

Below: Zdena, Tommy, Marta, Misa, and Dasa.

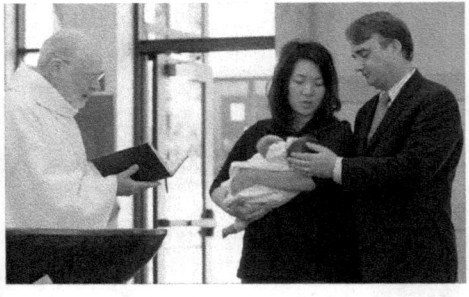

Tommy and Jenny and our great granddaugther Audrey at her baptism.

Above: Audrey

Above: Our grandchildren, Tommy, Brian, Jimmy Jr., Alyssa, Aurielle, Lauren, and David Jr.

Right: Jimmy Jr., David Jr., & Brian.

Above: David Jr. and David on the USS Abraham Lincoln.

Right: David Jr. in the Navy

Visiting David Jr. at Navel Base San Diego.

Family and friends in the USA from 1951 to 2010.

Early 1950's   Early 1960's building a cabin at Spirit Lake, WA.

Above From the left: Frank Schiller, Davy, Marta, Zdenek, Marney, Mrs. Schiller, Marta Ellen, Milan Blaha, Ellen Blaha, Frank Schiller's sister, and Mrs. Hausserman on the far right. (about 1968)

Hawaii 2006   Family gathering at Paul and Marta's in 2010

Appendix 2: USS Harry Taylor

Liberty Ship: Harry Taylor/Hoyt S. Vandenberg
Launched October 10, 1943 by Kaiser Co., Richmond, California.
Acquired by the Navy on March 29, 1944.
Transferred to Portland, Oregon on April 1, 1944.
Converted to a transport by Kaiser Co., Vancouver, Washington.
Commissioned on May 8,1944 in Portland, Oregon.
Served with the Army Transport Service.
Reacquired by the Navy on March 1, 1950 for use by MSTS.
Carried troops, dependents, and European refugees.
Placed in ready reserve on September 19, 1957.
Transferred back to Maritime Administration on July 10, 1958.
Placed in the National Defense Reserve Fleet, Beaumont, Texas.
Transferred to the Air Force on July 15, 1961.
Renamed General Hoyt S. Vandenberg
Acquired by the Navy on July 1, 1964.

Displacement: 17,250 tons (full load).
Length: 523', Beam: 72', Draft: 30'.
Speed: 15 knots (econ); 18 knots (max).
Armament: 4 5"/38 DP; 2x2 40mm; 15x2 20mm.
Complement: 449, Capacity: 3,600-4,000 troops.
Geared turbine engines; single screw; 2,250 hp.

In 1961 Harry Taylor was transferred to the Air Force and renamed General Hoyt S. Vandenberg. In 1964 she was acquired by the Navy and transformed into a sophisticated missile-tracking vessel.

In 1996 and 1997 Sea Star Productions filmed the movie *Virus* for Universal Studios, starring Jamie Lee Curtis, Donald Sutherland, and the *Gen. Hoyt S. Vandenberg* as the ship was possessed by an alien life form.

USN

Appendix 3: Liberator Memorial Project

This obelisk was erected in memory of the 10 bomber crew members of the US 15th Air Force, who perished in the Nepomuk-Dubec region of the Czech Republic during WWII. Ray Noury was the sole survivor of that crash. Ever since the February 1944 tragedy the local citizens could not show any respect until 1989 when the country was finally freed from the communist tyranny.

The citizens of the Nepomuk region have responded with commemorative acts at every years anniversary. The 60th was in 2004. I have personally witnessed the enormous heartfelt gratitude of everyone to the Americans who were present for this occasion, and was given the honor to be the interpreter.

In remembering the many thankful words from local representatives, these stand out: "these wonderful young men, they came so far to bring us freedom." It is comforting to know that America is still loved for its greatness. James V Frank

Right: Ray Noury, 86, in original uniform, at cemetary in Nepomuk region, in May, 2009.

The following are portions of the comments by Pavel Jiran, Mayor of Nepomuk, the principle planner and director of the commemorative act in May 2009. (translated by author)

"Raymond A. Noury returned to pay tribute to the memory of his fallen friends. He came to the friendly open arms of everyone, with knowledge that a big portion of his heart belongs here to us in Dubec, the place of the long ago tragedy...

p.j.

He became the messenger of the divine connection, between earth and heaven, at these moments, at this special place. He was the only one who could send a direct message of his heart, through the unveiling of the "leaning obelisk" up to heaven to his ten friends, whom he lost that tragic day of February 22, 1944.

Young women in traditional dress laid flowers at the monument   p.j.

Nepomuk – Dubec memorial to the Americans. Original display of gratitude by the people.

p.j.

p.j.

THANK YOU AMERICA

ON MAY 6TH 1945 THE CITY OF PLZEN WAS LIBERATED BY THE US ARMY

Bibliography & Recommended Reading

Agony and Ecstasy, by Irving, Stone Doubleday; 1961

Ahoy Sochy, by Olga Strusková, Spolelek pro realizaci Pomníku; 2000 (About Marie Uchitylova and her sculpture of the Lidice children)

American Caesar: Douglas MacArthur, by William Manchester. Little, Brown and Company; 1978

As He Saw It, by Elliott Roosevelt, Duell, Sloan and Pearce; 2nd ed. 1946 (forward by Eleanor Roosevelt)

Barbarossa: The Russian–German Conflict, 1941–45, by Alan Clark, William Morrow & Co.; 1985 (first published 1965)

Citizen Soldiers, by Stephen Ambrose, Simon & Schuster; 1997

The destruction of the European Jews, 3rd Edition, by Raul Hilberg, Yale Univ. Press; 2003, c1961.

Enemy at the Gates, by William Craig, Reader's Digest Press, 1973

F. L. Věk, by Alois Jirasek, (5 volumes, about the beginnings of the Czech National Revival)1888–1906

The Good Soldier Svejk: *and His Fortunes in the World War,* Jaroslav Hasek, illustrations by Josef Lada, Penguin Classics; 2005

The Greatest Generation, by Tom Brokaw, Random House; 1998

Jan Cimbura –(highly idealized depiction of peasant life), by Jindřich Šimon Baar. Prague: "Noviny" Publishing Co. 1940 (1st Ed. 1900)

Paměti, by Edvard BENEŠ, Praha 1947

Proti všem, by Alois Jirasek, 1893

The Rise and Fall of the third Reich, by William L. Shirer, Simon & Schuster; 1960

Robinson Crusoe, by Daniel Defoe, Penguin Classics, 2003. (first published in 1719)

The Two Germanys Since 1945: East and West, by Henry Ashby Turner, Yale University Press, 1987

The Second World War (Six Volumes), by Winston S Churchill, Houghton Mifflin/Riverside Press; 1948

Silent Spring, by Rachael Carlson, Houghton Mifflin; 1962

Ukrainian Refugees and Displaced People at the End of World War II, by M. Dyczok, Ph.D dissertation, Oxford University; 1995

Work hard, study-- and keep out of politics! by James Addison Baker III and Steve Fiffer, G.P. Putnam's Sons, 2006.

The World Must Know, by Michael Berenbaum, Little, Brown & Co., A publication of the United States Holocaust Memorial Museum; 1993

Yeager: An Autobiography, by Chuck Yeager and Janos Leo, Bantam, 1985

Zapadlí Vlastenci, by Karel Václav Rais, Praha : Albatros, 1974.

Index

air raid, 94, 107, 111, 113, 279
Alps, 6, 145, 239, 282
Americans, 90, 106-123, 153, 171, 182, 184, 202, 263, 272
Antochova, 150
Auschwitz, 83
Australia, 122, 209, 210, 237, 282
Austria, 73, 133, 191, 192, 239

B.P. John Furniture Company, 266
Baar, 161
Bagnoli, 194-208, 225-237
BBC, 89, 90, 107
Berlin, 79, 107, 120, 155
Big Eastern Brothers, 126, 140
Bismarck, 77
Bloch, 129
bombing, 60, 93, 107, 111, 152, 153
border, 3, 24, 87, 115, 126, 130, 142-158, 162, 167-182, 192, 276
Bremerhaven, 239, 241
Buffet, Warren, 106

Catholic, 2, 73, 158, 259, 261, 262, 267
Catholic Church, 73, 158, 261, 262
Christianity, 25, 230
Christmas, 24, 33, 48, 65-70, 85, 100, 136, 221, 254, 264, 265
Cizkov, 45, 51, 92
cold war, 133
communists, 24, 107, 111, 120-122, 130-140, 170, 189, 202, 203, 272, 274
concentration camps, 40
Corpus Christy, 24

Danube, 166, 171, 172, 183, 186
DDT, 187, 195
dog, 13, 68, 147, 158, 163-165, 180
Domazlice, 161, 174
Dutch oven, 7, 53

Easter, 24, 32-37
Eisenhower, 119, 120, 133
expulsion, 115

First World War, 2, 6, 78, 145
flailing, 64

290

Foreign Legion, 189
Frank, 1, 2, 8, 88, 166, 185, 220, 275
Furth im Wald, 151, 157, 173
Gates, Bill and Amanda, 106
Gestapo, 40, 82, 83, 84, 91
Goebbels, 89
Goethe Schule, 152, 184
Gottwald, 136

Hampl, 80
Heidelberg, 1, 40, 82, 118, 277
Helmut Kohl, 80
Heydrich, 79, 80, 82, 85
Hitler, 79, 121, 139, 220
holocaust, 118
Hood, 61, 77

inspector, 87, 88, 89
IRO, 197, 208
iron curtain, 136, 138

Jesi, 196, 204, 221
Jew, 59, 79, 130, 154

Kozina, 158, 161, 174
Krysl, 103

Liberators, 93
Lidice, 80, 220
Lounova, 37, 41

Masaryk, 136
Marshall, 105, 131, 132, 133, 156
McCarran, 208
Merchant Marines, 105
Mervart, 115, 116
Michelangelo, 227
Murmansk, USSR, 105
Myt, 1, 2, 37, 75

name days, 73
Naples, 194-202, 209, 210, 215, 221, 230, 231, 237
Nazi, 47, 89, 220, 236
Nepomuk, 23, 51, 56, 98, 117, 119, 130, 153, 154, 165, 175, 176
Noury, 153
Nyrsko, 142, 144, 145, 168, 169, 177, 178

Old Plzen, 94, 98, 101, 168, 175, 190
Oregon, 137, 235, 236, 253, 258, 261, 263, 270, 279

Pagani, 208, 210, 212, 213, 219, 221, 230, 238, 258
Patton, 119, 120, 123, 133
Pearl Harbor, 79
Plzen, 2, 277
plague, 186
pneumonia, 6, 54
Posviceni, 74
Prague, 1, 150, 151, 159, 164-168
prunes, 22
puppet, 58

Quonset huts, 205, 221

Radio Free Prague, 120
Rachael Carlson, 187
Red Army, 121, 122
Red Cross, 109, 173, 176, 187
refugee, 145, 151, 157, 177, 184, 190-198, 209-213, 231, 234, 246
Regensburg, 151, 153, 157, 166, 171, 172, 184, 187
Rome, 36, 159, 193, 218, 226, 227, 229, 230, 239
Roosevelt, 132
Russians, 114, 119, 120, 121, 126, 127, 132, 138

Saint Vaclav, 73, 74
Salerno, 219, 221, 225, 233, 236
scarlet fever, 56, 209, 236
Seaside, 255-258, 261
Schnitzer, 106
Siberia, 114
Skoda Works, 78, 94, 107, 108, 111, 134
sledding, 30
Smidova, 116, 117, 166, 167, 176, 177
soccer, 20, 22, 94, 107, 202
Soviet Union, 78, 121, 126, 138, 155
St. Nicholas, 23, 49, 66
St. Nicolas, 48
St. Mary, 198, 227, 248
St. Vaclav, 73
St. Vojtech, 34
Stalin, 120, 121, 127, 140
Stalingrad, 90, 114, 116
Statue of Liberty, 78, 161

Sudeten Land, 95

Third Reich, 87
Tillamook burn, 255
tonsillitis, 52, 241
Truman, 133, 140
tuberculosis, 208, 214

U.S.A., 86, 105, 191, 238, 247, 249
United Nations, 127, 208, 234
Uchytilova, 80, 82
uranium, 126, 137, 138
US Army, 113, 118, 120, 123, 183, 193, 204, 229

Vatican, 218, 226, 227, 228
Vlasov, 121
Voboril, 94, 99, 104-111, 122-129, 134-139, 144, 277

walnuts, 23, 48
Wannsee, 79
Wenceslaus, 73, 74, 254
White Mountain, 159
Winfrey, Oprah, 106

Yalta, 126

Zahradka, 2, 4
Zajicek, 1

www.ingramcontent.com/pod-product-compliance
Lightning Source LLC
Chambersburg PA
CBHW070637050426
42451CB00008B/199